The Art of
Social Conscience

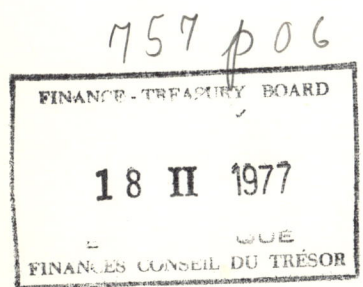

The Art of
Social Conscience

Paul Von Blum

Universe Books
New York

Published in the United States of America in 1976
by Universe Books
381 Park Avenue South, New York, N.Y. 10016

© 1976 by Universe Books

All rights reserved. No part of this publication may be reproduced, stored in a retrieval system, or transmitted, in any form or by any means, electronic, mechanical, photocopying, recording or otherwise, without the prior permission of the publishers.

Library of Congress Catalog Card Number: 76-2127

Cloth edition: ISBN 0-87663-228-2
Paperback edition: ISBN 0-87663-934-1

Printed in the United States of America

To Ruth

Contents

Foreword, by Peter Selz, ix
Preface, xi
1 Art and Social Conscience: Goya and Daumier, 1
2 Expressionism and Social Content: Rouault and Munch, 34
3 The Pivotal Role of German Social Art: Kollwitz, Grosz, and Heartfield, 58
4 Social Dimensions in the Art of Picasso, 83
5 The American Experience: Shahn, Gropper, Evergood, Albright, Blume, Cadmus, Tooker, Levine, and Baskin, 99
6 The Mexican Muralists: Rivera, Orozco, and Siqueiros, 137
7 Concentration Camp Art, 165
8 Photography and Social Content: Hine, Capa, Bourke-White, and Lange, 185
9 New Directions in Socially Conscious Art, 211
Bibliography, 229
Acknowledgments, 235
Index, 239

Foreword

Art, among other things, creates values, and this book focuses on traditional humanistic values in the art of the last two centuries. Humanity is not something with which man is born. It has to be learned and fought for, and often the artist becomes the individual in whom the struggle to maintain or achieve true humanity manifests itself, the man in revolt against accepted values, the guardian of nonconformity.

For too long the history of modern art has been couched in an academic system, a methodical and formalistic survey or "evolution" in style from Noeclassicism to Romanticism to Realism–Impressionism and on and on. Artists' critical views of the political order have often been slighted and their desire for social change, discernible in their work, overlooked. Many artists—painters and sculptors, printmakers and cartoonists, muralists and photographers—have been passionately engaged in using art as a weapon of censure. If artists cannot actually transform the social order, they can certainly function to alleviate man's alienation. Their work can act as an instrument toward a life of greater freedom and dignity. They can express and give form to social conscience.

Paul Von Blum assembles and discusses widely selected artists who share this attitude of engagement, from Goya's eloquent protest against the horror of war and Daumier's passionate, encyclopedic satire on the conditions of man (and woman) to Rouault's moral outrage based on deeply religious conviction and Munch's painting of anguish and despair. German artists like Käthe Kollwitz took a committed stand for the exploited working class, while George Grosz and John Heartfield were more biting in their powerful satire and more definite in their radical political message. Picasso's political stance took on the character of the more solitary protean genius. The "art of social conscience" is also traced in the work of America's leading socially conscious artists like Ben Shahn and Leonard Baskin and in the great mural painters of Mexico; it is seen in the powerful and terrifying recent political statements by Spain's Juan Genoves and in the social commentaries of the Black American artist Charles White as well as in the environmental sculptures of George Segal and Edward Kienholz. The book, however, does not limit itself to "high art." An outstanding chapter deals with the paintings and drawings made by prisoners in Nazi death camps—both adults and children—poignant communications of torture and confrontation with certain death. The work done in the American "relocation centers" for Japanese-Americans has its own pertinence. Von Blum discusses the potent photo-journalism of such giants as Lewis Hine, Robert Capa, Margaret Bourke-White, and Dorothea Lange and goes on to the radical political posters from Cuba, the United States, and 1968 Paris.

This is by no means an all-inclusive treatment of the subject. Many artists who partake of the author's conviction could not be included. Moreover, it does not touch on some of the most deeply felt art of this century, such as the truly revolutionary art of Surrealism or the work of abstract painters like Kandinsky or Mondrian, Pollock or Rothko, which can alter man's consciousness on a more subliminal and primary level without resorting to identifiable subjects. Von Blum deals rather with artists whose literary pictorial content is more readily accessible, whose feeling about the world and society is more clearly revealed, whose purpose is often more direct, and whose accusatory images are often laden with protest and revolt.

Albert Camus in *The Myth of Sisyphus* puts forth the theory that man's only response to the absurdity of life is revolt. In face of the futility of his mission, Sisyphus keeps rolling the rock up the hill. He becomes the hero because he will not resign himself but perseveres eternally in his revolt against his condition. Art, protest art, "art of social conscience" may at times affect the political situation, but often it is useless. Yet, as Camus explains, protest is "evidence of man's sole dignity, the dogged revolt against his condition."

Many of the artists discussed here had a purposeful concept in their revolt, while others merely expressed their social conscience because that is what they had to do. The artist's creative activity brings him closer to reality as he perceives it. The artists treated in this collection are direct in their response and revealing and compassionate in their humanistic comments on the injustices of life in our era. Clearly, if the world and our environment were at rest, if the human experience and the human condition were without mystery, without suffering as well as joy, the need for art would cease to exist.

Peter Selz
Berkeley, California
March 1976

Preface

This book was conceived as a result of several years of teaching experience at the University of California at Berkeley. It has become sadly apparent to me that university students are encouraged to pursue a comparatively narrow course of study at the expense of a wider educational background. The ever-increasing fragmentation of knowledge has resulted in the almost complete destruction of the ideal of the generally educated human being. The deplorable implications of this situation were eloquently and perceptively analyzed by José Ortega y Gasset forty years ago in his book *Mission of the University.* In that work he noted that the inability or unwillingness to examine the broader relationships of human knowledge gives rise to a class of half-educated technicians. The tragic personal and social consequences are all too clear.

A specific manifestation of the tendency toward fragmentation can be discerned in the attitude of university students toward the visual arts. It is no exaggeration to conclude that the overwhelming majority of undergraduate students in the humanities, social sciences, and natural sciences know little or nothing about the history of art, while art history students frequently know little about the historical and political context of art generally, particularly that strain of Western art that addresses itself to political and social topics. My response to this as a teacher was to institute a course that would address itself modestly to these deficiencies. I chose socially conscious art as my theme because the subject is inherently interdisciplinary. A serious consideration of this subject requires the thoughtful personal synthesis and integration of several fields of study. Neither history, nor art history, nor politics, nor sociology alone will enable a student to acquire a sufficient understanding of this particular theme.

The experience of having taught such a course convinced me that a survey on this aspect of art might advance the objective of a broader educational perspective. The themes that I emphasize in this book are generally treated only peripherally in the available literature. Few works consider the theme of social and political content in art directly, and then rarely in the form of a systematic survey. I have sought, therefore, to highlight a strain of art that is particularly valuable in raising broader social and ethical issues. My objective in this book is to use art as a source for the expansion of the social studies. My hope is that the visual arts, like literature and other creative activity, can add a humanistic dimension to the study of political and social phenomena.

Any survey is necessarily selective and replete with omissions. I have sought to deal with significant representatives of an artistic tradition within the past two centuries, with particular emphasis upon the 20th century. Except for the last two chapters, I have restricted my inquiry to paintings and graphics. Other media require comprehensive treatment beyond the scope of this effort. I have endeavored, moreover, to present an appropriate diversity of national artistic traditions, stylistic developments, and topical social issues. I recognize fully that the works of numerous men and women not covered in this book are fine representatives of the tradition of socially conscious art. I particularly regret the omission of such figures as Thomas Rowlandson, Gustave Courbet, Ilya Repin, Otto Dix, Max Beckmann, James Ensor, Reginald Marsh, and Edward Hopper. To a slightly lesser extent, I regret the omission of perhaps thirty or thirty-five other sensitive and insightful social artists. An author of a survey, however, must ultimately make a highly personal selection with the clear recognition that others have been excluded on grounds that can only be regarded as arbitrary.

I subscribe to no doctrinaire canon of critical interpretation. Instead, I have described and analyzed the various works of art in accordance with my considered judgment of the meaning of their content and of the broader social implications of the issues they raise. I have not been reluctant to offer speculative and controversial conclusions where I genuinely believed them to be appropriate. In so doing, I have not restricted myself to what may have been the specific intent of the artist. My view is that the ultimate value of art depends as much on the intelligent consideration of the observer as on the particular intention of the artist.

Finally, it should be obvious that the selection of a theme such as the art of social conscience is a reflection of the basic values of the author. I have chosen to present certain socially engaged artists in part because I am in sympathy with their objectives. I have tried to discuss their work with reasonable objectivity. I do not, however, purport that this effort is "value-free."

1-1. The Third-Class Carriage. *Honoré Daumier. Oil on canvas. Metropolitan Museum of Art, New York.*

1 Art and Social Conscience: Goya and Daumier

Social conscience is a major and recurring theme in the history of Western art. Throughout the ages there have been artists who, as perceptive observers of the affairs of mankind, have refused to remain indifferent to the social and political conditions affecting their fellow men. Over the centuries their work has stood as an impressive monument to the social and ethical conscience of humanity.

These artists have shared an awareness of the often harsh and unpleasant realities that make up the human condition. A serious consideration of their work reminds us of these realities, but at the same time, their work points to the possibility of social transformation and transcendence of those oppressive features of human existence.

The scope of social conscience is very broad indeed. Historically, men and women of conscience have reacted to social and political events in many ways. The manifestation of conscience in art is similarly broad, and it is desirable at the outset to define it with reasonable specificity. It is important, however, to avoid an overly restrictive view and thus establish too sectarian a definition as to what constitutes ethical conscience and social responsibility. The main premise of this book, therefore, is to expand the parameters of socially conscious art. Its primary definition is art which in its *content* sheds important critical insights on such broad concerns as society and its institutions and ethics, and perhaps even more broadly on the human experience and condition. The art of social conscience is vastly broader than political or protest art.

1

2 The Art of Social Conscience

The range of artistic expression that will be covered includes widely disparate artistic sources: from the painting of David Alfaro Siqueiros and Diego Rivera, reflecting their Marxist orientation; the more generalized empathetic view of the horrors of war and human suffering by Käthe Kollwitz; to the caustic satire of Honoré Daumier and George Grosz, in which they parody professions, social institutions, and specific individuals. It includes the sympathetic portrayal of the downtrodden by Georges Rouault, and the more private but nevertheless social vision of Edvard Munch, which encompasses loneliness, illness, death, and despair. It covers the anguished response of Picasso to the destruction of Guernica, the chilling view of modern bureaucracy by George Tooker, the compassionate photojournalism of Margaret Bourke-White, and the sensitive depiction of black Americans by Jacob Lawrence and Charles White. Whenever the artist uses his medium to offer a direct or implied ethical vision of the nature of social reality, the requirements of socially conscious art are fulfilled.

There are, of course, similarities that more specifically unite the artists discussed in this book. All share a critical outlook on major aspects of human society, and like all who criticize, they hope for some kind of qualitative change. This hope is frequently expressed directly. Often it is implied on the basis of the subject matter or the reasonable inferences that can be drawn from it. Moreover, all are united by their efforts to express their discontent in an aesthetic manner. Some of their work is unquestionably didactic; some more closely reportorial. It should be added that most of the art discussed here has in its time been considered radical, and in the modern era, politically left-wing.

The common bond of criticism shared by the artists of social conscience finds theoretical roots in a series of elaborate and sophisticated philosophical premises. These artists have all practiced what can be called the art of negativity—a pictorial counterpart to negative thought. This perspective is dialectical in character; a major assumption is that a critical or negative view of reality—the dialectical antithesis represented by the content of their art—is the beginning of a process in which qualitative change in the status quo may be effected. Within a dialectical framework, artistic content that initially negates a social reality is ultimately a higher form of affirmation. Theoretically at least, the antithetical nature of the content of socially conscious art sets the stage in criticism for action that can address itself to the evils that have been artistically depicted. It is clear, of course, that most of the artists have been far from effective in using their art directly to alter the social realities they criticized. Some, perhaps, helped modestly to change the political or social climate, while others hardly conceived of their art as a political lever. Any political consequences emerging from the ethical content of a work of art, however, must be seen as fortuitous. Nevertheless, the dialectical foundation remains, and in any case the ethical content of a work of art is independent of its possible political consequences.

There are a few qualifications that serve to place the art of social conscience in a clear perspective. Some of the artists to be discussed were *primarily* socially conscious artists. For others, that theme was merely one of many, or appeared as

Art and Social Conscience: Goya and Daumier 3

a minor manifestation in their work. Of course, the artists here vary greatly in personal philosophy and artistic style. None, however, could detach himself from the world and none could abstract his art from the grim realities of the human experience.

This book focuses on the content, rather than the form, of art. Scholarship in art history places substantial emphasis on form and style. The focus on content here is not intended as a condemnation of formalism. Although occasionally restrictive in scope, formalism remains a valuable approach. In the case of the art of social conscience, however, the specific thematic content often outweighs the formal considerations.

The emphasis on content in this book must be viewed against the background of the largely contentless nature of much of modern art. Contentless art, which has gained in popularity and has received major critical acceptance, is largely a 20th-century phenomenon, and in America it has generally resulted from the influence of Abstract Expressionism. An important emphasis in recent years has been painting about painting, painting for catharsis, painting for the sake of painting, and numerous variations thereof. Many of these works are valuable, aesthetically pleasing, and highly craftsmanlike, and they are undeniably a major contribution to modern art. Contentless art has further encouraged, however, a view that treats form as the only critical consideration. Other artistic forms, notably literature and especially poetry, have exhibited this tendency for half a century or more. The visual arts, in fact, are a comparatively recent convert.

More importantly, the rise of contentless art has encouraged some art criticism to become so formally oriented that content considerations have largely faded into insignificance. There are academic and journalistic critics today for whom the mere mention of content is regarded as heretical. Other critics, less strident and dogmatic, frequently intimate that a preoccupation with artistic content lacks academic respectability. One unfortunate consequence is that some works of art, which are important for their content, tend to be viewed in formal terms alone. This results in the emergence of a repressively narrow meaning that removes the work of art from its historical and social context. To that extent, the fullest appreciation of these limitations can be seen in the following view of Goya's masterpiece, *The Third of May, 1808* (see Fig. 1–8):

> As in the case of many Baroque narrative paintings, strong chiaroscuro stresses the dramatic climax of a continuing action in his *Third of May*. The white shirt of the man raising his arms and the light projected by the lantern provide islands of vivid brightness in the otherwise gloomy setting. The painterly technique is Baroque and the flame-like handling of the surfaces of the figures and the trembling quality of the setting, which do much to convey the full horror of the scene, go further back to the manner of El Greco. Baroque, too, is the relationship of figures and space. The line of soldiers, curving gradually beyond the right edge of the frame, is a line of force linking the scene to the far distance. The raised arms of the man facing the guns similarly link the prisoners to the sky above. The ridge on

4   The Art of Social Conscience

the left counters the curve of the row of soldiers with another dynamic accent.*

As valid as this may be, the analysis ignores the broader and more significant issues depicted by Goya in this painting. The background of the Napoleonic occupation of Spain is absent, as are the difficult moral issues of responsibility for possible war crimes and atrocities. These issues, which are treated in depth later, show the limitations of formal analysis alone. More importantly, they suggest that the pendulum has shifted precariously to the side of form alone.

It is important to bring the pendulum back. There has been a long and highly respectable tradition of art criticism that has had a strict content orientation. Many art historians in this tradition were similarly disturbed by the overemphasis on formal considerations. This view was expressed a generation ago by Frederick Antal, one of the more erudite of the content-oriented critics:

> In defining a style, I believe that contemporary art-historians frequently devote too much attention to the formal elements of art at the expense of its content. They only too often overlook the fact that both form *and* content make up a style. . . . Moreover, it is the content of art which clearly shows its connection with the outlook of the different social groups for whom it was created, and this outlook in its turn is not something abstract, it is in the end determined by very concrete social and political factors.†

Such a view will be pursued in the following chapters. The primary premise is that art should *not* be separated from the wider context of life. In other words, form and content are also ultimately inseparable. A mature consideration of art takes both into account and avoids arbitrary and artificial distinctions. Clearly, even the most admirable content is worthless as a work of art if it is inferior in technique. A rigorous consideration of formal elements is a precondition of fine art. At the same time, however, form and content are not merely equal components in a work of art. Professional competence is of course prerequisite to artistic achievement, but it should not be regarded as an end in itself. Rather, form should be, as Ben Shahn so eloquently noted, the shape of content. It should be used to express and emphasize a specific content that is the product of the artist's thought and imagination. It should shape and mold the object of expression, and when properly executed, it genuinely creates the fusion of form and content.

The presence of these assumptions implies a hierarchy of values that should be elaborated briefly in the interest of intellectual candor. The art of social conscience is by definition *content art*. The choice of emphasizing this theme in Western art is meant to imply that, in certain respects, it is more valuable than

*Henri Dorra, *Art in Perspective* (New York: Harcourt Brace Jovanovich, 1972), p. 178.
†Frederick Antal, "Reflections on Classicism and Romanticism," *Burlington Magazine*, Vol. 66 (April 1935), p. 159, quoted in Donald Egbert, *Social Radicalism and the Arts* (New York: Knopf, 1970), p. 565.

Art and Social Conscience: Goya and Daumier   5

other themes and other artistic content. This is hardly to suggest that nonsocially conscious art is to be denigrated as worthless or irrelevant. Rather, the object here is to reveal the particularly valuable features of socially conscious art.

The critical dimension of this art has important ramifications. It can contribute simultaneously to moral engagement and intellectual advancement and curiosity. It creates a consciousness of human problems far more effectively than other artistic means. Since man is an incontrovertibly social animal, social art encourages a more comprehensive understanding of the complex realities of human life. The critical element, moreover, encourages the viewer himself to evaluate these social and political realities more objectively. The engaged posture of socially conscious art also stimulates ethical controversy and resolution, which in itself is an admirable effect in a world that is often pervasively indifferent.

In a perfect world, it would be difficult indeed to assert the higher value of any particular artistic content. Under these conditions, virtually any subject would seem to have little claim to priority over any other. The world as we know it, however, is far from perfect. Warfare remains a primary means of resolving human contention, and in fact has posited a more awesome level of barbarism by means of our 20th-century technological advancement. Meanwhile, millions of people continue to starve while conditions of political oppression dominate our geographical space. These and related factors affect the entire character and future of the human race. Consequently, it is clear that certain topics in art, literature, and other related endeavors have a higher probability of raising human consciousness than others. The art of social conscience performs this function.

A final comment on the subject of social art is useful here. It has been fashionable for some time to disparage art that contains or implies a message, particularly when it involves an element of sociopolitical propaganda. It is necessary to concede that a great deal of protest and related art has been inferior in quality. All too frequently, passionate involvement in political affairs has encouraged artists to ignore or compromise the first technical principles of professional work. The highest stratum of socially conscious art, however, is not subject to this criticism. The quality of the work that is to be discussed here is rarely affected negatively. Frequently, artists' passion or personal commitment has stimulated them to even greater artistic achievement. In communicating through their art thoughts and feelings directly contrary to majority sentiment, many artists have acted with courage. Moral engagement coupled with thoughtful dissent should be regarded as a higher form of human endeavor in a world that is too often beset with conformity and apathy. The passionate engagement of the artists to be discussed can only serve to emphasize and heighten their vital importance.

The art of social conscience has many honorable antecedents in the history of art. From the beginning of man's artistic expression, critical commentary appears in the content of art. Satire has been a significant feature in art virtually since its inception. Examples can be found in the Greek and Roman civilizations, where satirical treatments of the gods appear in paintings and ceramic art. A major thrust of more modern satire has been artistic protest against the evils and excesses of organized religion. Other facets of socially conscious art have involved protests against military atrocities, commentary on human folly, and dissatisfaction with the class structure of society.

There were numerous artists of social conscience before the 19th century. Some, of course, are of transitory interest, while others created work of enduring value. The work of some of these artists is especially significant as it relates to developments in the 20th century. The artistic themes of such disparate figures as Brueghel, Callot, Rembrandt, and Hogarth are particularly pertinent to ideas developed throughout this book. The work of these artists not only indicates historical continuity but also sets the stage for the more modern manifestation of similar themes. Each artist is from a different historical period, from a different national origin, and more importantly, the work of each reveals different aspects of the art of social conscience. A cumulative view of the socially significant features of their art suggests a defective world badly in need of change. It suggests, furthermore, that art has the capacity to illuminate broad areas within the social spectrum.

Pieter Brueghel the Elder (1525–69) is an early major representative of this tradition in Western art. One of the great figures in Flemish painting, he was a close and perceptive observer of human affairs. While his art was multifaceted and embraced varying themes, a significant percentage of his work falls into the broad category of social conscience as previously defined. Brueghel had an amazing capacity to discern the darker side of human nature: its folly, vice, brutality, and delusion. There is some controversy as to whether he intentionally portrayed these situations specifically in order to offer criticism, or whether he merely recorded such events without judgment. That question is irrelevant here, for even the latter view conforms to the requirements of socially conscious art in that the specific content clearly requires an inferential judgment and socially conscious response on the part of the viewer.

Some of Brueghel's paintings have an obvious political content. In *Massacre of the Innocents (Fig. 1–2)*, it seems highly probable that his intent was one of artistic protest. At the time of this painting, the Spanish had obtained control over the Low Countries. Spanish rule was brutal and oppressive, and on occasion Spanish troops had repressed rebellions with an unthinkable savagery. Whether or not Brueghel meant this particular work as political allegory is perhaps debatable, but the painting clearly depicts a scene in which innocent people suffer gratuitously. The helplessness of the victims is the timeless message of the work. Here the viewer is compelled to move from a specific event to an insight of more lasting significance—that it is impossible to avoid the painful human consequences of war and oppressive military action. In every era, these consequences are thrust upon innocent people who neither understand nor influence the political events around them.

1-2 Massacre of the Innocents. *Pieter Brueghel the Elder. c. 1566. Oil on canvas. Kunsthistorisches Museum, Vienna.*

The work of the French artist Jacques Callot (1592-1635) similarly serves as an important progenitor of the modern art of social conscience. Callot is a major graphic artist whose most remarkable work portrays the horrors and barbarism of war. He is best known for the series of engravings *Miseries of War,* one of the most powerful indictments of war in the history of art.

The historical setting for this masterpiece series was the Thirty Years War of 1618-48, which involved most of the states of Europe and had both religious and political dimensions. Devastation, destruction, death, and massive human suffering pervaded the Continent, while looting, rape, and executions were commonplace. These events were to become the specific focus of Callot's artistic skill.

In 1633 French soldiers entered Nancy, the home of the artist and then the capital of the independent Duchy of Lorraine. After the fall of that province, the soldiers acted as an army of occupation. Violence and brutality against the local populace were prevalent. Callot recorded this infamous spectacle in a series of engravings. Executed with objective precision, the act of recording speaks clearly for itself, and the strength of the message is indisputable. Done in story form, the linear progression of the story emerges relentlessly: the battles, the pillaging, the burning of a village, the subsequent revenge of the peasants against the soldiers.

8   The Art of Social Conscience

The most dramatic examples in the series involved Callot's depictions of executions. Perhaps the most famous is *The Hanging (Fig. 1–3)*. In this engraving, a score or more people are hanging from a large tree. Although they seem to be soldiers who are being punished for their own brutal excesses, the effect of the total view creates an impression of the inherent senselessness and savagery of war. A serious confrontation with the explicit content of Callot's art destroys any remaining vestige of the romantic glorification of war.

The work of the greatest of all Dutch artists, Rembrandt van Rijn (1606–69), is not usually considered to be political or even social in character. There is nothing that specifically touches the social realm in any area of his work. Nevertheless, a careful examination of his art reveals his implicit awareness of the needs and feelings of others. This human sensitivity serves an important historical influence on the more direct expression of socially conscious art. Few artists have had such depth of human compassion and sympathy. Indeed, his work is replete with a generalized humanism that continually reveals a socially coherent view of life. This humanist orientation led him to a highly sympathetic view of the humble and downtrodden, and this attitude occasionally found direct expression in his art.

Although primarily a painter, Rembrandt was also a great graphic artist. It is in his engravings that most of his socially conscious work can be found. At recurring intervals in his career, his inherent humanism impelled him to portray beggars, cripples, and other members of the lower social and economic classes. This deeply moving work conveys a powerful sense of the ravages of poverty and deprivation. In 1630, for example, he executed *Beggar with a Wooden Leg (Fig. 1–4)*, a ragged figure whose lonely and unhappy life is expressed with unforgettable clarity. As the crippled outcast hobbles along, the viewer is encouraged to consider the broader implications of his plight. Rembrandt assigns a quality of

1–3. The Hanging. Jacques Callot. Etching. Metropolitan Museum of Art, New York.

1-4. Beggar with a Wooden Leg. *Rembrandt. Etching.*

dignity to a person who might ordinarily be considered superfluous or beneath one's attention. Perhaps more important, he implies that compassion is far superior to callous indifference.

The very portrayal here and in other etchings of social outcasts is in itself the exercise of an important choice. Rembrandt's view, artistically expressed in such work, is that everyone is entitled to a basic recognition of his humanity. Such an attitude runs counter to the actuality (if not to the professed ideals) of his, and subsequent, societies. The same theme became a major facet of the art of social conscience in the centuries to come. The influence of Rembrandt can be found in such diverse figures as Honoré Daumier, Georges Rouault, Käthe Kollwitz, and Diego Rivera. The ethical conscience of the great Dutch artist clearly rivals in importance the formalist aspects of his art.

Social commentary is a hallmark of the work of the English painter and engraver William Hogarth (1697-1764). His art is an interesting amalgam of social history and critical analysis. Some of his work deals with specific 18th-century English political events, but most of his content involves universal social situations. Hogarth lived in London during a time when it was a bustling, jostling, overflowing, and thoroughly fascinating city. Crime, poverty, and alcoholism were rife, and Hogarth captured the spirit of his time. His pictures depict the crowded streets, the boisterous pubs, the bleak prisons, and the decadent style of the wealthy in contrast to the precarious conditions of the poor.

Hogarth was essentially a storyteller in pictures. He was a liberal moralist who was indignant about many of the problems and evils of the time. Although much of his art reveals the bias of the emerging 18th-century middle class, he often came to terms with the social ills of the day, and his message has assumed a timeless relevance. A major element of his social commentary involves a critique of social institutions, the professions, and some of the prevalent values of social life. A good example is his sardonic treatment of an arranged marriage whose primary raison d'être was pecuniary gain and social advancement. *The Breakfast Scene* (Plate II of the series *Marriage à la Mode*) (*Fig. 1-5*) reveals the boredom and vacuity of a marriage that lacks a continuing process of serious communication. The dull look on the faces of both parties indicates the underlying emptiness of their situation. No conversation occurs, and the viewer is stimulated to think about the reasons for such a crippling relationship. Even more important, Hogarth seeks to connect private despair with a social reality. The work far transcends a mere criticism of the institution of marriage. The artist successfully indicts a society that values social position beyond a more humane and enduring personal relationship. Hogarth at once criticizes and urges reform, for to him the gap between the ideal of love and the socially engendered mercenary reality was intolerable.

The themes that occupied at least the partial attention of the four artists presented here find full and direct expression in the 19th and 20th centuries. The evils exposed by Brueghel, Callot, Rembrandt, and Hogarth would seem to be an

Art and Social Conscience: Goya and Daumier

1–5. The Breakfast Scene. (*Marriage à la Mode: Plate II.*) William Hogarth. Etching. National Gallery of Art, Washington, D.C.

omnipresent feature of man's social being. Many artists who followed responded with sensitivity to these realities. Foremost among them are Francisco Goya and Honoré Daumier, whose art constitutes a direct historical link to the socially conscious art of the 20th century. Both artists have been enormously influential in the work of the artists to be discussed in subsequent chapters. Each must be discussed in some depth in order to understand adequately the character of socially conscious art in our era.

Goya: The Master as a Social Critic

Francisco Goya y Lucientes had a remarkable ability to fuse great art with trenchant social criticism. One of the masters of Spanish painting, along with El Greco and Velázquez, Goya was an artist of extraordinary versatility; during the course of his career, he created drawings, etchings, lithographs, paintings, and frescoes. The range of his subject matter was equally diverse. He handled such noncontroversial subject matter as picnics, bullfighting, and commissioned portraits, but he also made controversial studies of war, terror, and human folly. His work provides a major transition from the work of the great masters to more modern conceptions of art. In the most obvious and dramatic way, his work serves as the point of departure for the modern art of social conscience.

Goya was born in 1746 in Fuendetodos, a small village in the Spanish province of Saragossa. He lived in a time of massive political turbulence, social unrest, and glaring social inequities. These factors profoundly influenced his career as an artist, for they created in Goya a consuming disillusionment with the character of Spanish social life. Like Brueghel and Hogarth, he painted and drew people as he saw them, even when their actions and concerns horrified him. He carefully observed and recorded their follies, their pettiness, and their brutalities. There is no neutrality in these portrayals. His art makes it clear that he is assuming a stance on issues of fundamental human importance. His deep belief in a secular and rational humanism served as the foundation for the critical content of much of his work, and he was not afraid to employ his particular vision as an act of personal advocacy on behalf of those ideals.

A historical background is crucial for a serious consideration of Goya's art. When the artist was about thirty years old and beginning to establish a major reputation, Charles III was the king of Spain. He was perhaps one of the few enlightened monarchs Spain has ever had. A progressive autocrat, he had a widely different outlook from his royal predecessors. Charles III was conscientious, a hard worker who attempted to elevate Spain from a backward and repressive country into a modern European state. The country had been dominated by the Church, the effects of the Inquisition, and the large landholders, to the harsh spiritual and economic detriment of the majority of the population. For years, stultifying custom and submission to authority were the rule in Spain. Unlike many European countries, where tolerance and a more modern outlook were developing, Spain continued the tradition of religious persecution. At the same time, the material conditions of the peasants and urban proletariat remained on a scant subsistence level.

Goya had a basic respect for Charles III. He was sympathetic to his efforts to effect at least a modicum of change in the structure of Spanish society. The ideas of the French Enlightenment were becoming more influential, and the more progressive Spanish intellectuals borrowed heavily from the ideas of neighboring France. The primary feature of this influence involved a belief in the value of reason as a controlling factor in human affairs. Although intellectuals frequently disagreed as to how effective a force reason should be, many were openly sympathetic to the ideals of the Enlightenment. Goya had several friends and acquaintances who shared these values; consequently, he developed an intellectual underpinning for his art that infused the body of his work.

The brief ascendancy of rationalist philosophy and modernity in Spanish politics was abruptly halted by the death of Charles III in 1788. His successor, Charles IV, was a stunning and depressing contrast. He was a dull, boorish man who was dominated by his neurotic and promiscuous wife, Maria Luisa. One of her lovers, Manuel Godoy, was eventually elevated to a position of prominence and power. Together, they managed to destroy most of the progressive features of the Spanish Enlightenment. The decline of rationality in Spain became increasingly evident as corruption and intrigue came to dominate the Royal Court. Against this background of incompetence and social decay, the cataclys-

Art and Social Conscience: Goya and Daumier   13

mic events of the French Revolution and its aftermath affected Spain both intensely and painfully.

Goya was initially sympathetic to the new king, particularly since he had achieved his goal of becoming Painter to the Chamber, a post that brought him both fame and pecuniary reward. It was not long, however, before the regressive tendencies of the time became apparent to the artist. This regression, linked with a series of personal affairs and tragedies, engendered a gloom and despair that fundamentally affected the direction and social content of Goya's art.

Goya suffered a devastating personal blow in 1792 when a serious illness left him completely deaf. This malady necessarily limited his communication with others and its impact on his life was incalculable. His personal troubles were exacerbated by the trials and tribulations of his famous relationship with the Duchess of Alba. Ill, lonely, and emotionally distraught, Goya sought a deep emotional relationship with the Duchess, while she desired only superficial involvement. Goya was unable or unwilling to gauge her true character. This affair, which has fascinated scholars and novelists, ended unhappily for the artist. The cumulative effect of these events and the increasingly deteriorating political situation led Goya to express his chillingly depressive view of the world.

A great graphic artist as well as a painter, Goya turned to etching in order to explore artistically the darker side of the human condition. In 1797 he embarked upon one of the monumental projects of his career. The full series of *The Caprices (Los Caprichos)* was published in 1799. It contained eighty prints and is one of the most important contributions to the history of socially conscious art. In this

1–6. The Sleep of Reason Produces Monsters.
Francisco Goya. Etching.

series Goya explores an impressive range of human folly and irrationality. His etchings deal with vanity, greed, superstition, promiscuity, delusion, and, indeed, the vast complex of human aberrancy. His targets have become familiar objects of critical scrutiny: marriage, prostitution, the law, and especially the Church. The artist underscored his etchings with pungent and satirical captions, which added even greater force to their impact.

The basic and recurring theme of *The Caprices* is that when man's reason is permitted to retrogress, his irrational tendencies emerge and undermine all that is valuable and humane in the human experience. This unifying thesis joins the widely disparate subjects found in the series. Perhaps the best example of this jointure is found in Plate 43, *The Sleep of Reason Produces Monsters (Fig. 1–6)*, in which Goya depicts the symbols of irrationality as a warning. The consequences of a diminished rationality are made unmistakably clear. Bats, demons, and monsters have assumed control and a grimly hostile cat assumes an ominous focus. Appropriately, Goya added a further caption in order to underscore his philosophical intent and to emphasize the intensity with which he held it: "Imagination abandoned by reason produces impossible monsters; united with her, she is the mother of the arts and the source of their wonders."

There is little doubt that this work is a graphic embodiment of Enlightenment philosophy. As valuable as these principles are, they should not be disjoined from the clear and direct political and social implications of his attitude: Unrestrained irrationality invariably encourages negative social consequences. Goya was obviously aware of the causal relationship between the diminution of the force of reason and his country's regression as a social entity. (Over a century later, the German artist George Grosz would discern many of the same tendencies in Weimar Germany and would record with equal horror a similar retrogression.)

Goya went even further; he expressed the view that the superstitiousness that characterized his countrymen must be removed as a precondition to any serious social and political transformation. He believed that as long as the symbolic bats and demons prevailed, Spanish society would be destined to deteriorate still further. The thoughtful viewer of this work, finally, is stimulated to conclude that a rational philosophical framework is a first principle of a humane and progressive social ideology.

One feature of *The Caprices* involves very specific topical political satire, always a significant element in the art of social conscience. There are several plates in which Manuel Godoy appears, literally, as an ass. In one example, Goya portrays Godoy purporting to minister to a man on a deathbed, possibly representative of Spain itself. Since Godoy is an ass, the artist's prognosis for political recovery is far from hopeful. In the way that medical quackery can only exacerbate the problems of the sick, so, too, does the ambitious quackery of the influential lover of Maria Luisa effect the detriment of the political health of the nation.

In spite of the artist's frequent dismay and his artistic disapproval of sociopolitical developments in his country, he continued to be well received at the court

Art and Social Conscience: Goya and Daumier 15

1-7. The Family of Charles IV. Francisco Goya. Oil on canvas. Museo del Prado, Madrid.

of King Charles IV. Having achieved respectable stature and comfortable material prosperity, Goya was named First Painter to the King in 1799. Shortly after his appointment, he was commissioned to paint a group portrait of the royal family. The result was a masterpiece of savage satire and one of the few instances in the history of socially conscious art in which commissioned portraiture has resulted in such acerbic social commentary. Traditionally, of course, official portraits of royalty display their subjects in all their pomp, magnificence, and splendor, either real or imagined. Truth is invariably sacrificed to an ideal. *The Family of Charles IV (Fig. 1-7)* is a notable exception. In this painting Goya eschewed all image-creating artistic exaggeration and dishonesty. Instead, the realism of his portrayal clearly reveals the royal family's lack of character and substance. Their clothing, of course, glitters with the resplendent tokens of wealth, position, and power. The faces of the king and queen, however, reveal a drab couple who look little different from thousands of petty shopkeepers, civil servants, and other representatives of the petite bourgeoisie. It is strongly indicative of the loathing Goya must have felt, his personal response to what he viewed as a betrayal of the ideals of the spirit of Enlightenment.

The portrayal of the queen, Maria Luisa, is especially uncomplimentary. Goya emphasizes her unattractive double chin, thick neck, and fat arms. Her expression is grossly harsh, even to the point of fatuity. The eldest son Ferdinand—later to become the tyrannical successor to his father, and to be himself the object of Goya's satirical portraiture—is presented in a thoroughly unflattering posture. His haughty adolescent arrogance clearly reveals the artist's personal distaste.

Most significant of all, the queen occupies the center focus in the portrait—a realistic reflection of the power realities of the royal family. What is perhaps most surprising is that the family raised no objections to the final product. Presumably, only an artist of Goya's stature and talent could effect so powerful a satire without severe sanction or public reproval.

Goya enjoyed his new-found leisure for several years, occupying himself with the wealth and public respect he had come to enjoy. Meanwhile, internal and foreign political developments were moving rapidly, and the outcome was a war that would give rise to the best work of Goya's artistic career and solidify his reputation as one of the greatest artists of all time. Charles IV, his wife Maria Luisa, and their son Ferdinand began to feud and quarrel about who was to rule. Napoleon, who had always coveted Spain, was eager to take advantage of the strife in the Spanish royal family. Charles IV abdicated in favor of Ferdinand, who vainly hoped that Napoleon would favor his regime. Instead, Napoleon exploited the situation and personally assumed the Spanish throne. He made use of troops that were already in Spain under the pretext of marching to Portugal, and simply took control, installing his brother Joseph as monarch. Thus, in 1808, the stage was set for a brutal war that would last for six years.

The rule of Joseph was actually more liberal than that of his Spanish predecessors. Many members of the Spanish intelligentsia, including Goya, thought that his accession would effect major changes and bring Spain into the mainstream of modern European life. Joseph abolished some of the repressive features of Spanish life and had intended to return, at least partially, to the ideals of the Spanish Enlightenment. His rule was one of force, however, and the people of Spain rose up against the French occupation. The events of the next six years engendered a wave of terror and bloodshed, which Goya was to immortalize.

The precipitating events occurred in May 1808. On May 2, Napoleon ordered the removal of the last member of the royal family from Spanish soil. A large and anxious crowd gathered in Madrid, disturbed by the flood of rumors circulating in the capital. Some were concerned that the royal family would be massacred, while others were troubled by vague rumors of other forms of betrayal. Mob action in times of political tension is often rife with danger, and this was to be no exception. The restive and nervous Spaniards turned against the French guards, French reinforcements and mercenary troops in their employ were enlisted, and there were many casualties on both sides. Six years later, in 1814, Goya vividly re-created this incident in the painting entitled *The Second of May, 1808*.

The next day, May 3, the French retaliated by executing, without trial, all Spaniards thought to be involved in the previous day's uprising. Some of the people killed had in fact been involved, but there were also many innocent victims of this retaliation. This event catalyzed the guerilla war that followed and was later immortalized by Goya in one of the most famous paintings in the history of art. *The Third of May, 1808 (Fig. 1–8)*, like its companion work, was painted six years after the actual event. It was a commemorative painting presented to the government after Napoleon's retreat. It is clear that Goya was

Art and Social Conscience: Goya and Daumier 17

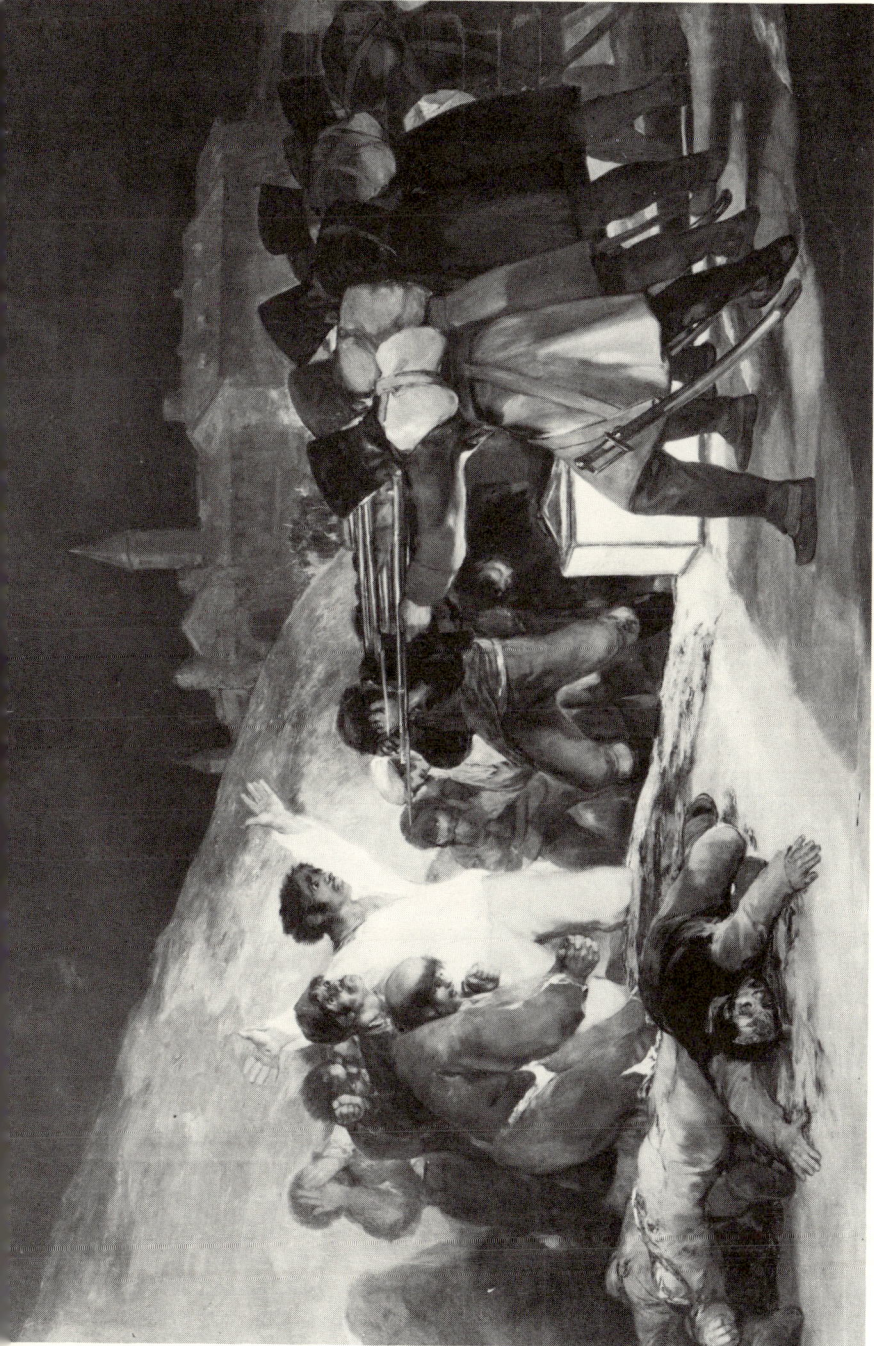

1-8. *The Third of May, 1808.* Francisco Goya. Oil on canvas. Museo del Prado, Madrid.

not an eyewitness, although he, like most residents of Madrid, certainly had direct knowledge of the events. The content of *The Third of May, 1808* has universal implications that transcend the gruesome massacre of the Spanish civilians. A close examination of this masterpiece should convince the thoughtful viewer that its theme, regrettably, is as applicable to the American bombing raids in Southeast Asia in the 1960s and '70s as it was to the specific event in 1808.

The painting focuses on the victims of the French executioners. The central figure is the man with his arms upraised. The whiteness of his shirt hints at the innocence that accompanies his impending death. The fusion of horror and resignation on his face is tragically universal in scope. Goya underscores the horror of the event by vividly emphasizing the bloodshed and corpses, which dominate the lower left portion of the work.

At the right, the soldiers are presented as anonymous executioners, blindly obeying the orders of their superiors. Directly or by clear implication, Goya's masterpiece presents a social and ethical issue of the gravest importance. Significantly, the faces of the soldiers are not shown; all act in unison, a token of the mindless automatons who have blindly served in military organizations throughout history. No one questions the immoral orders of superior officers, and each member of the firing squad presumably has no compunctions about performing the task assigned to him. Since all fire at their victims simultaneously, individual responsibility for the atrocity is conveniently avoided.

This is perhaps the greatest tragedy of all, and the observer must ponder the complex ethical problems which Goya presents: Who, after all, is to blame for the murder of these innocent human beings? It is naive, certainly, to think that the individual soldiers involved were ever encouraged to become autonomous and responsible individuals capable of ascertaining the moral implications of their conduct. At the same time, however, to hold only their superiors culpable, and to excuse the men who executed the orders on the basis of their cultural and military conditioning tends only to increase the probability of the recurrence of similar acts. Goya's painting encourages the viewer to determine the propriety of institutionalizing a higher and more rigorous standard of individual responsibility.

The ensuing years of war were years of deep personal anguish for Goya. His own reactions were painfully mixed, for he had joined a love for his own country with an admiration for the ideals of the French Enlightenment. He recoiled at the senseless and ubiquitous brutality that characterized this war, and the art he produced clearly reveals this reaction.

Both the French and the Spanish tortured and mutilated prisoners and innocent victims. Barbarism dominated the land, and the most grotesque tortures became commonplace. Hunger and disease ravaged the population of Spain, and Goya was impelled to record their horror in a series of etchings that were to stand at the pinnacle of graphic art. *The Disasters of War* is cumulatively as powerful an antiwar statement as has ever been produced. The eighty-two plates illustrate the panoply of horrors: rape, murder, looting, destruction—indeed, all the atrocities that human beings are capable of inflicting on their fellows. As with the finest socially conscious art, its implications are universal, and it is interesting to note that over a century later another Spaniard would repeat the message with equal force in his monumental painting *Guernica (see Fig. 4-8)*.

Most of the individual plates in *The Disasters of War* speak clearly for themselves. The collection, which was published thirty-five years after Goya's death, contains intimate views of the prevailing horrors. Several subsidiary themes emerge, but the cumulative impact assures its permanence in the history of socially conscious art. Many of the plates exhibit specific atrocities that occurred during the war. It is difficult to select any that are especially revealing, for each represents a stark depiction of real events. Typical, however, is Plate 28, *The Populace (Fig. 1-9)*, in which Goya shows the reaction of the Spanish as they retaliate against the French. Here, their revenge is savage as they subject a slain French soldier to a series of physical indignities. Once again, warfare breaks down the ordinary controls over human behavior, and individual conduct reverts to primal savagery. The approval of the onlookers is evident, indicating Goya's pessimistic view of these basic human realities.

The tone of the series is a dramatic contrast to and a healthy tonic for the tendency in art to portray war in romantic and heroic terms. Goya knew well that there is nothing romantic about war. He knew that pervasive suffering is the end result, whoever the victor and whatever his cause. Throughout the series the artist reveals the final effects of armed conflict in a dramatic human context. His portrayals of civilian refugees demonstrate convincingly that innocent people

1-9. The Populace. (*Disasters of War: Plate 28.*) *Francisco Goya. Etching.*

20 The Art of Social Conscience

1-10. The Prisoner. *Francisco Goya. Etching. Private collection.*

pay the highest price and suffer the most intimate personal sorrow. The poignancy of the work is obvious; it is difficult to imagine an unaffected viewer.

With the retreat of Napoleon across the Pyrenees, the arrogant Ferdinand returned from France and assumed the throne. He quickly restored the authority of the old conservative institutions. The Church and the major landholders soon dominated the life of Spain once again. Liberals were forced out; some were persecuted and executed. Lethargy became the distinctive response. Ferdinand was even more backward than his father, more insensitive to the plight of the majority of the Spanish people. Censorship was restored and Spain quickly resettled into spiritual darkness.

Goya, who had also executed numerous nonsocial works during the war years, retreated to a more private personal world. In the years following he created his famous series on bullfighting, his allegorical works known as the Black Paintings, and a major graphic series *The Proverbs (Los Proverbios)*. The latter two contain a major recapitulation of themes that informed his earlier work: studies of human folly, disturbing allegorical views of human terror, and related topics that further revealed his pessimistic and despairing mood.

In 1820 there was a successful although short-lived revolt of the liberals against the repressive absolutism of King Ferdinand. With the help of the French, the king returned in 1823, and the familiar political retrenchment ensued. During the period 1818–24, Goya returned to art that was directly socially conscious in its content. In a series of ink drawings, he delineated victims of the Inquisition, the persecution of liberals, and the ill-treatment of imprisoned men and women. The latter theme, in fact, is a significant feature of Goya's socially conscious art. A typical example is an individual etching entitled *The Prisoner (Fig. 1-10)*, in which the artist condemns the inhumanity of penal servitude in Spain and the barbarous treatment of prisoners. The victim is shown in chains in a dim and miserable cell, and the critical character of the artist's presentation suggests that the punishment is at least as reprehensible as the crime the prisoner may have committed. Like Hogarth, Goya frequently used his artistic talent to protest the conditions of prison life.

After the return of King Ferdinand, Goya, old, deaf, and ailing, left for France, where he remained for the rest of his life. His death in Bordeaux, in 1828, brought to an end one of the most enduring chapters in the history of the art of social conscience. His career demonstrated that passionate social advocacy was far from incompatible with the highest requirements of artistic excellence. That principle would be demonstrated once again by another important socially conscious artist of the 19th century, Honoré Daumier.

Daumier and the Political Vision

The life and career of Honoré Daumier (1808–79) coincided with an amazingly turbulent period of European history. During his artistic prominence, Daumier lived through or witnessed the revolutions of 1830 and 1848, the ascension of Louis Napoleon, the Crimean and Franco-Prussian wars, and the

Paris Commune. These and other events supplied him with a wealth of subject matter, which he was to turn to satirical account.

Any discussion of the role of the politically engaged artist or socially conscious art would be sadly deficient without a substantive treatment of Daumier. Like Goya, he was an artist of immense range and versatility, and he produced during his career 4,000 lithographs, 1,000 woodcuts, several hundred paintings, and some remarkable sculptures. His subject matter was as diverse as his choice of medium: His topics ranged from the most savage and biting satire in the history of art to a wide spectrum of nonpolitical subjects. The satire includes specific commentary on actual political events and personalities and a more general view of French and Parisian life. The latter category includes his depiction of the foibles of the bourgeoisie, the squabbles between landlords and tenants, and his well-known treatment of the professions, most notably lawyers, whom he ridiculed so memorably. In his paintings and lithographs he passionately defended freedom of speech and the press, expressed a strong belief in the dignity of labor, and displayed a sympathetic consideration of the poor and lowly, which was unrivaled since the days of Rembrandt.

Daumier was a modest man whose artistic vision was timeless. Although, like Goya, he employed the events of his times as a point of departure for his art, his work has endured precisely because he concerned himself with universal human problems. His insightful treatment of war, middle-class fatuity, and political duplicity and oppression are as pertinent to contemporary life as they were to 19th-century France. His satirical treatment of the Parisian bourgeoisie sounds wider echoes of human frailty. For those reasons, he is a figure of major artistic recognition rather than merely a political cartoonist whose impact fades with the news of the day.

Daumier's lithographic output remains the primary source for his fame and importance as an artist of social conscience. These lithographs, which he produced with impressive regularity throughout his career, were the primary source of his income. His life was lived on the edges of poverty, and his massive artistic output was a matter of basic personal necessity. Unlike Goya, Daumier never achieved "success" as traditionally defined, and at the time of his death he was almost blind and nearly a pauper.

The July Revolution of 1830 is the most important historical point of departure in the social content of Daumier's art. That revolution was directed against the regime of Charles X, who had ascended the throne in 1824, a decade after the fall of Napoleon I. Charles was a personable and graceful reactionary whose policies inevitably served to mobilize his political opposition. His affection for the Church led him to restore to that institution vast controls over education. The effect of this policy was to strengthen the opposing forces of anticlericalism. The limited electoral processes then extant in France continually returned majorities against him, which he ignored with impunity. Finally, on July 26, 1830, he issued a series of extreme royalist decrees, and this became the catalyst for the revolutionary events that were to follow. Barricades went up

Art and Social Conscience: Goya and Daumier 23

1-11. Gargantua. Honoré Daumier. 1831. Lithograph. Bibliothèque Nationale, Paris.

24 The Art of Social Conscience

throughout the city of Paris. The small government forces were attacked by a coalition of students, workers, and middle-class republicans. Four days later, Charles X abdicated and fled into exile, bringing to an end the restored Bourbon monarchy. The revolution resulted in a victory for the more conservative interests in the rebellious coalition. The upper bourgeoisie prevailed, to the bitter disappointment of the radical and moderate republicans. The result was the assumption of power by the "citizen-king" Louis-Philippe, who seemed most tolerable to the diverse political factions which then divided the nation. Louis-Philippe, a good family man, of royal blood, was sympathetic to business and industrial interests, and he professed a number of liberal ideals. It was not long, however, before his true character emerged. He quickly became the symbol of materialist triumph, mediocrity, and still another monarchical form of government.

The reign of Louis-Philippe coincided with and facilitated the development of a new class of capitalists, economic speculators, and ruthless entrepreneurs. The identification of the citizen-king with that class was complete, and he assisted its members in helping themselves to the public and private wealth of France. The conditions of workers and peasants remained grim: Long hours, widespread unemployment, and terrible housing were the commonplace conditions for the lower classes of the nation.

1–12. *The Legislative Belly. Honoré Daumier. 1834. Lithograph. Metropolitan Museum of Art, New York.*

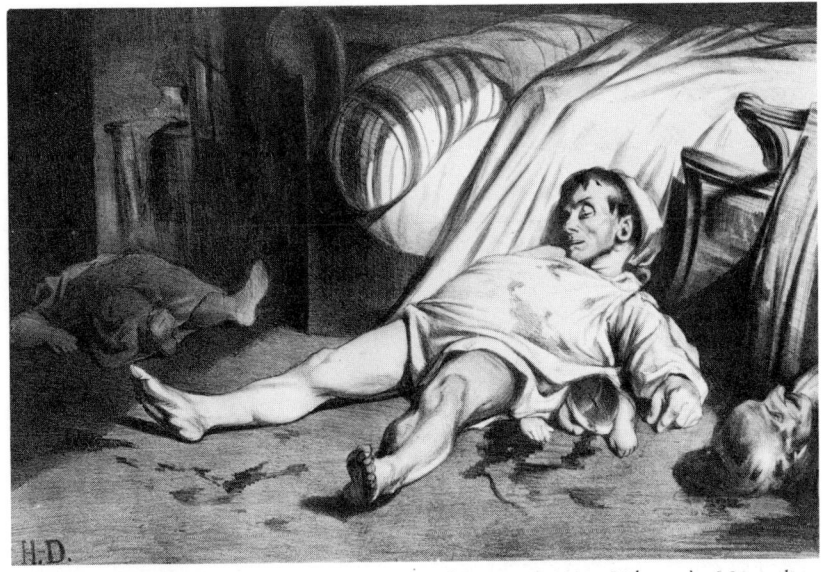

1-13. Rue Transonain, April 15, 1834. *Honoré Daumier. 1834. Lithograph. Metropolitan Museum of Art, New York.*

The new class was not without substantial political opposition, however. Republicans, social reformers of various ideologies, radicals, students, and other oppositional groups were horrified at the mercenary inclinations of Louis-Philippe and his supporters. Among the opponents was Charles Philipon, a publisher whose record of political dissent was to span several decades during the 19th century. His most famous employee was Honoré Daumier, who produced over 3,000 lithographs for Philipon's newspaper *Charivari*.

Daumier began with *La Caricature*, the first of Philipon's journals in 1831, when he was twenty-two years old. That year he created his *Gargantua (Fig. 1-11),* a biting and scatological satire of Louis-Philippe, which portrayed the king as the gluttonous hero of Rabelais's book. The head of the king looks much like the shape of a pear. This was hardly accidental, for that had become the symbolic weapon of artists opposed to the regime. As slang, the French word for pear, *poire,* means "blockhead" or "fathead." Daumier's insult, therefore, was certainly intentional.

This lithograph depicts the king as he exacts tribute from the poor of France. The tribute money is conveyed up a ramp to the ravenous mouth of Louis-Philippe. Most dramatically, he sits on a toilet instead of a throne, and the people's money is subsequently excreted in the form of rewards for his faithful sycophants. These people, whom Daumier obviously loathed, emerge from the stock-exchange building in the background, eager for the king's excremental spoils.

The picture blatantly attacks the government of the citizen-king. Not un-

26 The Art of Social Conscience

1-14. You Are Free to Speak. Honoré Daumier. 1835. Lithograph. Bequest of William P. Babcock, Museum of Fine Arts, Boston.

expectedly, some critics have been offended by the gross vulgarity of Daumier's assault. Doubtless the work is in poor taste insofar as it departs from the ordinary strictures of satirical decorum. There are times, however, when such grossness is strikingly appropriate. It must be recalled that the government of Louis-Philippe was characterized by greed and corruption. A few cronies of the king profited at the expense of thousands of people who were forced to endure oppressive poverty.

The creation of *Gargantua* caused criminal charges to be brought against Daumier. He was charged with fomenting disrespect for the government and was sentenced to six months in prison. Fortunately, prison life was comparatively easy, and Daumier managed to avoid the harsher treatment that generally characterized penal servitude.

Upon his release, Daumier continued his artistic agitation. In 1834 he executed the lithograph *The Legislative Belly (Fig. 1-12)*, which combines a specific topical subject with a more universal theme. At that time, the French Assembly was full of men who were far more concerned with their own pecuniary rewards than with the welfare of the country. Daumier found these members of the assembly to be especially suited for artistic condemnation. The result is a work of political art in which the greed and personal slovenliness of the subjects merge to produce a sense of more than justifiable disgust in the minds of the audience.

By 1834 massive tensions clouded French political life. The oppositional press had been plagued by continuing censorship, judicial harassment, and its own

Art and Social Conscience: Goya and Daumier 27

1-15. He Defends Orphans and Widows. *Honoré Daumier. 1846. Lithograph. Private collection.*

28   The Art of Social Conscience

financial precariousness. Daumier was much concerned with the threat to free expression. As usual, responding with artistic fury, he produced a famous lithograph whose specific object was to warn the king not to meddle with the press. Subsequent events would indicate that Louis-Philippe was not about to listen.

The year 1834 was politically important for other reasons. Legislation was enacted that prohibited associations of even small groups. Its primary objects were workers who were engaged in labor organizational activity in Lyons. The influence of the manufacturers in obtaining such legislation was obvious, for the government of Louis-Philippe was perpetually interested in the preservation of the economic interests of the developing capitalist class. As a result of this law, workers in Lyons, fearful of the possible arrest of their leaders, took to the streets. A few days later, a massive insurrection occurred.

Paris joined the rebellion, but there it was quickly and brutally suppressed. During the fighting the police were fired upon by snipers in a working-class district of the city. In retaliation, they entered the building at number 12, Rue Transonain, where snipers were thought to be hiding. The authorities proceeded to slaughter the occupants of the house, including men, women, and children. This vicious act impelled Daumier to create a magnificent lithograph in indignant response.

Rue Transonain, April 15, 1834 (Fig. 1–13) indicts not only the particular instance of violence and brutality, but any and all senseless and gratuitous political murder. The vision of the dead body, the central figure, evokes memories of Goya's *Third of May, 1808* (Fig. 1–8). Daumier further adds dramatic poignancy to the picture by portraying corpses of a small child and an elderly man.

Many of the insurrectionist leaders were arrested and imprisoned. The government accelerated its assault against the labor movement, while Daumier continued his artistic offensive. A year after the massacre at Rue Transonain, the government rounded up "subversives" throughout France and conducted a mass trial against them. The defendants were not permitted counsel of their own choosing and were forced to use advocates appointed by the Tribunal. It was evident that the defendants' guilt was predetermined and that the judicial process was only meant to formalize that result. Daumier responded in characteristic fashion. In the lithograph *You Are Free to Speak* (Fig. 1–14), the artist lambastes the fraudulent character of political "justice." The judge's smirk combines with the bound and gagged defendant to reveal the deceit of these legal proceedings. The ironic title further underscores the loathsome character of the trial, while the impending execution in the center of the picture may represent a sardonic view of the government as a whole. This lithograph, too, is part of Daumier's continuing attack on legal institutions, which reached its fullest expression several years later in the famous series *The Gentlemen of Justice*.

In July 1835, there was an attempt on the life of the king. The government promptly used this as a convenient pretext to enact harsh laws directed against the oppositional press. This constituted a severe blow to the republican cause and

1–16. You've Lost Your Case, It's True. *Honoré Daumier. Lithograph. Private collection.*

30 The Art of Social Conscience

changed the character and direction of Daumier's artistic career. Since overt political commentary, particularly that directed against the king, became exceedingly dangerous, Daumier was compelled to direct his satirical art at more general subjects.

His works of the next dozen years constitute a phenomenal contribution to the art of social conscience. Their range was immense. He caricatured virtually every aspect of bourgeois life in Paris. While no major profession escaped his merciless scrutiny, he pursued lawyers with a special venom. Among the thousands of lithographs executed during his career are numerous works that

1–17. The Republic. Honoré Daumier. Oil on canvas. The Louvre, Paris.

pertain directly to lawyers, judges, and courts. These superbly executed and powerful works of art have become especially popular in law offices throughout the world.

It seems especially ironic that Daumier has achieved such a monumental popularity among lawyers, since his graphic treatment of lawyers and judges was savage. Convinced that the quest for justice was not the primary objective of lawyers and courts, he viewed most lawyers as cynical and callous charlatans whose motivations were transparently pecuniary. He repeatedly portrayed the chicanery, hypocrisy, and amorality of the lawyers and the roguery and corruption of the judges.

Both Daumier and his father had been involved in extensive litigation because of their chronic inability of pay their debts, and Daumier himself had been a defendant in a criminal action arising out of the difficulties with *Gargantua*. In each case Daumier observed the law from the vantage point of its victims—a recurring characteristic and attitude of socially conscious art.

One of Daumier's primary objections to lawyers involved their tendency to abuse their verbal talents. In a lithograph from *Gentlemen of Justice (Fig. 1-15)*, he portrays a lawyer who defends orphans and widows one day and attacks them the next. Utterly cynical, the lawyer represents the worst of the legal profession as he substitutes cleverness for fairness. The viewer can only conclude that the lawyer, perhaps within the week, may with equally contrived passion present an opposite and contradictory argument to the same court.

You've Lost Your Case, It's True (Fig. 1-16) is a forceful presentation of a scene that the artist himself observed on numerous occasions. The lawyer has just lost his case, but as he and his client and her child leave the courthouse, he piously deflects attention from the loss of the suit by suggesting the magnificence of his performance. Obviously, he is impervious to the agony and despair of his client. Compassion and concern are entirely absent, and the lawyer's attitude only compounds her pathos and bewilderment.

The year 1848 was a period of crisis throughout Europe. Precipitated by financial and agricultural difficulties, demands for reform intensified. The barricades in Paris were manned by a loose coalition of students, workers, and middle-class liberals with republican sympathies. Louis-Philippe was forced to abdicate, but this time the rebels would not accept another monarch. Despite the creation of a republic, many severe problems continued to exist, and some political groups wanted to consolidate the gains of the Revolution while others pressed for more radical social transformation.

There were, however, substantial gains. The strict laws against free expression were repealed, and again a wide range of journalistic freedoms became possible. At the same time, some measures were taken to remedy the problems of unemployment and unhealthy and hazardous working conditions. Universal suffrage for adult males was established. To encourage the development of the arts, the new provisional assembly sponsored a national competition for a work of art to serve as a symbol for the new order. Daumier, at the urging of friends, entered a sketch that eventually culminated in the painting *The Republic* (Fig. 1-17), an important work of social conscience as well as a significant contribution to art history. The central figure is a sturdy female seated majestically on her throne with the tricolor in her right hand. Two children lean forward to nourish themselves at her breasts. A third child sits at her feet with a book, a symbol of the free expression of ideas in a republican form of government. This is a painting of hope, idealistic in conception and eternally inspiring.

Unfortunately for France, and for Daumier personally, the brief period of freedom did not endure. Political divisions intensified and the national assembly was dominated by a conservative coalition of monarchists, Bonapartists, clerical forces, and others. In the years 1849–51 Daumier executed a series of satirical lithographs entitled *The Face of the Assembly*, in which he portrayed the foolishness, pomposity, and stupidity of its members.

Elected president in December 1848, Louis-Napoleon gathered power and political strength and prepared to consolidate his authority. Alarmed at these developments, Daumier mounted an artistic attack against the emergence of Napoleonism. Creating a sculptural and lithographical figure, "Ratapoil," to signify the impending order, Daumier used this character to warn his audience of what was to come. But his efforts were unsuccessful. In 1851 Louis-Napoleon seized power, and his coup d'etat was validated by the electorate. Censorship was resumed and Daumier fell back on more general social satire and commentary. Unable to use his art to express his dislike of the new emperor, Daumier in the next few years returned to themes he had treated during the repressive days of Louis-Philippe. While many of the works of this period are fine contributions to socially conscious art, few achieved the force of previous series such as *The Gentlemen of Justice*.

Daumier's separation in 1860 from the staff of *Charivari*, itself the subject of some controversy and interest, gave impetus to his serious painting. Relieved of the pressures of having to produce so many lithographs, Daumier created paintings, which are remarkable examples of the theme of social conscience as well as major contributions to 19th-century art. Perhaps his most famous painting of the period is *The Third-Class Carriage* (Fig. 1-1), in which he moves from trenchant social criticism to a sympathetic portrait of working-class people. The central figures, of various age groups, show patience in the face of uncomfortable, class-discriminatory travel. Executed with quiet force, the work is really a general affirmation of working-class life, and the image evokes memories of Rembrandt in the underlying compassion of the artist for the tired and weary.

In 1864 Daumier returned to *Charivari* because he needed the income he could obtain from regular lithographic production. Deeply worried that war was imminent, he repeatedly issued artistic warnings in the form of cartoons showing peace balancing precariously on bayonets and depicting the increased expenditure of funds for armaments, diplomatic machinations devised solely for purposes of expediency, and related topics pertaining to the general political crises. Too topical to be as enduring as other aspects of his artistic production, many of these works are, however, extremely effective in illuminating the tension of the era.

War broke out between France and Prussia in the summer of 1870, and six weeks later, Louis-Napoleon was resoundingly defeated. The French suffered thousands of casualties, and the aftermath of the war caused massive starvation throughout the capital city of Paris, where citizens held off Prussian troops for several months. Embittered, Daumier recalled that a decade earlier Louis-Napoleon had proclaimed that peace would be an enduring feature of the Second Empire.

The Commune, which followed shortly after the fall of Paris, included, among others, moderate and radical republicans, democratic socialists, and members of the more radical First International. Daumier was personally involved in the Committee of Arts of the Commune, but little of his own work involved a direct artistic response to the Commune itself. The conservative interests that dominated the new government in nearby Versailles overwhelmed the Commune, and government troops executed thousands of Parisians. For the first time in his long career, Daumier's artistic indignation was lacking; perhaps it had been overwhelmed by the terrifying bloodbath that occurred.

As Daumier grew older, his eyesight failed and he retired to the countryside, where he died in 1879. Without the passionate social commentary of an artist who never wavered in his desire for a humane social order and the dignity of human life, the world would be a poorer place indeed.

2-1. Man and Woman. *Edvard Munch. Woodcut. Oslo Kommunes Kunstsamlinger, Munch-Museet, Oslo.*

2 Expressionism and Social Content: Rouault and Munch

The horizons of socially conscious art have been deliberately broadened in this survey to the widest but most reasonable limits. The artistic content of the work of Georges Rouault and Edvard Munch adds two new dimensions to the modern expression of this theme. Unlike Goya or Daumier, Rouault and Munch are not specifically political artists. Munch, in fact, is largely a painter and graphic artist of the sad and tragic features of the individual caught in an alien social world and of the concomitant psychological significance of that entrapment. Rouault, on the other hand, predicates his social commentary on a deeply religious foundation, thus establishing a unique iconography. Both men, however, are easily identifiable as artists of considerable social significance, and there are compelling reasons to group their work together in one chapter.

Georges Rouault (1871–1958) and Edvard Munch (1863–1944) were contemporaries, but each reacted differently to the tenor of social and personal life. Remaining outside any formal group of aesthetics, each evolved his individual style within the broad category of Expressionism. Both rejected the narrow range of academic painting, and while they experimented with form, it was rather "expression" that they sought. The obsessive focus of their lives and careers was the marginal existence of man. Each was inner-directed: Rouault by his religious faith and piety and Munch by his melancholia. The depth of their different but complementary perceptions helped to make Expressionist style a powerful vehicle for social commentary.

Expressionism became a main current in early 20th-century art, and its influence can be seen in literature as well as in the visual arts. Although the movement began as a reaction to Impressionism, the main thrust of it was given impetus by the social upheaval and spiritual unrest in Europe. Expressionism sought to convey the artist's inner passions and feelings. Careful attention to precise visual realities was subjugated to the more important "expressive" qualities of mood or obsession. Expressionism involved both a new attitude and a new artistic methodology. It sought to transcend what it perceived to be a 19th-century scientific world view, which encouraged an objective perception of everything, including the arts. In order to dramatically reveal the innermost sentiments of the artist, distortion and exaggeration were employed. Among the techniques used to accomplish this objective are fierce and vigorous color, exaggerated outlines, crude texture, and simplicity of drawing. Such devices were used to convey a strong emotional impact. For Rouault, Expressionist techniques heightened the incredible moral anguish he felt, and for Munch they evoked his pervasive despair and heightened the emotional quality of his work. Expressionism is broad enough to include scores of prominent artists, including figures such as Käthe Kollwitz and the Mexican muralists José Clemente Orozco and David Alfaro Siqueiros. The paramount feature of Expressionism was a consistent subjectivity that encouraged a new, virtually unlimited freedom. For both Rouault and Munch, the subjective emphasis assumes a critical importance.

Although predicated on vastly different premises, the artistic content of the deeply religious Rouault is similar to some of the work of Goya and Daumier, notably in its sympathy for social outcasts. Georges Rouault was born in Paris in May 1871, during the bombardment of the Paris Commune by troops of the Versailles government. As a youth, he led a poverty-stricken existence. He left school at an early age and became apprenticed to a stained-glass maker, a factor that would eventually influence his stylistic development as an artist. As a young man, he also encountered the work of Daumier, and it is reasonable to assume that he was also a significant influence.

More importantly, Rouault's childhood was dominated by the Catholicism of his family, and his basic perspective remained devoutly Christian throughout his life and career. For Rouault, this was a much more important factor than the specific political events that occurred during his lifetime. The socially conscious dimension of his work is usually general in scope. It deals with the eternal problems of human suffering and social inadequacy. By way of contrast, both

Goya and Daumier used specific events as a point of departure for artistic commentary whose implications assume more universal proportions.

The Christian perspective of Rouault led him to identify with the poor and oppressed. He abhorred the sins of man, but his religious feelings prevented him from hating man himself. Rather, he pitied man and hoped for his spiritual redemption. As a Christian, he believed deficiencies of social life and political injustice could only be remedied through religious salvation rather than political organization and activity. This is essentially the view that personal moral change is the ultimate foundation for more humane social relationships, an attitude that has received increasing public acceptance in major intellectual sectors during the 20th century, although many theoretical objections have been raised to it.

The artist's fervent Catholicism led him, furthermore, to use his creative talents to proselytize for his faith. His art was consciously rhetorical. He hoped that the viewer's reaction to his paintings and graphic work would engender so powerful a feeling of Christ that it would lead to conversion. Rouault was also cognizant that reason was directly inimical to religious intensity. He detested rationalism and science. Here it is important to recall that his views ran counter to the prevailing belief in scientific rationalism among the intelligentsia at the beginning of the 20th century. The foundation for Rouault's art, therefore, is dramatically opposite to Goya's, for whom Enlightenment philosophy was inseparable from the character of his work.

Intense religious conviction frequently results in a fundamental retreat from worldly concerns, and while Rouault had a sympathetic regard for this stance, he never disengaged himself from the secular realities of human life. He retained a basic relationship with social reality in his work, while many of his contemporaries were involved in abstract problems of line and color or were producing work of predominantly ornamental value.

Rouault's thematic depictions included social corruption, the horrors of poverty and human degradation, the abusive power of legal institutions and the insanity of war, and the human suffering each produces. Many of these topics found powerful expression in the early years of the 20th century. One of the major devices Rouault employed in order to confront society with its failings was his use of clowns as an ironic symbol of human sorrow. A clown, of course, represents happiness and gaiety in the common consciousness. In showing the clown in an unmistakable aura of suffering, however, Rouault exposes the gap between the pleasant external image and the melancholy internal reality.

An impressive early example is *The Tragic Clown (Fig. 2-2)*, executed in 1903. The expressionist lack of detail adds immeasurably to the intensity of sadness that pervades the painting. The work stimulates the viewer to consider the broader implications of Rouault's message. All too frequently, what is wrong with society is not apparent on the surface. Instead, it is sometimes carefully hidden by a commonplace facade that conceals the defects and problems. To compound the problem, people rarely pierce this veil, for unpleasant truth is profoundly disturbing to the personal security that is so dominant a human

2-2. The Tragic Clown. Georges Rouault. Private collection.

aspiration. Still, Rouault's painting is not overt and reform-oriented social criticism in the manner of Daumier. It is rather a lament for the ills of the world, an exercise in the pity that characterized the artist's religious ideology.

An even more powerful example visually, *The Clown (Fig. 2–3),* appears several years later. The facial expression symbolizes the tribulations of life in general by revealing the sorrow that characterizes so much of life. Indeed, the picture is a moving comment on the human condition as it passionately mourns the unhappy lives of the majority of mankind. One need hardly agree with the artist's religious objectives in order to sympathize with his compassionate involvement.

The early period of Rouault's artistic career was similarly distinguished by his depiction of prostitutes. There are numerous examples in both his painting and graphic art. Without exception, all are haunting and memorable commentaries on the basic structure and underlying values of society. These paintings constitute a damning criticism of the socioeconomic conditions that force these women to eke out such a marginal existence. Forced for the most part by circumstances beyond their control, prostitutes are continually degraded and their lives are fraught with tragedy and intermittent violence. A poignant example is *Four Prostitutes (Fig. 2–4),* in which years of squalid brothel life are abundantly evident. Remnants of corrosive bitterness are especially apparent in the facial expression of the woman at the left. The painting, moreover, reveals

38 The Art of Social Conscience

2-3. The Clown. *Georges Rouault. Stedelijk Museum, Amsterdam.*

2-4. Four Prostitutes. Georges Rouault. Private collection.

the humiliation of women forced to exist as sexual commodities. Rouault's pity emerges clearly in this portrait, and the condemnation inherent in the work is directed not at the female subjects but at the society that has produced the unsavory conditions of their plight.

The same themes of degradation, debased sexuality, and socially induced personal despair are reiterated in several other paintings during the years shortly after the turn of the century. Another element of Rouault's work, equally inspired by his active social conscience, appears in the years 1911–12. Some of his art reveals a movement from personal sorrow to topics traditionally viewed as more social in character. The underlying religious philosophy, of course, remains.

40   The Art of Social Conscience

Refugees (Fig. 2–5) is a good example of the work of this period. The influence of Daumier's humanism is apparent here as Rouault depicts a scene that has been a tragic constant in the history of mankind. Whenever there is war, civil turmoil, or other catastrophic political events, the ordinary people bear the brunt of the cost and suffering. Far too frequently political activists and analysts alike neglect the human consequences. That factor, however, is the central focus of Rouault. His painting reminds us unfailingly that the true subjects of adverse social actions are human beings. This humane emphasis is a refreshing antidote to the chilling tendency to forget that politics is a process inseparable from its human consequences.

In 1912 Rouault addressed the ubiquitous problem of poverty in a painting known variously as *Slum, Poor Quarter,* and *Homes of the Wretched (Fig. 2–6).* The substance, however, is far more important than its formal designation. The reaction against Impressionism is obvious as the artist represents the burdens of the poor and disinherited. The faceless inhabitants of the Parisian slum could be people anywhere who are trapped by economic insecurity. The wretched quarters in which they endure loom over them in a way that suggests even further entrapment. The buildings form a veritable prison wall, which serves to underscore the hopelessness of their situation. While the painting is not in itself a plea for social and economic reform, it is impossible to avoid the accusation inherent in its content.

2–5. Refugees. *Georges Rouault. 1911. Distemper on cardboard. Kunsthaus, Zurich.*

2-6. Homes of the Wretched. *Georges Rouault. Private collection.*

42 The Art of Social Conscience

Similarities to Daumier are evident in other major examples of Rouault's work. As a young man, Rouault closely observed court sessions and the sometimes sordid atmosphere of judicial proceedings. Like Daumier, he believed that lawyers were frequently unscrupulous and judges frequently corrupt. The result was a series of works over the years that constitute a powerful critique of legal institutions and personnel. These paintings usually protray judges as insensitive oppressors who are representatives of a degenerate bourgeois society. An early significant example of this perspective is *The Condemned Man (Fig. 2-7)*. The smug expression of the judge—significantly the central figure—contrasts pointedly with the condemned prisoner, who is consigned to his fate with a flippancy that negates even an elementary respect for justice. The artist expresses his indignation as he confronts his audience with the universal nature of his indictment. At the same time, however, it is well to recall Rouault's proposed alternative: When men judge men, only injustice can occur; therefore, only God shall judge.

The greatest socially conscious art produced by Rouault is his graphic series *Miserere et Guerre*. The fifty-eight etchings are a modern classic of humanitarian concern and are powerful social commentary. The works are a religious counterpart to Callot's *Miseries of War* and Goya's *Disasters of War*. Most of the plates were executed during the 1920s, but they were not published until 1948. Rouault's efforts to create the series were remarkable. Constantly dissatisfied, he reworked some of the plates as many as fifteen times.

In the manner of his distinguished predecessors, Rouault created works of art that contain messages of everlasting importance. The first part, *Miserere,* is a

2-7. The Condemned Man. *Georges Rouault.*

2–8. It Is Hard to Live. (Miserere et Guerre.) Georges Rouault. 1922. Etching, aquatint, drypoint, and roulette over heliogravure. Collection, The Museum of Modern Art, New York. Gift of the artist.

comprehensive treatment of human suffering. Rather than a substantive reaction to specific topical events, it is a more general view of man's fate. That fate is linked inseparably with that of Christ, and the pity and faith that dominate Rouault's work reach new levels of expression in *Miserere*. The second part of the series is devoted to war. It is infused with eloquent feelings of intense pain, yet the Christian view of suffering is apparent. Like the similar work of Callot and Goya, *Guerre* is replete with scenes of horror, and the impact engenders a gloomy view of man's capacity to alter this recurring feature of his social and political experience.

Typical of the central tone of *Miserere* is the plate entitled *It Is Hard to Live* (Fig. 2–8). Rouault uses the Expressionist idiom effectively in communicating his

44 The Art of Social Conscience

2–9. The Society Lady Fancies She Has a Reserved Seat in Heaven. *Georges Rouault. 1922. Aquatint, drypoint, and roulette over heliogravure. Collection, The Museum of Modern Art, New York. Gift of the artist.*

Expressionism and Social Content: Rouault and Munch   45

pessimistic view of human existence. Like most of Rouault's work, however, the message is far more than a mere analytic statement adduced from years of observation. It is a powerfully emotional reaction as well, an expression of the most severe anguish experienced by the artist throughout his own life. The work fuses emotional engagement and intellectual acuity in a synthesis of remarkable artistic achievement.

Rouault also attempted a satirical tone in *Miserere*. The best example is a denunciation of bourgeois society, for which the artist had a continuing enmity. *The Society Lady Fancies She Has a Reserved Seat in Heaven (Fig. 2–9)* is a rare instance of artistic ridicule in Rouault's art. The exposure of the woman's arrogance reveals the artist's belief that the fortuity of one's social and economic position

2–10. This Will Be the Last Time, Little Father. *(Miserere et Guerre.)* Georges Rouault. 1927. Aquatint, drypoint, and roulette over heliogravure. Collection, The Museum of Modern Art, New York. Gift of the artist.

2-11. Arising from the Dead. (*Miserere et Guerre.*) *Georges Rouault. Aquatint and roulette over heliogravure. Collection, The Museum of Modern Art, New York. Abby Aldrich Rockefeller Purchase Fund.*

affords no special status in the Kingdom of God. The portrayal of the "society lady" inevitably invites comparison with his far more sympathetic treatment of the degraded prostitutes.

The most famous single plate of *Guerre* is *This Will Be the Last Time, Little Father* (Fig. 2-10), where Rouault's bitter denunciation of war depicts the terrible human consequences with a force reminiscent of Goya. The reality of the father's grief as he bids farewell to his son, who is about to depart for his inexorable fate, vividly displays the senselessness of war. The triumphant grin of Death pervades the picture and intimates to the observer that this will *not* be the last time. The prophetic irony of the artist is depressingly substantiated by subsequent events in the 20th century: World War II, Korea, Vietnam, and other conflicts only add to the poignancy of this engraving.

Another and equally bitter example in this series is *Arising from the Dead (Fig. 2-11).* The sardonic use of the battle cry of French soldiers at Verdun as the title underscores the reality of armed conflict. The message of the picture is all too evident as it articulates a timeless message about human irrationality.

Rouault's most savage accusation against man appeared in the twilight of his career. The major Expressionist techniques combined to create a masterpiece of social commentary. *Man Is Wolf to Man (Fig. 2-12)* is one of the most disconcerting paintings in modern art. Completed in 1944, the simple composition, with its lack of precise detail and powerful use of symbolic color, invites an unassailable comparison of human conduct with that of animal predators. The burning houses in the background exhibit the recurring effects of human savagery. The blood-red sun hovers over the scene as if to remind men of their perpetual propensities toward violence. The dark, foreboding sky warns of things to come unless people seize the opportunity to change the errors of their ways. The hanging man is the final comment on the current condition of man. It is clear that Rouault meant to permit no possible misinterpretation of his message: He inscribed at the bottom of the painting in bold letters the Latin version of the title of the work, *Homo Homini Lupus.*

Rouault died in 1958. It is unquestionably reasonable to view him as a major contributor to the art of social conscience. His passionate commitment to the moral uplifting of mankind must strike a responsive chord in anyone who professes a belief in humanitarian ideals. Similarly, the insightful nature of his social criticism can only add positively to the consciousness of the viewers of his work.

There are troubling features, however, in some of the premises that underlie his work. Rouault's theme of pity for suffering humanity may have consequences that are inimical to some of the objectives of social criticism. Pity can be viewed as a passive response to the intolerable conditions produced by oppressive social, political, and economic institutions and it frequently discourages an active, energetic response to such institutions. Instead, pity implies an attitude that what is presently tragic will remain so. Social life may indeed remain abominable, but Rouault's apparent passivity here seems unduly defeatist. His belief, moreover, that spiritual redemption is the ultimate hope of mankind fortifies this attitude. Rouault's art often fails to recognize that social life is complex and that love alone will not solve its problems. On balance, however, the moral fervor of this humble Christian artist should be viewed with sympathy.

Edvard Munch, the most distinguished Scandinavian artist, was another pioneering figure in modern art. His Expressionist style imparted an intensity of content rarely found in the visual arts. Although that content is ultimately social

48 The Art of Social Conscience

2-12. Man Is Wolf to Man. (*Miserere et Guerre.*) Georges Rouault. 1927. Aquatint, drypoint, and heliogravure. Musée National d'Art Moderne, Paris.

in character, it is nevertheless a substantial departure from the themes developed by such artists as Brueghel, Hogarth, Goya, Daumier, and Rouault.

Born in Norway in 1863, Munch was a lonely and deeply troubled man. His early life was characterized by great misfortune, and the atmosphere of his entire life seemed only to amplify this misfortune. There was constant illness and death in Munch's family. These factors inevitably affected the development of the themes that would dominate his work. Those themes are intricately related to the difficulties and fears of his personal life: death, illness, loneliness, panic, despair, and the stormy relationships between the sexes. The same subjects were explored by August Strindberg and Henrik Ibsen in the literature of the period and related to the Christian existentialism of Kierkegaard and the development of psychoanalytic theory by Freud. The work of Munch, therefore, is a significant component of this general intellectual ferment.

It is important to stress the significance of Munch's personal life and his recurring moods of melancholy. This aspect is as crucial to Munch's art as other factors were to the artists previously examined: the political circumstances of 18th- and early 19th-century Spain and Goya's high regard for the values of the French Enlightenment; the specific events of 19th-century France and Daumier's republican sympathies; and the deeply religious orientation of Georges Rouault.

Although Munch lived to be eighty years old, the tragedy of death and sickness persisted throughout his life. His mother and sister died of tuberculosis while the artist was a young boy, and Munch himself was frequently sick. The accumulated contact with these tragedies weighed heavily on Munch, and he would later remark that nothing but illness and death characterized his family life and that his family must have been born to it. His art, often moody and macabre, does much to reveal the deeper meanings of death.

The prolific Munch constantly returned to the subject of death in his work. With the possible exception of Käthe Kollwitz, no modern artist has treated the topic so poignantly. One of the notable examples is the lithograph *The Death Chamber* (Fig. 2-13), executed in 1896. The work is a pictorial study of the sociology of dying and the tormented ambiance is presented with chilling accuracy. The mourners await silently the impending death of their relative as they realize, all too well, how helpless they are to postpone the inevitable. What emerges is a

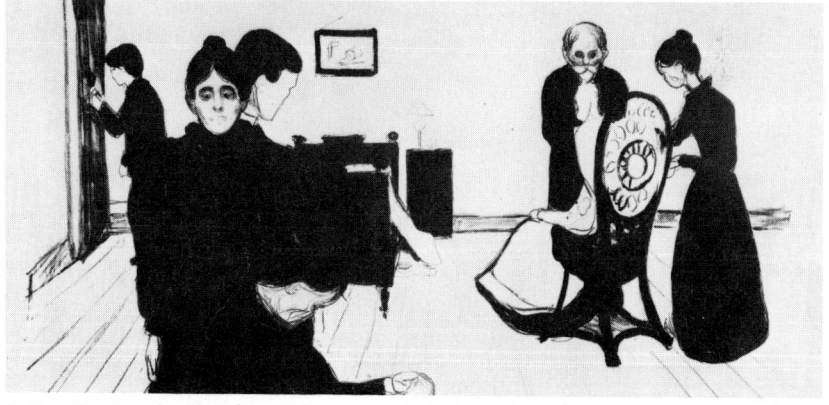

2-13. The Death Chamber. *Edvard Munch. Lithograph. Oslo Kommunes Kunstsamlinger, Munch-Museet, Oslo.*

50 The Art of Social Conscience

picture of despair, dramatically emphasized by the young boy at the extreme left, who is so overwhelmed by the situation that he seeks a discreet exit.

That Munch is able to capture the personal realities of a deathbed scene in such gripping terms is obvious. Such realities, however, should be understood in a broader social context. Munch's lithograph encourages the viewer to pursue for himself the implications of its content. Individuals do not exist in a vacuum, and their responses to the grim occurrences of life, however personally tragic, affect

2-14. The Dead Mother and the Child. *Edvard Munch. Oil on canvas. Kunsthalle Bremen, Bremen.*

both their individual outlook and their relationships with other people and with social institutions.

Munch similarly confronts death in a painting done a few years later. *The Dead Mother and the Child (Fig. 2-14)* is one of the most emotionally haunting works of art of the past hundred years. The horror of the mother's death is reflected in the child, who covers her ears in shocked disbelief. The viewer can only share the child's agony and empathize with her desire to turn her back on such a frightening event. That Munch confronts his audience with this reaction suggests that no one can view death without irrationality. It is as terrifying to the adult as to the child. Once again, there are broader implications to the content of Munch's work. Death can, and frequently does, lead to massive personal delusion, as it did with the artist himself. This in turn affects the nature of society, for there is constant interaction between the ability of individuals to cope with life either with reason or with delusion.

Much has been made of Munch's preoccupation with death and his inability to cope with it throughout his life. Those factors make it doubtful that he sought to use his art to encourage a mature attitude toward death. Nevertheless, an objective perception of *The Death Chamber* and *The Dead Mother and the Child,* apart from Munch's personal obsessions, can generate a stronger attitude toward the subject. Such an attitude would at once accept the inevitability of death and shift one's focus on living a more active and vigorous life.

The relationship between the sexes is another area in which private realities must be understood within their broader social setting. That theme, too, occupied the artist repeatedly throughout his career. His own relationships with women were short-lived and his ambivalence toward women is reflected in his work. However, his paintings transcend his personal anxiety and are objective comments on the painful nature of sexual relationships.

An expressive example of this ambivalence can be seen in the woodcut *Man and Woman (Fig. 2-1),* executed in 1899. The scene conveys the fragility of the relationship, and with consistent emotional force, the artist portrays a situation that is repeated daily thousands of times throughout the world. A man and a woman, obviously intimately involved, are undergoing the pain and aggravation that so often accompany human relationships. The man holds his head in his hands in obvious despair, possibly as a result of rejection by his lover. Munch exposes the anguish of both parties in a vision that is stark and unromantic. It reminds the viewer that human affairs are precarious at best and that an idealized view of those affairs most likely will be shortsighted and potentially painful.

Munch was cognizant of the destructive forces that often lie beneath the surface of male-female relationships, and several works offer impressive insights into those forces. Jealousy, for example, is universal in human emotion. Frequently, it is a major source of tension in personal affairs and is sometimes responsible for the termination of relationships. Munch expressed the powerful impact of jealousy in a painting of that name in 1895 *(Fig. 2-15).* The nude body of the woman represents the wildest fantasies of the man at the right. He is

52 The Art of Social Conscience

2–15. Jealousy. Edvard Munch. 1895. Oil on canvas. Rasmus Meyer's Collection, Bergen, Norway.

obsessed with the possible betrayal of his lover. Quiet rage, bewilderment, and despair are reflected in his expression. He becomes the victim of his own hallucination. Munch captures the unconscious of the man in conflict with his own irrationality.

Unsavory attitudes toward sex also exacerbate the difficulties between men and women. Munch underscores this factor in the lithograph entitled *Lust* (Fig. 2–16). This common situation is portrayed with obvious repugnance by the artist.

2–16. Lust. Edvard Munch. Oslo Kommunes Kunstsamlinger, Munch-Museet, Oslo.

Expressionism and Social Content: Rouault and Munch

The picture is a study of debased sexuality as the three men leer vulgarly at the prone female figure. The implication of Munch's portrayal is clear: The men's lust serves only to deny the humanity of the woman. Even more importantly, lust inhibits the emergence of a mature attitude, which must underlie a fulfilling personal relationship. The critical content of this work, therefore, points at least theoretically to a healthier and superior form of human conduct.

2-17. The Scream. *Edvard Munch. 1893. Mixed media on paper. Nasjonalgalleriet, Oslo.*

54 The Art of Social Conscience

Like Rouault, Munch was deeply concerned about the suffering and anguish of mankind. In his most famous painting, he depicted the ultimate in human agony: *The Scream (Fig. 2–17)* is a view of unmitigated terror. The most expressionistic of his paintings, it is a visual counterpart to the theme of the precariousness of existence treated throughout 20th-century existentialism. The victim, with skull-like face, holds his hands to his head as his body convulses in unfathomable fear. Approaching on the bridge are two gaunt and ominous figures reminiscent of the brutal minions of the law in Kafka's novel *The Trial*. Waves of grief reverberate around the subject, and the observer can only speculate about the specific source of his anguish. Whether it is applicable to this instance or not, the effects of alienation and social isolation can lead to the qualitative kind of psychic pain depicted by Munch in *The Scream*.

No more powerful example of that suffocating alienation is evident than in *Spring Evening on Karl Johan Street (Fig. 2–18)*. Truly, this painting reveals a parade of the living dead on the main boulevard of Oslo. The ghoulish scene is no mere imaginative fantasy. Millions of people live lives, in Thoreau's term, of quiet desperation. Munch captures this aura well in a pessimistic vision of human existence. Personal life is inseparably connected to the social context of life. Where the preconditions of rewarding personal life are socially absent or unavailable, there is accordingly a higher probability of the acute personal anguish as in *The Scream*. Taken together, the content of both works reveals a powerful indictment of the social order.

2–18. Spring Evening on Karl Johan Street. *Edvard Munch. 1892. Oil on canvas. Rasmus Meyer's Collection, Bergen, Norway*

Expressionism and Social Content: Rouault and Munch

2-19. Thanks to Society. *Edvard Munch. Lithograph. Oslo Kommunes Kunstsamlinger, Munch-Museet, Oslo.*

A minor but nevertheless significant strain of Munch's work involves a satirical thrust that is similar to many of the efforts in the mainstream of the art of social conscience. Always aware of the hypocrisy and decadence that sometimes characterized middle-class life, Munch occasionally turned to caricature to express his views. His objects were the rich, the art critics, and the facade of bourgeois respectability. A typical example is an 1899 lithograph entitled *Thanks to Society* (Fig. 2-19), in which he satirizes the various members of the upper social classes. The carping chatter of the participants reveals the vacuousness of their lives. Sharply critical of their insensitivity toward others, Munch is far from subtle in communicating his own displeasure. Perhaps significantly, a police officer stands by as if to protect their meaningless but socially pernicious conduct.

Later in his career, Munch began to portray workers from a sympathetic perspective, similar in some respects to some of the work of Daumier. He believed that workers were constantly exploited, and he even expressed the view that the workers' movement would be the wave of the future. There are numerous examples of this subject in the artist's work, and a typical portrayal is found in a painting of 1915 entitled *Workers Returning Home* (Fig. 2-20). Here the forward surge of the workmen indicates both the sympathies of the artist and the broader political consequences that will shortly ensue.

56 The Art of Social Conscience

2–20. Workers Returning Home. Edvard Munch. Oslo Kommunes Kunstsamlinger, Munch-Museet, Oslo.

An overview of Munch's work indicates a gloomy sense of the human condition. The most valuable feature of that work, insofar as it relates to the vision of socially conscious art, is its sustained capacity to provide cogent insights into matters of basic human importance. The critical dimension of his work simultaneously engages the intellect and the emotions. It can stimulate his audience to consider carefully the intimate themes he depicted so powerfully. Ironically, one of the most fruitful consequences of Munch's art lies in its power to suggest the personal solutions that eluded the artist himself throughout his life.

3–1. Memorial to Karl Liebknecht. *Käthe Kollwitz. 1919. Woodcut. Philadelphia Museum of Art. Given anonymously.*

3 The Pivotal Role of German Social Art: Kollwitz, Grosz, and Heartfield

Germany has produced some of the greatest and most enduring social and political commentary in 20th-century art. The first half of the century in Germany was a period of monumental political conflict, social turbulence, and military horror, and consequently a period of extraordinary artistic ferment. While the work of the German Expressionists and the art of the Bauhaus were the major part of that ferment, many other artists combined excellent artistic quality with moving, powerful, and savage commentary.

Two of these artists, Käthe Kollwitz (1867–1945) and George Grosz (1893–1958), are indispensable to any survey of socially conscious art. Major figures in modern art, they are, like Goya and Daumier, colossal representatives of the art of social conscience. Several other artists advanced this critical vision, including John Heartfield (1891–1968), who was responsible for the creation of an impressive body of socially significant art fused with the development of a new and major artistic technique.

Once again, the work of these artists must be examined against the background of the political, social, and cultural history of their era, in this case the tragic but fascinating period of the Weimar Republic. This short interval between the end of World War I and the rise of Hitler was a time of frenzied political and cultural activity. Both the war and the Nazi period are relevant, however, because the content of some of these artists pertains directly to those events.

The career of Käthe Kollwitz spans almost a half-century. A graphic artist of the highest quality, she is also one of the finest woman artists of all time. She was born in 1867 and lived through World War I, the Weimar Republic, and most of the Nazi era. Her entire life was dedicated to a profoundly compassionate concern for humanity. Her personal commitment was inseparable from her work, and her background is especially significant for a deeper comprehension of the socially conscious art she would produce during her career. Her family situation was conducive to the class-conscious and politically left-wing nature of that art. Her grandfather was a minister who founded his own religious sect, a 19th-century German counterpart to American Quakerism or Unitarianism. Her father also held radical views and infused the family life with an abiding sense of social responsibility. The young artist herself was an avid reader who was early influenced by a complex of socially progressive ideas. Artistically, her contact with the engravings of Hogarth was influential in her choice of the print as a medium and in the critical character of its content.

In 1891 she married Dr. Karl Kollwitz, a physician who maintained a medical clinic in Berlin for workers and their families, who paid a modest weekly sum. Naturally a doctor who practiced this kind of medicine was not about to become a wealthy man, but this was the life they chose, and they remained in Berlin for half a century. Meanwhile, Kollwitz developed her artistic talent, beginning with etchings and drawings and experimenting with various styles and subjects. Her early career was especially notable for her self-portraits, which would be a recurring theme in her work throughout her life.

Kollwitz's first major exercise in socially conscious art was undertaken in the late 1890s. A few years earlier, she had attended a performance of *The Weavers* by Gerhart Hauptmann. The play concerned an abortive strike in 1844 by the Silesian weavers, whose desperate economic plight was emphasized by the author. Kollwitz decided to create her own graphic version of the event.

The revolt of the weavers in the 1840s was a part of the Industrial Revolution and its consequences, which were felt throughout the Continent. Silesia was then the most economically distressed region in Germany. Poverty was rampant, wages for weavers were low, and the situation was ripe for insurrection. On June 3, 1844, a group of workers gathered outside the house of one of the mill owners. One demonstrator was arrested, and rioting erupted the next day. The property of one of the owners was destroyed and the demonstrators marched to neighboring towns to engage in similar agitation. Troops were called and the incident resulted in the death of eleven workers. About a hundred workers were arrested and most were sentenced to terms of imprisonment.

Kollwitz executed *The Weavers*, a series of six etchings relating to the incident. She chronicled the progressive stages of the story in the manner of

60 The Art of Social Conscience

Hogarth's famous series, such as *The Rake's Progress* and *Marriage à la Mode*. The series is characterized by an obvious partisan sympathy, but a more universal human empathy emerges. The plight of the workers was powerfully portrayed and the classic clash of labor versus capital was highlighted.

The first plate in the series, *Poverty (Fig. 3–2),* depicts the desperate plight of the weavers with stunning force. The wretched economic conditions of the Silesian weavers are transformed from an abstract and remote historical event to a vivid, concrete reality. The artist hauntingly conveys the impact of poverty in human terms. The distraught expressions on the faces of the victims show that their poverty consumes their lives. Kollwitz captures the horrifying personal despair not only of the 19th-century weavers, but of everyone caught in the vice of economic insecurity. The fullest appreciation of poverty's horror, like the horror of war, can occur only with personal experience. This work by Käthe Kollwitz, however, provides a remarkable vicarious counterpart.

When this series was shown in the Berlin Art Exhibition of 1899, it caused a sensation. The series was awarded the gold medal, but it was later canceled by

3–2. Poverty. *Käthe Kollwitz. 1897. Lithograph. Philadelphia Museum of Art. Given by Lessing J. Rosenwald.*

3-3. Outbreak. *Käthe Kollwitz. 1903. Etching. From "The Peasant War." Library of Congress, Washington, D.C.*

the Kaiser, who, in his capacity as critic of the arts, regarded the work as "gutter art." Decades later, the Nazis would similarly "honor" Kollwitz by including her work in the broad category of "degenerate art."

Kollwitz followed *The Weavers* with a similar theme. *The Peasant War* series, based on early 16th-century revolts by oppressed peasants, portrayed another major category of the downtrodden—the peasantry. Her objective was to show sympathy and solidarity for the classes of people who were crushed in their struggles to achieve a better life.

A good example from *The Peasant War* is the plate entitled *Outbreak* (Fig. 3-3), in which Kollwitz portrays the violence that characterized the events of the period. The central figure is a charismatic woman who incites her fellow peasants to armed conflict. The forward surge of the mob underscores their resolve to achieve liberation from their oppression. This passionate portrayal of the angry peasant woman discloses without question the partisan sympathies of the artist. The series as a whole is a modern classic of class-conscious art.

A few years after the completion of *The Peasant War*, Europe became embroiled in the conflict that would erupt in world war. The shooting at Sarajevo and its grisly aftermath intimately affected both the life and the art of Käthe Kollwitz. Few people escaped personal contact with the war, and it had a

3–4. *Killed in Action. Käthe Kollwitz. 1921. Lithograph. Philadelphia Museum of Art. The Print Club Permanent Collection.*

powerful effect on many artists whose perspective and work would be permanently altered in forthcoming years. The war also brought tragedy to the Kollwitz family. Her eighteen-year-old son had enlisted in the army and was killed in action only a few weeks later. His death left her with a passionate hatred of war for the remainder of her life. Her aversion to war also emerged in the content of her art and left the world with examples of antiwar art that were magnificent in conception and execution.

As with other memorable artistic endeavors in the past, the artist refused to treat war in the abstract. Real people suffer real pain, and Kollwitz destroys the facade of the patriotic fervor that causes so much grief. A striking example is the lithograph *Killed in Action* (Fig. 3–4). Inspired by her own tragic loss, the work shows the panic and grief of a mother and her children as they learn of the death of their husband and father. The mother clasps her hands to her head in overwhelming despair. Her children cling to her, not yet comprehending the fate that has befallen them.

The Pivotal Role of German Social Art 63

Kollwitz also turned to the poster as a medium through which she could express her commitment to pacifism. In *Never Again War (Fig. 3-5)*, she employed Expressionist techniques to convey the depth of her feelings. The poster combines absence of detail and vigorous strokes in its depiction of a figure who dynamically condemns the brutality of war. The power of the work is underscored by the addition of the verbal message. More than a transitory piece of political propaganda, the poster achieves the level of durable art through its expression of a sensible human aspiration.

3-5. Never Again War. *Käthe Kollwitz. 1924. Lithograph. Photo Galerie St. Etienne, New York.*

64 The Art of Social Conscience

The defeat of the Germans in World War I set the stage for the creation of the Weimar Republic, an era that is crucially relevant as background to a major body of Kollwitz's socially significant art. The period also serves as the focal point for the work of George Grosz, whose artistic treatment of Germany's problems is different from but thoroughly complementary to that of Kollwitz. Taken together, in fact, their art is extremely valuable as a historical source for that vital period of German history.

In 1919 Germany was compelled to sign the Treaty of Versailles, which dictated the conditions of peace. Severe economic, political, and psychological burdens were imposed on an exhausted Germany. Territory was distributed to other nations, the army was reduced, and substantial reparations payments were ordered. The proclamation of the Republic made Germany, in theory, a democratic European republic. Theory and practice diverged markedly, however, for the long tradition of authoritarian and antidemocratic rule caused substantial opposition to this new political experiment. Many were aghast at the prospect of democratic government, while others, including influential segments of the intellectual community, were lukewarm and unenthusiastic.

3-6. Germany's Children Are Hungry. *Käthe Kollwitz. 1924. Lithograph. Rosenwald Collection, National Gallery of Art, Washington, D.C.*

3-7. Old Man with Rope. *Käthe Kollwitz. Woodcut. Rosenwald Collection, National Gallery of Art, Washington, D.C.*

3-8. Solidarity: The Propeller Song. *Käthe Kollwitz. 1931-32. Lithograph. Reproduced from Prints and Drawings of Käthe Kollwitz, selected and introduced by Carl Zigrosser (New York: Dover Publications, 1969).*

The Weimar period was characterized by extraordinary internal political turmoil and confusion. Political extremists of all ideologies abounded, while the left frequently fought among itself with more ferocity than it struggled against the right. Political assassinations and violent street disorders became an everyday reality. The discriminatory treatment of political prisoners by the judiciary only added to the political crisis. Sentences meted out to leftists were generally more severe than those to rightists. Hitler, for example, served less than a year in prison after his abortive attempt to assume power in the Munich *putsch*.

The divisions on the left were bitter. The moderate socialists were opposed by more radical socialists known as Spartacists. The schism was intense and bloody fighting was commonplace. Thousands of persons were armed and prepared to kill their opponents. After a rebellion in Berlin in January 1919, the leaders of the Spartacists, Rosa Luxemburg and Karl Liebknecht, were arrested, imprisoned, and murdered shortly thereafter. In response, Kollwitz executed a woodcut entitled *Memorial to Karl Liebknecht (Fig. 3-1),* which is a moving visualization of bitterness and mourning. The Expressionist technique lends intensity to the emotion of the workers as they stand before the funeral bier. While Kollwitz was not specifically a political follower of the Spartacists, this woodcut clearly reveals the general direction of her political sympathies.

Economic miseries compounded the political turmoil of the Weimar Republic. In April 1923, a major economic crisis occurred. Inflation reached fantastic levels as people literally used wheelbarrows to transport their worthless paper currency in exchange for the minimum necessities of life. A devastating depression ensued and brought with it food riots, starvation, and financial speculation

The Pivotal Role of German Social Art   67

wherein a few people grew rich while millions lost their life savings. As usual, Kollwitz was sensitive to the plight of the populace. She observed the misery in powerfully personal terms, among her husband's patients and elsewhere, and she transformed the sufferings into works of empathetic art, executing several works that reflected the mood of the period. Her works, unfortunately, are not exaggerations.

A poignant example is a lithograph completed in 1924 entitled *Germany's Children are Hungry* (Fig. 3-6). Kollwitz reduces social events to the more basic human realities, which are presented with a compassion possibly unrivaled in the history of art. The helpless expressions on the children's faces reveal again how the innocent suffer in times of economic depression. The eyes especially convey the pathos of the situation. *Old Man with Rope* (Fig. 3-7) completes the sad picture. The old man, his left hand unsteadily gripping the chair with fear, has resolved to terminate the misery of his existence. The darkness of the print emphasizes his hopeless condition. This, perhaps, is the ultimate human implication of hunger, unemployment, and economic insecurity.

In 1932, at the end of the Weimar Republic, Kollwitz created the large lithograph *Solidarity: The Propeller Song* (Fig. 3-8), which expressed her support for the people of the Soviet Union. It is important to recall that the Soviet Union at

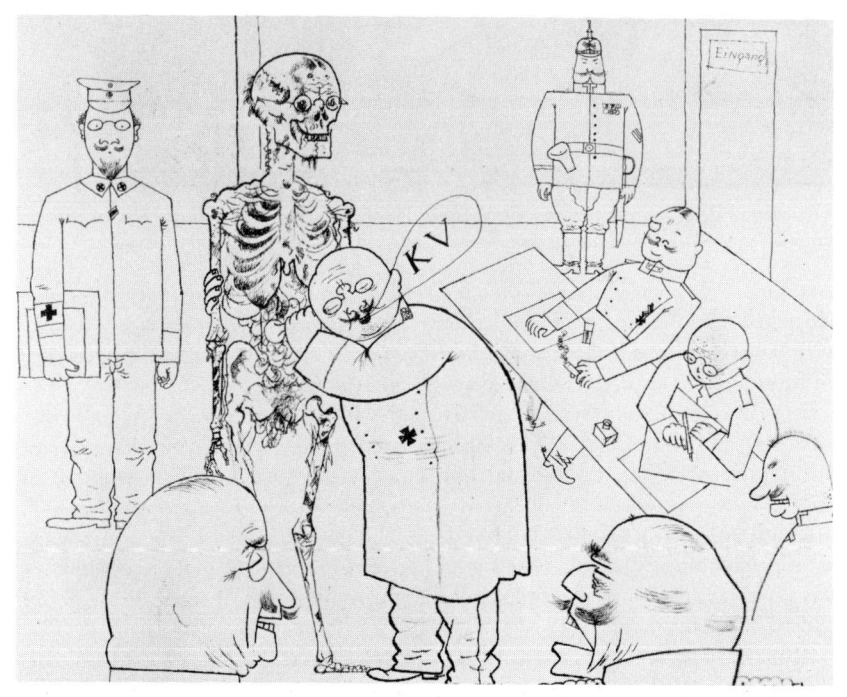

3-9. Fit for Active Service. *George Grosz. 1916-17. Pen and brush and India ink. Collection, The Museum of Modern Art, New York. A. Conger Goodyear Fund.*

3-10. Republican Automations. George Grosz. 1920. Watercolor. Collection, The Museum of Modern Art, New York. Advisory Committee Fund.

that time still represented the ideal of socialism, to which many progressive artists, literary figures, and intellectuals throughout the Western world looked with favor and hope. *Solidarity* was done as a poster and it expressed a determined position against an imperialistic war against the USSR.

In 1933 one of the darkest periods in the history of man cast its pall over Germany and the world. After Hitler seized power, the entire character of cultural, artistic, and intellectual life was transformed into an instrument of Nazi policy. As works of an artist of the left, Kollwitz's art was banned, although personally she was not harassed. She was offered a home in America, but she stayed in Germany, an exile in her own country. Among her last work was a powerful group of graphics on death, reminiscent of some of the art of Edvard Munch.

Kollwitz died in Germany in 1945, but her legacy was to inspire many socially conscious artists, including some of the major figures of the contemporary era. More important, her art remains a moving reminder of the human dimensions of history.

The Pivotal Role of German Social Art   69

George Grosz, born in 1893, chronicled the Weimar period with savage fury, and his work ranks with that of the greatest satirists. Grosz turned to art as a young man, experimenting with various styles and subjects as he roamed amid the seamy and exciting nightlife of prewar Berlin. It was not, however, until World War I that his familiar style and content emerged.

His experiences as a soldier were embittering and disillusioning. He found himself caught within a vacuous and dehumanizing military organization. Although he received a medical discharge from the army, he was redrafted in 1917 and eventually ended up in a military asylum before his discharge. These experiences provided abundant source material for the satirical work he produced during this time, most of which involved an attack on the military institutions and personnel he had come to hate.

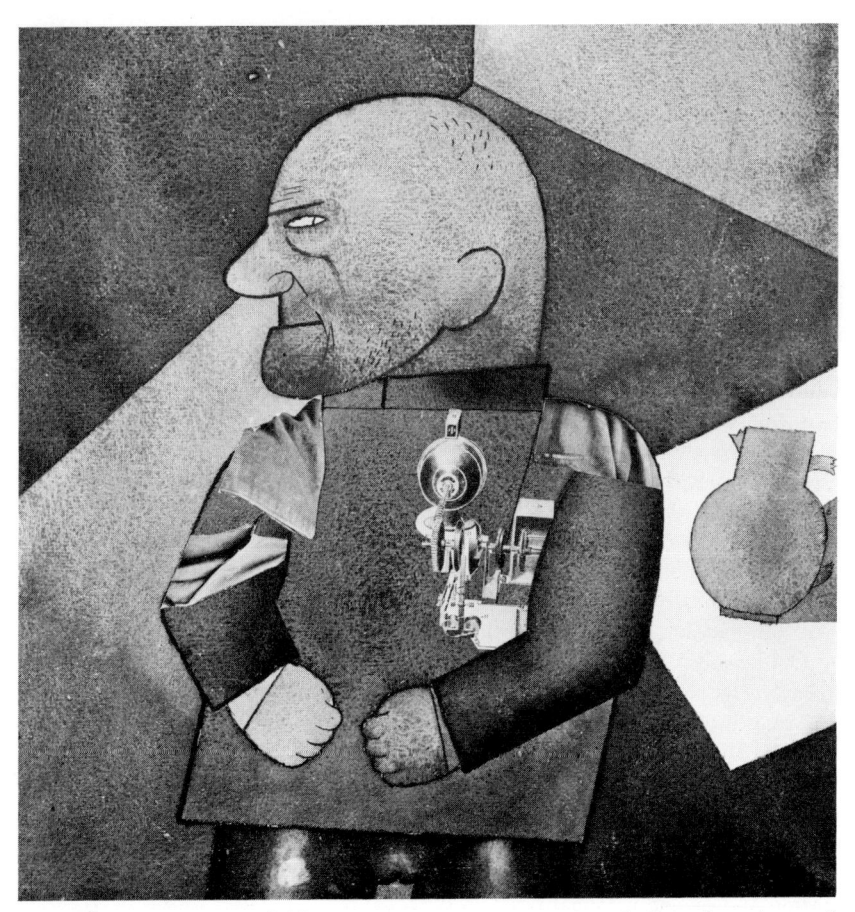

3-11. The Engineer Heartfield. George Grosz. 1920. Watercolor and collage of pasted postcard and halftone. Collection, The Museum of Modern Art, New York. Gift of A. Conger Goodyear.

70 The Art of Social Conscience

A fine example can be found in his famous drawing *Fit for Active Service (Fig. 3-9)*, possibly the most acerbic commentary ever on the idiocy of military life and practice. A veritable skeleton, clothed in remnants of rotting flesh, has been pronounced medically fit, as arrogant Prussian officers look on smugly. Even more sardonically, Grosz portrays the enlisted men who assist in this process as vacuous minions who will obey any orders for any purpose at any time. The work is applicable not only to the military mentality but to bureaucratic ineptitude everywhere.

Grosz later joined in the chaotic life of postwar Berlin. He became a member of the Dadaist movement, which, in Germany, had a politically left-wing orientation in contrast to other less political strains of the movement throughout Europe. Grosz himself became a revolutionary. He engaged in substantial agitation, worked on behalf of the Spartacists, and became sympathetic to Communism, although he never formally joined the Party. During this period he painted vicious satires on the German bourgeoisie in the immediate aftermath of World War I. A marvelous example, *Republican Automatons (Fig. 3-10)*, offers a powerful critique of his fellow Germans. The most prominent feature of the painting is the blankness on the faces of the two figures. The absence of intelligence which that implies, however, does not prevent them from parading automatically to the polls. Flag in hand, the man in the center has been programmed to be patriotic. He would support the government anywhere, and the German banner he holds is a token only of the fortuity of his present locale. This work goes beyond political satire by commenting more generally on the robotlike tendencies of human nature.

Grosz carries his vision a step further in *The Engineer Heartfield (Fig. 3-11)*, which provides a view of a sinister engineer whose heart is as mechanical as the patterns of his thought. Engrossed in his own schemes, the viewer can only speculate on the horrors he is concocting. The facial expression, so typical of Grosz's satirical portraits of the period, reveals the artist's revulsion at the inhumanity of the people who, just a few years later, would rise to the pinnacle of political power. The engineer, whose only "contact" with the external world is the newspaper, which serves as his surrogate window, is the supreme example of the technically competent barbarian whose influence in the industrial life of the 20th century has been as pernicious as it has been dominant.

Unlike most of his colleagues on the left, Grosz was somewhat of a misanthrope. His pessimism contradicted any romantic illusions about the purity of the working class or about the perfectability of human nature. Essentially, he sought to use his art to express this pessimistic view. The cultural life of the Weimar Republic afforded him many opportunities to expose the soul of the bourgeoisie and, at the same time, to create enduring works of social conscience. The political turbulence and the shock of economic disaster followed by a miracle of economic recovery had a profound effect upon the cultural life of the nation and on the personality of its citizens. It is the latter aspect of Weimar society that became the focal point of Grosz's artistic brutality.

The Pivotal Role of German Social Art 71

Weimar Germany was an era of astonishing intellectual and artistic productivity, unparalleled in recent history. It was, at the same time, a period of unparalleled anti-intellectualism and antirationalism. Rarely has there been a society with so many internal contradictions. One of the most salient factors, both culturally and psychologically, was the urgent and massive personal subjectivity that prevailed, and which found expression in the art of the period. The aggressive use of color and primitive subject matter of so much of German Expressionist art reflected the underlying character of the cultural life. Expressionist plays, novels, and films, moreover, seemed to crave desperately for some sort of religious transformation. Thousands of people seemed to long for some nebulous cultural renewal that would end their isolation and spiritual malaise. This was accompanied by outbreaks of anti-Semitism, which often occurred at the major German universities. As Peter Gay so appropriately notes in his book *Weimar Culture*, "whatever most Germans hungered for, evidently it was not reason, whether in its conciliatory or its critical form."[*]

The society's rejection of rationality was accompanied by a resurgence of sectarian cultural movements with obvious religious overtones. Poetry became a matter of cult worship and it exercised a curious power over thousands of Germans. Mysticism also abounded as people sought after some kind of oceanic feeling. The occult became increasingly popular; astrology, numerology, and assorted superstitions enjoyed a renaissance in what was supposed to be the enlightened 20th century. In times of increasing social complexity and personal confusion, people often turn to simple and secure answers in order to escape confrontation with an uncomfortable reality. Germany in the 1920s was perhaps the textbook example.

Other related tendencies emerged that would ensure that George Grosz would never lack relevant subject matter for his vehement artistic denunciations. Sexual deviance increased and in some places became ostentatious. Incest, for example, was often proudly flaunted as the old controls of internal repression and sublimation began to deteriorate. Such activity, once considered shameful, became almost ideological in character as thousands sought to justify their aberrant behavior as socially beneficial and personally liberating. Boisterous drunkenness also became more evident, while attitudes of personal narcissism, at the expense of social obligation and political responsibility, dominated the epoch. The life of Weimar Germany was as fascinating as it was perverse. It is, accordingly, to George Grosz to whom one must turn for a remarkable pictorial presentation of the agony and upheaval of the times.

Grosz's art is not pleasant, it is obsessed with the sordid details of bourgeois moral decay. His topics include lust, greed, drunkenness, prostitution, incest, the pursuit of money, crime, and barbarism. Grosz forces his audience to confront the smug and greedy who cared only about their own pursuits and viewed with callous disdain the suffering of those around them. Grosz portrays the cheap cabarets in Berlin in order to reveal the hypocrisy of the era. At every level he

[*]Peter Gay, *Weimar Culture* (New York: Harper and Row, 1968), p. 45

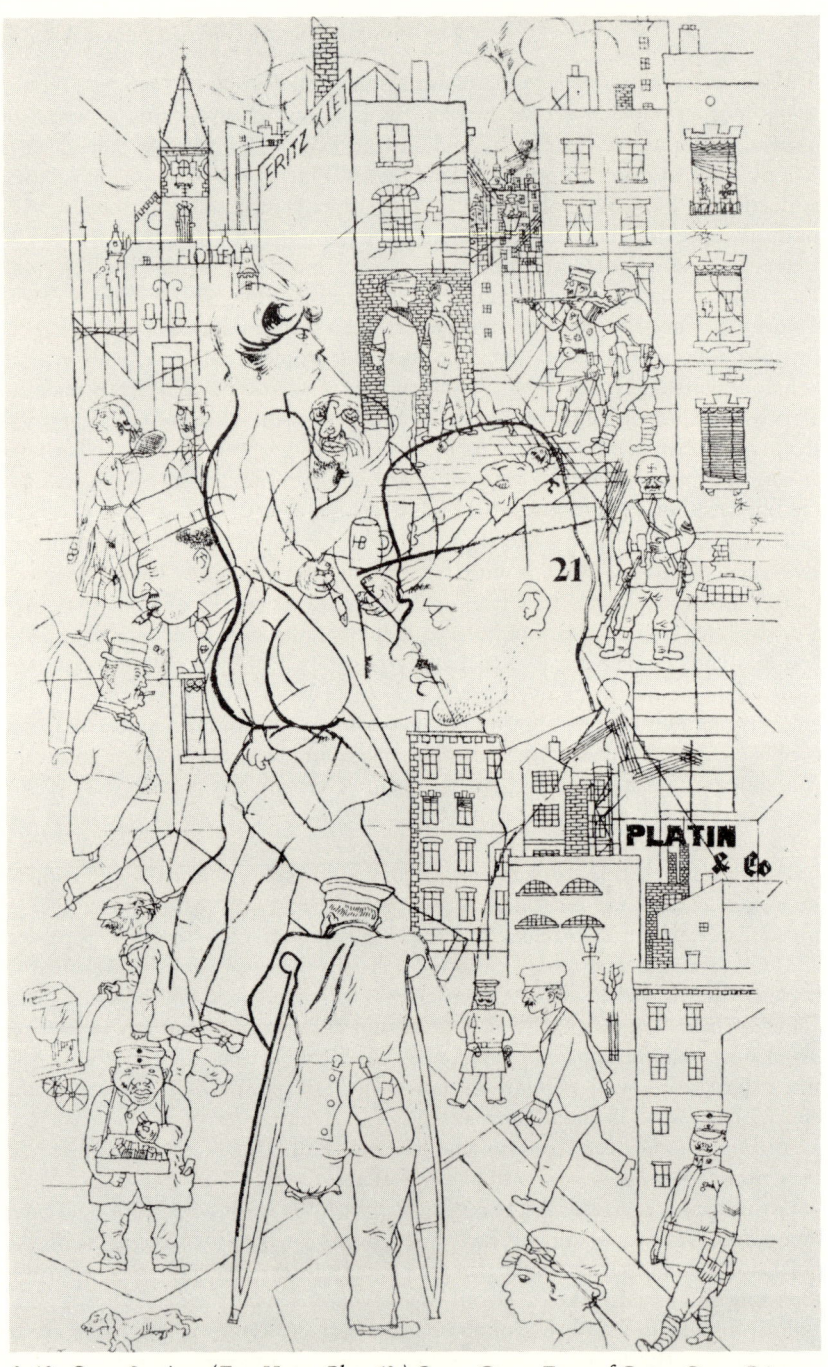

3-12. Cross Section. (*Ecce Homo: Plate 68.*) George Grosz. Estate of George Grosz, Princeton, N.J.

3-13. Beauty I Will Cherish You. (*Ecce Homo: Colorplate III.*) George Grosz. Estate of George Grosz, Princeton, N.J.

exposes the participants in activities that emphasize their essential ugliness. Over and over again, he strips people naked, literally, in order to strip away their veils of respectability.

Grosz is probably most famous for his series *Ecce Homo*. Because of this series, he was charged with the criminal offense of defaming public morals, for which he was required to pay a substantial fine. Most of the individual works are

74 The Art of Social Conscience

brutally self-evident and require little additional commentary. They are perhaps the most significant period pieces in the history of art, although their insights far transcend the Weimar Republic. Interestingly, Grosz's art became popular among the nouveau riche of German society during the late 1920s and early 1930s. His works were eagerly purchased by the very groups he so viciously condemned, thus once again revealing the curious dialectical irony wherein

3-14. Evening Party. (*Ecce Homo: Colorplate IX.*) George Grosz. Estate of George Grosz, Princeton, N.J.

The Pivotal Role of German Social Art 75

lawyers buy Daumier's critical legal lithographs, and Hauptmann's socialist drama found its greatest success in the bourgeois West End of Berlin.

The critical message of *Ecce Homo* emerges only after a confrontation with all of the works it contains. Nevertheless, individual works within the series pertain to major—if repulsive—features of Weimar life. The drawing *Cross Section (Fig. 3-12)* provides a broad overview of the confused and perverse atmosphere of

3-15. Spring Awakening. (*Ecce Homo*: Plate 26.) George Grosz. Estate of George Grosz, Princeton, N.J.

76 The Art of Social Conscience

3-16. Sex Murder on Ackerstrasse. (Ecce Homo: Plate 32.) George Grosz. Estate of George Grosz, Princeton, N.J.

postwar Berlin. Dated 1920, the picture is an uncanny composite of the realities that were so prevalent: crippled veterans of World War I, fat-headed capitalists on their way to further economic speculation, executions by firing squad, prostitution, paramilitary representatives in the streets—indeed, the whole collage of the chaotic life in Berlin at the time. The technique employed in this drawing—the overlaying of numerous scenes in the composition—lends itself perfectly to the presentation of the society he perceived.

Grosz's insightful vision of that society enabled him to move with ease from general to specific topics. Weimar society, and especially Berlin, was characterized by an active cabaret life in which the baser human propensities emerged without the ordinary protective facade. The watercolor *Beauty I Will Cherish You*

The Pivotal Role of German Social Art 77

(Fig. 3–13) is a caustic view of the dissolute nature of Berlin nightlife in the early 1920s. Grosz literally strips the woman naked in order to show her ugliness and that of the leering male bystanders. Alcohol and cheap sex dominate the scene as any pretensions to civilized life fade into obscurity. In a companion work, *Evening Party* (Fig. 3–14), the artist moves from a sordid cabaret to an eminently respectable restaurant. In this watercolor all the trappings of high bourgeois life are present. Everything is proper, from the deferential treatment of the restaurant personnel to the correct handling of the bottle of champagne. The thick, bullet-headed man and the nakedness of the woman, however, reveal the true situation. The patrons are as decadent as their counterparts in the cabaret. The only distinction is that in the latter work the participants have an added layer of hypocrisy. In piercing this hypocrisy with such obvious glee, Grosz also reveals the cultural preconditions for the eventual emergence of the era of Nazi barbarism.

Spring Awakening (Fig. 3–15) intensifies his ferocious social criticism. Here Grosz portrays what he perceived as a dominant feature of the "secret life" of

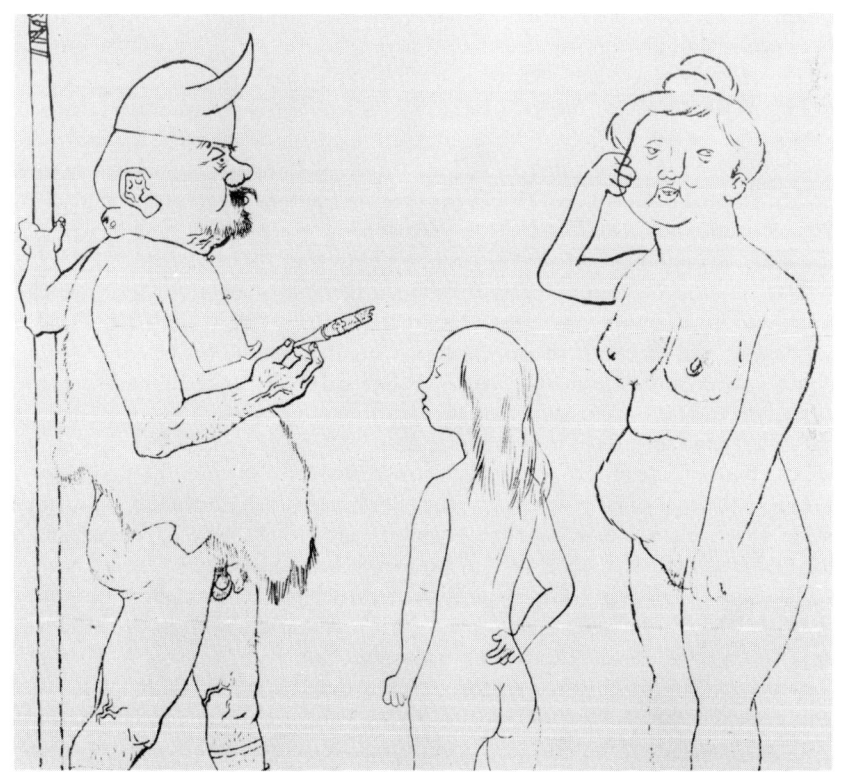

3–17. In Memory of Richard Wagner. (*Ecce Homo: Plate 60.*) George Grosz. Estate of George Grosz, Princeton, N.J.

Germany. The leering man is a study of debased sexuality, a critique of a culture that encourages perversion. The man's treatment of the girl as a mere sexual object represents a total negation of all that is valuable in human relationships. Grosz knew well that people fantasize the most unsavory activities. In Berlin during the Weimar period, however, fantasy was frequently transformed into reality.

Unfettered expression of instinctual desires often leads to the gruesome, as Grosz vividly depicts in *Sex Murder on Ackerstrasse (Fig. 3-16)*. Almost ghoulish in conception, the work conveys a sense of the savagery of a society that is incapable of redemption. This grotesque crime mirrors the violence that occurred in the streets of Berlin, dominating the brief life of the Weimar Republic.

The drawing *In Memory of Richard Wagner (Fig. 3-17)*, sums up the whole era. It is Grosz's ultimate commentary on the German character and the perpetual human propensity toward irrationality. The curious mixture of sex and mythological fantasy is indicative of the romanticism that dominated the era, and Grosz captures the perverse excesses of unchecked personal subjectivity. As much as any other single work in *Ecce Homo,* this drawing serves as a warning of things to come only a decade later, for the connection in Grosz's mind between seemingly innocuous personal perversion and a social order premised on principles of racial annihilation was all too apparent.

In 1932 Grosz left for America as the Nazi takeover became imminent. He was eager to leave behind the troubled times he observed so shrewdly. The work he produced in the United States lacked the force and satirical content of the work he had created in Germany in the face of such ubiquitously perverse stimulation. His innocuous nudes and landscapes were done in an effort to forget the past and concentrate on the task of adapting to the contours of American life. His horror of Nazism impelled him to return once again to socially conscious art, where he expressed his bitterness and hatred for what was occurring in Germany. He also worked on the theme of the madness of war. In those works he expressed an apocalyptic vision of human destruction. Beyond those concerns, however, the early fire and fury were gone, and most of the latter work of George Grosz is artistically and socially of lesser significance. Invariably, a negative political and social context is required as a stimulus for powerfully expressed artistic opposition. In the case of George Grosz, all the problems of American life and society could never begin to match the grotesque character of the society from which he had departed. In 1958, on a visit to his native land, he died.

The bitter personality of George Grosz was such that he undoubtedly enjoyed some of the perversity he portrayed in his art. His obsession with human degeneracy suggests an unusual personal fascination with the subject. To assess the man and his art on that basis, however, would be unjust. Of much greater importance is the consistent critical accuracy of his artistic vision. His personal bitterness notwithstanding, Grosz genuinely abhorred the irrational features of society and politics in Germany. At every level, the content of his art implies his desire for a more decent and civilized social order. The increased fury of his later

The Pivotal Role of German Social Art 79

German work indicates his pessimism regarding any serious chance of social transformation. That he would create some of the most bitterly satirical work in the history of art only underscores his abhorrence of the society he observed.

The work of John Heartfield is different from Grosz both in subject matter and technique. Born Helmut Herzfelde in 1891, he studied art in Munich, and in 1915 he decided to anglicize his name. Along with his brother (who would later write the definitive book about Heartfield's life and art), he became involved in

3-18. Goering, the Executioner. *John Heartfield. 1933. Photomontage. Reproduced from John Heartfield, by Wieland Herzfelde (Dresden: VEB Verlag der Kunst, 1964).*

3-19. The Reichsbishop Shapes Up the Church. *John Heartfield. Photomontage. Reproduced from John Heartfield, by Wieland Herzfelde (Dresden: VEB Verlag der Kunst, 1964).*

Communist activities in Germany. Like Grosz, both were deeply involved in the Dadaist movement in postwar Berlin. Heartfield eventually joined the Communist Party, and he maintained the affiliation for the rest of his life.

Both politically and artistically, Heartfield worked in close collaboration with Grosz, and it is probable that together they developed the technique of photomontage. That process involves the combination of a photograph and elements of drawing that produces a collagelike vision, and the technique lends itself particularly well to political commentary. The photographic component

The Pivotal Role of German Social Art   **81**

draws immediate attention to topical issues, while the flexibility of the composition enables the artist to express his personal response. After Hitler's rise to power, Heartfield had to leave Germany. At first, he went to Czechoslovakia. Later, when that land was swallowed by the Nazi machine, he fled to England. During the period of his exile, he created a collection of antifascist works based on the photomontage principle. The content of this work deals exclusively with the ugly and vicious conditions existing in his homeland. The political message is unambiguous; it is a brutal condemnation of Nazism. Although obviously propagandistic in scope, the power of the work transcends mere sectarian political opposition. Instead, it serves to illuminate and horrify the audience by exposing the viciousness of the Nazi regime.

Most of the works are entirely self-explanatory. Probably the most famous example of Heartfield's art is the photomontage *Goering, the Executioner* (Fig. 3-18). The burning Reichstag in the background is associated with the man who rose to a position at the highest echelon of Nazi leadership. The picture brutally portrays the Nazi mentality as the symbolic meat cleaver and the blood-laced

3-20. Through Light to Dark. *John Heartfield. Photomontage. Reproduced from John Heartfield, by Wieland Herzfelde (Dresden: VEB Verlag der Kunst, 1964).*

apron are featured in the center of the composition. There is no subtlety in the work, for there was nothing subtle about the character of Nazi terror.

Heartfield adds another dimension to this vision in *The Reichsbishop Shapes up the Church (Fig. 3-19)*. The artist moves from personal to institutional attack as he records an ugly historical fact. The way in which organized Christianity quickly assumed its "proper" place in the scheme of things in the Third Reich was scandalous. Not only does Heartfield use his art to reveal the general capacity of institutions to adapt to any political situation, but he also belies Christianity's often-repeated claim to humanism and opposition to persecution. The implications are devastating on a variety of levels.

The artist is unrelenting in his powerful pictorial response to the Nazi period. His reference to the infamous book burning episode is among the most effective of his works. The photomontage *Through Light to Dark (Fig. 3-20)* records Dr. Goebbels overseeing the destruction by fire of many of the major classics of Western literature and philosophy. The books in the picture tell the story with gruesome accuracy of how the masterpieces of thought were sacrificed in pursuit of monolithic control over the thoughts of men and women. Not only the works of Marx, Lenin, and Ehrenburg, but also *The Magic Mountain* by Thomas Mann and *The Good Soldier Schweik* by Jaroslav Hašek join other distinguished works on the literary funeral pyre. Heartfield's portrayal of this event was a dark portent of the logical outcome of this affair: Auschwitz, Dachau, and Buchenwald.

In 1950 Heartfield returned from England to take up residence on the Continent. He came back to Eastern Germany, which by then had become the German Democratic Republic. There he worked until his death in 1968. Although his political commitments encouraged a limited range of subject matter, he remains one of the finest antifascist artists of the 20th century.

4-1. Dove. Pablo Picasso. 1949. From the poster for the World Congress of Peace, Paris, 1949. Courtesy of the Daily World and permission of SPADEM 1975 by French Reproduction Rights, Inc.

4 Social Dimensions in the Art of Picasso

Pablo Picasso, who died in April 1973 at the age of ninety-one, is one of the giants of modern art. Responsible for many major stylistic innovations, Picasso was an extraordinarily prolific artist whose works span three quarters of a century. His scope was enormous, and both his work and his life have been a constant source of interest and critical consideration.

It would be both erroneous and misleading to identify Picasso as a social protest painter. In very basic ways, he is not the heir of Goya or Daumier or other artists whose work reflects a consummate ethical and political commitment. The vast majority of Picasso's works, fascinating and magnificent in their own right, have virtually no political or social significance. Despite his early anarchist leanings and his later and sometimes nominal membership in the French Communist Party, Picasso's reputation as an artist does not rest on the strength and character of his political life. This exciting, contradictory, creative man was only marginally a political creature. His turbulent personal life was characterized by a consistent self-indulgence that lasted throughout his career. It has, in fact, been reasonably alleged that his later left-wing political motivations were a consequence of his own narcissism. Although that is not the premise here, it is clear that Picasso was never a serious political thinker. In fact, his lifelong dealer, Daniel-Henry Kahnweiler, described the artist as the most apolitical man he had ever known.

84 The Art of Social Conscience

Having stated these severe restrictions and qualifications, it is important to note that the history of socially committed art would be seriously deficient without a fair treatment of a small but highly significant strain of Picasso's oeuvre. A modest but persistent undercurrent in his work, it reaches its apex in the monumental work *Guernica* (see Fig. 4–8), the greatest political painting of all time and in the view of many authorities, Picasso's single greatest painting. That effort alone would justify the inclusion of Pablo Picasso in a general survey of socially conscious art. At the same time, however, there are other works of art, although admittedly minor, that help to underscore that facet of Picasso's production.

Picasso was born in 1881 in Málaga, Spain. His father, a successful painter and art instructor, provided an early artistic environment for his son. Picasso's own talents became quickly apparent. The young prodigy received his earliest training in Barcelona, where many of his early works are now housed in the Picasso Museum. As a young man he experimented with many styles and embarked on important journeys to Paris to further his experiments. Most of his early life was spent in Barcelona, a city with a strong anarchist tradition until the days of the Spanish Civil War. The young Picasso was involved with people who professed a general left-wing and anarchistic perspective. Some of his earliest works, even before his twentieth birthday, had an anarchist orientation. A typical example is a drawing of an anarchist meeting, probably done in 1897 (*Fig. 4–2*). It captures at once the anarchist spirit in the city at the turn of the century

4-2. Drawing of an Anarchist Meeting. Pablo Picasso. c. 1897. Drawing. Courtesy of SPADEM 1975 by French Reproduction Rights, Inc.

4-3. The Frugal Repast. Pablo Picasso. 1904. Etching. Collection, The Museum of Modern Art, New York. Gift of Abby Aldrich Rockefeller.

and the artist's own early sympathy for this ferment. Although the primary interest of the work is historical, the militancy among the workers comes through with clarity.

Early in his career, Picasso became familiar with the work of several artists who would exert various influences on him. Perhaps most important, the works of Toulouse-Lautrec and Van Gogh served to engender a strong sympathy in Picasso for the poor and downtrodden of the world. Between 1901 and 1904 he executed a series of works that expressed that sympathy. One theme during that time involved the portrayal of beggars. In works such as *Beggar on a Crutch* and *Beggar's Meal,* Picasso is able to convey in dramatic human terms the tragedy of being poor.

An etching done in 1904, *The Frugal Repast (Fig. 4–3),* is an even more powerful

4-4. Woman Ironing. *Pablo Picasso. 1904. Oil on canvas. Solomon R. Guggenheim Museum, New York. Thannhauser Collection.*

expression of that general theme. Picasso reveals a genuine empathy as he portrays an emaciated couple looking forlornly at another slim and debilitating meal. In *Woman Ironing (Fig. 4-4)*, also done in 1904, Picasso expresses another facet of his sympathetic view of the world's lowly and poor. Like Daumier's *Washerwoman,* the artist reveals the wretched working conditions of a poor laboring woman. In this painting, the stoop of the woman indicates her never-ending exhaustion. She is a universal symbol of personal despair and unhappiness, for the viewer knows well that her lot has been predetermined.

During this part of his artistic career, Picasso expressed a highly generalized compassion for the downtrodden. In the manner of Rembrandt, Rouault, or Kollwitz, it is clearly a contribution to socially conscious art. For the next three decades, however, Picasso was involved in the pioneering stylistic innovations that were to make him the most renowned artist of modern times. His youthful anarchism and his compassion for the poor were subjugated to the development of his art. Perhaps his most significant creation was Cubism. Developed with his friend Georges Braque and practiced primarily by Braque, Picasso, and Juan Gris, Cubism changed the course of modern art in Europe and throughout the Western world.

Picasso's political sentiments, which had remained latent, were not to become manifest until the mid-1930s, when Spain became embroiled in a brutal civil war, a preview of World War II. It is essential to emphasize that Picasso, despite his long years of residence in France, was always a Spaniard. The soul of Spain evoked powerful passions in him until his death. The Spanish Civil War stimulated Picasso into a spirited and passionate defense of his land. That reaction was soon to be immortalized in *Guernica.*

It is absurd to view *Guernica* in a vacuum. It can be understood only in the context of the political history of the era and specifically in light of the civil war, which lasted from 1936 until 1939 and cost 600,000 or more lives. The Spanish Civil War was the opening battle of World War II, the first major military confrontation with the emerging specter of fascism in Europe. Since 1931 Spain had been, for one of the few times in its history, a democratic nation. In 1936 the parties of the left won a narrow electoral victory. The coalition included socialists, anarchists, and Communists. These parties grouped together under the designation of the Popular Front. There were, of course, vast differences between the parties on the left, and these differences would emerge, sometimes with fury, during the civil war itself.

The Spanish Republic, thus, had a democratically elected left-wing government. Several disgruntled right-wing generals, however, began almost immediately to plot the overthrow of that government. Their intention had been to stage a quick coup d'etat, but this did not occur. Instead, the nation was plunged into three years of bloody civil war. For several months prior to the actual outbreak of armed hostilities, there were various conspiracies and attempts to effect ad hoc coalitions directed either against or in defense of the Spanish Republic.

The civil war broke out in earnest in July 1936. Under the leadership of General Francisco Franco, and supported by Generals Mola, Varela, and Queipo de Llano, the Nationalist insurgents began their march on Madrid. These were the famous four columns and, as Franco boasted, the "fifth column" contained the Spanish fascists and their supporters in Madrid and in other territory held by the Republic.

Political divisions became quickly apparent. The fascist character of the nationalist rebellion led to military and political support from Nazi Germany and fascist Italy. The Soviet Union aided the Loyalist government. The major world democracies were responsible for a calculated indifference toward the conflict in Spain. Without undue oversimplification, Franco's rebellion stood for the darkness that had characterized the life of Spain for centuries: clericalism, military dictatorship, and a rejection of modernity and rationalism. For all its internal conflicts and occasional political cynicism, the Republic nevertheless sought to extend liberty throughout the nation, and for that and other reasons the Spanish anarchists were among its strongest supporters.

A related historical development involved the sense of outrage throughout the intellectual communities of the world. It is difficult to convey the depth of the importance of the Spanish Civil War to many artists, intellectuals, and others in America and Western Europe. For thousands of people the war raised the issue of fascism versus democracy. Many were unable to avoid a personal stand on the conflict. Poets, artists, musicians, scholars, politicians, and workers found themselves irrevocably committed to the defense of the Spanish Republic against the Nationalist attack under Franco. In various capacities, eminent people throughout the world rallied to the cause: André Malraux in France, George Orwell in England, Pablo Casals and Joan Miró in Spain itself, and countless others. For millions of people, Spain was the paramount issue and the supreme moral crisis.

The commitment in many cases went far beyond the merely verbal. Outraged by the blatant military and bombing support of the Axis powers, men from fifty countries, young and old alike, journeyed to Spain to fight as volunteer soldiers for the Spanish Republic. They were intellectuals and artists, workers and students; Communists, Catholics, socialists of various stripes, liberals; and men of no discernible political or religious belief. Their only common bond was a hatred for fascism. Their involvement in the International Brigades was a story of heroism and tragic idealism, for many were to die in battle for their cause.

As the war continued, atrocities abounded on both sides. It took the Nationalists, however, to shock the world with their particularly savage acts of brutality. In Nationalist-held territory, executions of political opponents were usually summary affairs, without trials and without appeals. Many were simple acts of murder. The most infamous involved the death of Federico García Lorca, the most notable Spanish poet and playwright of the 20th century. Although he was not a member of any of the parties of the left, he was sympathetic and therefore vulnerable to Nationalist retribution. The Church, which had allied itself with the Nationalist cause, was guilty of the grossest complicity with regard to these slaughters.

As horrifying as these atrocities were, the worst was still to come. Until April 26, 1937, Guernica, a small Basque town located near the city of Bilbao with a population of about 7,000, was not especially noteworthy. On that day, a market day in the town, the German Air Force, acting under the direction of General Franco, bombed the defenseless citizens for over three hours. This was the first example of mass bombing of a civilian population and, in fact, was viewed as an experimental procedure for possible future military strategy.

At the end of the raid, most of the town lay in ruins and over a thousand people were dead. More than anything else, the brutality of this event mobilized Picasso to use his artistic talent to express with eloquent force both his outrage and his passionate partisanship in the Spanish Civil War. Thus Picasso, like the members of the International Brigades and thousands of others, felt compelled to make public his personal stand in a powerful and dramatic fashion.

At the outset of the war, rumors had circulated that suggested that the artist was in favor of Franco's rebellion. In May 1937, however, he made his position clear in a public statement:

> The Spanish struggle is the fight of reaction against the people, against freedom. . . . How could anybody think for a moment that I could be in agreement with reaction and death? When the rebellion began, the legally elected and democratic republican government of Spain appointed me director of the Prado Museum, a post which I immediately accepted. In the panel on which I am working which I shall call "Guernica" and in all my recent works of art, I clearly express my abhorrence of the military caste which has sunk Spain in an ocean of pain and death.*

In addition, even before the atrocity at Guernica, Picasso had executed an etching entitled *Dream and Lie of Franco (Figs. 4–5a and b)*, a double work that contains eighteen panels in a form similar to a comic strip. That work indicated both Picasso's fervent contempt for Franco and his willingness to use his creative powers to express that feeling. *Dream and Lie of Franco* is an effective piece of political propaganda. In the first panel, Picasso exhibits his distaste for the Nationalist leader by portraying him as a strange and bizarre monster. The panel, which reads from right to left, shows the future dictator in a series of vile disguises. In the first scene, the monster rides to war on a horse, destined to obliterate the sunshine of the Spanish republican government. In scene number 6, center-left, Franco is portrayed in ecclesiastical garb, symbolic of the overwhelming support given his rebellion by the Church.

In the first scene of the second panel, Franco is shown triumphing over a dead horse, a symbol that later appears in *Guernica*. The next scene shows a slain figure, which possibly represents Spanish progress slain by the insurgent fascists. Many of the other scenes are reminiscent of figures that appear throughout *Guernica*.

In January 1937, Picasso accepted an invitation from the Spanish government

---

*Quoted in Alfred Barr, *Picasso: Fifty Years of His Art* (New York: Museum of Modern Art, 1946), p. 202.

4-5a. Dream and Lie of Franco. Pablo Picasso. 1937. Etching and aquatint. Collection, The Museum of Modern Art, New York. Gift of Mrs. Stanley Resor.

4-5b. Dream and Lie of Franco. Pablo Picasso. 1937. Etching and aquatint. Collection, The Museum of Modern Art, New York. Gift of Mrs. Stanley Resor.

to paint a mural for the Spanish Pavilion at the World's Fair, which was to be held in Paris the following summer. No particular subject matter for this project had been specified. The bombing of Guernica in April, however, made that topic compelling. The artist began work on his masterpiece only a few days after the event. He worked furiously, and the entire painting was completed in a few weeks. He also made about a hundred preliminary sketches, drawings, and paintings in preparation, and the painting itself went through several stages.

Social Dimensions in the Art of Picasso 91

These preliminary works are themselves significant examples of socially conscious art. They are closely related to the final product and each is valuable independently. In these works the artist portrays the horrible suffering of the people of Guernica and his own passionate outcry against the senseless bombing and terror. These themes, of course, reach fullest maturity in the final version of *Guernica*. What is significant about the preliminary works is the specific detail of the artistic vision.

An impressive example is the study for the horse's head, an oil painting done on May 2, 1937 (*Fig. 4-6*). The study captures the piercing shriek of the injured horse in much the same way Munch captured the agony in *The Scream*. In Picasso's painting the viewer cannot avoid the sheer terror the bombing raid must have brought to Guernica on that infamous day in April 1937. The horse becomes a disturbing symbol for all that is terrible about military destruction.

Another powerful example is a preliminary drawing done a few days later,

4-6. Horse's Head. (*Guernica Studies and "Postscripts": May 2, 1937.*) Pablo Picasso. 1937. Oil on canvas. On extended loan to The Museum of Modern Art, New York, from the artist.

which is a study of a horse and a mother with a dead child (*Fig. 4–7*). Picasso returns to the horse as a symbol of terror. The mother and child are an extraordinary portrait in human anguish. The mother's expression reveals an uncomprehending grief as she peers upward, wondering why, without answer, the terror from the sky has murdered her child. The still body of the child emphasizes the innocence of the victims at Guernica.

Guernica itself (*Fig. 4–8*) is a monumental and complex work. The two most immediately striking features of the painting are its immense size—ll feet 6 inches by 25 feet 8 inches—and the color scheme. It is executed solely in blacks and whites and various shades of gray—colors that instill a dominating sense of somberness and mourning. The work is a spectacular fusion of brilliant style with social content, a magnificent synthesis of Cubist form with an Expressionist intensity. The purpose of *Guernica* is frankly propagandistic. The artist's intent was to point out the inhuman character of Franco's fascist rebellion. Like Goya's *The Third of May, 1808* (*Fig. 1–8*), it accomplishes the most important objective of socially conscious art: to comment on the horror of a specific occurrence in a work of universal significance. *Guernica* simultaneously condemns the senseless bombing of the peaceful Basque town and stands as an eternally transcendent protest against war.

Picasso portrayed the victims' agony by using both human and animal figures. The bull and the horse signify the bullfight, a recurrent theme in Picasso's work. The general scene is only vaguely reminiscent of the actual town. Instead, there are marginally featured buildings in the picture. At the top of the painting, slightly to the left of center, there is a lamp in the shape of an eye, with an electric light that illuminates the entire scene.

The most obvious human characters are the women, whom Picasso portrays as

4-7. Horse and Mother with Dead Child. (*Guernica Studies and "Postscripts"*: May 8, 1937. Pablo Picasso. 1937. Pencil on white paper. On extended loan to The Museum of Modern Art, New York, from the artist.

the primary victims of suffering and despair. They serve as symbols of defenseless humanity in general. The woman at the extreme left is screaming, with a dead baby in her arms, not unlike the view in the previous preliminary drawing. At the other end, there are three additional female figures: At the bottom, a woman is shown rushing in, hands clasped in the greatest possible fear. Directly above her to the right is another woman, screaming in anguish as her home is enveloped in flames. The last woman leans out of a window and holds a lamp, perhaps to represent the forces of truth or light in a situation seemingly devoid of hope. The only male victim appears at the bottom left, a warrior who lies fallen and dismembered.

The animals are integral facets of the complex allegorical nature of the work. Picasso's own explanation for the symbolic meaning of the various figures was revealed in an interview conducted in 1945. He noted that the horse represented the people. Once again, the theme of the bullfight becomes significant; the horse is often the innocent victim in the clash between bull and matador. In the painting, the viewer can clearly see how the shrieking pain signifies innocent people in the midst of war. The bull in its ominous appearance at the top left was thought by many to represent fascism. In that same interview, however, Picasso said that the bull represented brutality and darkness. It is reasonable, certainly, to take the artist at his word. His explanation goes beyond the specific events of April 26, 1937, but at the same time it takes them into account. Picasso himself sought to elevate his achievement into an artistic monument for the victims of military brutality everywhere.

Controversies remain, of course, about the precise meaning of the complex symbolism of *Guernica*. There is substantial ambiguity in the painting, and eminent authorities have differed in their interpretations of significant aspects of the work. What no one can dispute, however, is that *Guernica* is a supreme moral statement.

Guernica marked the starting point of a brief but noteworthy political period of Picasso's artistic life. The themes of war and, especially, peace were to be elaborated by Picasso. For several years he was more or less actively involved in organized Communist political activity. In 1945 he issued an eloquent statement about the social role of the artist:

> What do you think an artist is? An imbecile who has only his eyes if he's a painter, or ears if he's a musician, or a lyre at every level of his heart if he's a poet, or even, if he's a boxer, just his muscles? On the contrary, he's at the same time a political being, constantly alive to heartrending, fiery, or happy events, to which he responds in every way. How would it be possible to feel no interest in other people and by virtue of an ivory indifference to detach yourself from the life which they so copiously bring you? No, painting is not done to decorate apartments. It is an instrument of war for attack and defense against the enemy.*

*Quoted in Herschel Chipp, *Theories of Modern Art* (Berkeley: University of California Press, 1971), p. 487.

94 The Art of Social Conscience

4-8. Guernica. Pablo Picasso. 1937.
Oil on canvas. On extended loan to
The Museum of Modern Art,
New York, from the artist.

Many of Picasso's works of the late 1940s and early 1950s had a specifically political or more generally a social and ethical content. On several occasions he attended various peace congresses, which gave rise to his well-known portrayals of the Dove of Peace. The example entitled *Dove (Fig.4–1)* rapidly appeared in Communist publications throughout the world, and it evoked considerable hostility because of its association with Communist-sponsored political activity.

In fact, however, the dove is a symbol for peace. *Dove* has value as a work of art far transcending its particular sectarian setting. It is interesting to add that for all of his involvement with the Communist Party, Picasso had repeated difficulty with the orthodox nature of Soviet aesthetic dogma. At the same time, Picasso also executed several posters for the various peace conferences.

In 1950, when the war in Korea began, Picasso expressed his hostility for the

96 The Art of Social Conscience

American position in *Massacre in Korea (Fig. 4-9).* Here Picasso adapted his familiar style to a Goya-like version of the Korean conflict. Several soldiers, obviously Americans, are shown butchering innocent Asian civilians who stand naked and helpless in front of their rifles. As in *Guernica,* women are depicted as the primary victims. While the painting clearly lacks the force of either Goya's or Picasso's great masterpieces, it has often been downplayed as an aberrant and unimportant piece of propaganda. The reason, presumably, is largely political, because it has not been as acceptable to criticize American involvement in Korea as it has been to condemn American involvement in Vietnam. Intelligent

4-9. Massacre in Korea. *Pablo Picasso. 1952. Oil on canvas. Courtesy of SPADEM 1975 by French Reproduction Rights, Inc.*

criticisms of the earlier war have been made and, as in all wars, innocent civilians were slaughtered by robotlike soldiers. *Massacre in Korea*, therefore, stands as a strong general indictment of war.

Shortly thereafter, Picasso painted two massive murals in Vallauris in southern France. These were done in two parts, *Peace* and *War*. American military aggression was the stimulus, but the work also transcends the Korean War in its more general advocacy of peace. For a short time, Picasso continued to be active politically. In 1953, for example, as a part of the worldwide protests against the execution of Julius and Ethel Rosenberg, he drew a portrait of those victims of

98 The Art of Social Conscience

Cold War anti-Communist hysteria in the United States. Shortly thereafter, Picasso abandoned his political activity. He remained a Communist in name only. For the next two decades he returned to other artistic endeavors, mainly graphics and ceramics, and remained for the most part in the seclusion of his villa in the south of France. He continued to be amazingly prolific until his death. With his passing, a major epoch in the history of art ended. So, too, had an important era of the art of social conscience in the 20th century.

5-1. Scott's Run, West Virginia. *Ben Shahn. 1937. Tempera on cardboard. Collection of the Whitney Museum of American Art.*

5 The American Experience: Shahn, Gropper, Evergood, Albright, Blume, Cadmus, Tooker, Levine, and Baskin

The history of 20th-century America is as fascinating as it is turbulent. The Depression and the events that followed serve as the primary background for the consideration of several artists and the social content of their work. The postwar prosperity of the 1920s turned quickly into unprecedented economic disaster, and the situation became desperate for millions of people. In addition, agriculture deteriorated dramatically and the once-fertile land turned into dustbowls, with all the attendant human displacement and suffering described by John Steinbeck in *The Grapes of Wrath*. In 1933, at the time of the first inauguration of President Franklin D. Roosevelt, twenty-five percent of the labor force in America was out of work. The grim pattern of urban bread lines and the consequent personal despair became the hallmark of American life. Meanwhile, in Europe, the increasing power of fascist totalitarianism became an ever more frightening force.

In response to these conditions, a group of artists became involved in the social issues of the times and used their talents to express their opposition to the prevailing political, social, and economic realities. Influenced by the political content of the Mexican murals of the 1920s and the social orientation of much of the WPA art, these artists resolved to merge their work with their social concerns. Unlike most of their contemporaries in the world of art, they were not reluctant to express an engaged, partisan position.

This group of artists, who opposed the formal aesthetics that dominated much of European painting, were designated "Social Realists." This is a vague and highly imprecise term, since the artistic styles of the various people varied substantially. Realism in the visual sense, in fact, is somewhat of a misnomer, for serious attention was rarely paid to visual detail. Frequently, the Social Realists exaggerated the features of human figures, landscape, and objects in the manner of Expressionism. Color, too, was used to heighten the emotional impact of the social content of their art. The "realism," therefore, concerned their preoccupation with "real" human events. Yet even here the designation has connotations of objective, dispassionate reportage. The Social Realists, however, were not dispassionate. They shared a common bond of compassion for the poor, the oppressed, and the working class, and they sought political and social reform.

"Social realism," furthermore, sounds uncomfortably like "socialist realism." It is crucial to distinguish between them. "Social realism" is oppositional, critical art. "Socialist realism," which became the official art in the Soviet Union in the aftermath of the Bolshevik Revolution, is quite the contrary. "Socialist realism" is dogmatic and lacks both the stylistic distinction and moral fervor of the Social Realists. The Social Realists were not the only American artists of considerable social merit. Historically, the pungent cartoons of Thomas Nast, the earthy paintings of the Ash Can School, and the militant graphics of *The Masses* and *The New Masses* were important precursors of American socially conscious art. The Social Realists, however, are the major emissaries of this tradition.

The finest American representative of the artists who merged art with ethical and political commitment is Ben Shahn. Born in Lithuania in 1898, he grew up in Brooklyn in an atmosphere of social radicalism and with a strong Jewish repugnance toward injustice. This background would affect his art throughout his career. For many years some critics and art historians viewed Shahn as a mere propagandist, and he received only passing reference in books and art journals. Fortunately, that attitude has now largely vanished and Shahn has received the major critical acclaim he richly deserves. Much of his art is unquestionably propagandistic, but it is also art in the best sense of the word. Shahn combined an outstanding technique with lasting themes, premised upon a complex intellectual foundation. He is as important to this tradition as Goya, Daumier, Kollwitz, and Grosz.

Ater studying at New York University and City College, Shahn went to Europe for further training. While he was there, two Italian immigrants and anarchists, Nicola Sacco and Bartolomeo Vanzetti, were executed in Massachusetts for the murders of a paymaster and a guard in a hold-up. This case was to have an enormous impact on the future direction of Shahn's art.

During the 1920s the "red scare" was dominating the public consciousness. Anyone different was suspect; not only Communists but socialists, anarchists, union organizers, and immigrants, who were feared to carry the seeds of the nation's destruction. The fear of radicalism reached almost pathological levels. Earlier, from 1919 through 1921, the attorney general under President Woodrow Wilson, A. Mitchell Palmer, was responsible for one of the most notorious and disgraceful episodes in American history. Palmer devoted his time and energy to fighting labor unions and chasing real, or imagined, domestic radicals. During his time in office thousands of people were rounded up, frequently beaten, often summarily deported if they were foreign-born, or held for months without trials or hearings. For these people there was no due process of law. These actions, known as the Palmer Raids, were patently illegal, yet they were conducted with impunity by government officials.

The two immigrant anarchists were doubly suspect: They had been personally involved in labor agitation and, in 1917, both fled to Mexico to avoid military conscription. Both factors would eventually seal their fate. The actual crime for which Sacco and Vanzetti were executed was committed on April 15, 1920. After their arrest they produced witnesses who testified that they were miles from the scene of the robbery-murder. The merits of the defense witnesses notwithstanding, the prosecution's case was transparent and flimsy. The judge never concealed his animosity for the defendants, his rulings were flagrantly biased, and he repeatedly permitted the prosecutors to remark about the defendants' radical social views. Under these circumstances, both men were found guilty and sentenced to death.

For several years the defense lawyers sought to obtain a reversal of the conviction and a new trial. Sacco and Vanzetti, meanwhile, remained on Death Row at the Massachusetts State Prison. Eventually the governor of Massachusetts, Alvan T. Fuller, refused to commute the death sentence. That decision was largely predicated on the report of a special committee named to investigate the case, headed by President A. Lawrence Lowell of Harvard University. The report concluded that the trial had been fairly conducted and that the sentence was just.

Governor Fuller's refusal to act served as the catalyst for protest demonstrations throughout America and the rest of the world. Millions of people concluded that Sacco and Vanzetti were to go to their deaths because of their political beliefs and as a result of the anti-immigrant sentiment in the United States. Intellectuals, artists, and literary figures rallied to the cause. Ben Shahn, too, viewed the Sacco-Vanzetti case as a miscarriage of justice. His stay in Europe had revealed to him the magnitude of the opposition to the execution of the two men. When he returned to America, Shahn became actively involved in the controversy. He went to Boston to picket and demonstrate. He also came to

102 The Art of Social Conscience

believe that another reason for the persecution of Sacco and Vanzetti was that many of the people in New England were resentful of immigrants who had prospered economically.

Shahn decided to portray his version of the case artistically. This was an immensely important step in his emergence as a painter of social protest. Earlier, in Europe, he had completed numerous paintings that were professionally executed. Yet, as he later indicated in his book *The Shape of Content,* mere technical proficiency was not enough, for there was really little of Ben Shahn in those works. The Sacco-Vanzetti case aroused in him the need to combine his art with the essence of his moral consciousness, and that consciousness required, at every level, a political commitment.

The case quickly solved that problem for the artist. The works to emerge were not, however, Shahn's first social paintings; a few years earlier he had painted a series of thirteen watercolors on the Dreyfus affair in France, where the specter of anti-Semitism had arisen once again. Shahn's decision to do the Sacco-Vanzetti series, however, was even more significant. In 1931, when he began work, abstract art was enjoying an immense public popularity. Even then, for some critics, art was seen as purely line, form, and color. Shahn, however, thrived on unpopularity; he was determined to tell the story as he saw it, without regard for the opinion of the established art world. His series of twenty-three paintings was a highly partisan treatment that stands as a monument against all acts of injustice.

The most notable and important painting in the series is *Sacco and Vanzetti* (Fig. 5–2). At the left of the work, Shahn portrays a group of workers demonstrating against the unfair trial. In demanding the freedom of the persecuted victims of injustice, the workers pointedly dwarf the figure to their right, Governor Fuller of Massachusetts, who is self-righteously denying a commutation. His comparative height in the painting is a measure of the artist's assessment of his stature

5–2. Sacco and Vanzetti. *Ben Shahn. Tempera. Courtesy of Kennedy Galleries, New York / © Estate of Ben Shahn.*

5-3. Six Witnesses Who Bought Eels from Vanzetti. *Ben Shahn. Tempera. Courtesy of Kennedy Galleries, New York /* © *Estate of Ben Shahn.*

and worth. The figures of the defendants themselves dominate the center of the work, as if to further emphasize the smallness of the governor. At the right, standing in mock piety over the corpses of Nicola Sacco and Bartolomeo Vanzetti, are the members of the Lowell Commission. Shahn is far from subtle here in allocating a major share of the responsibility for the executions to these three cowardly men. In the back is a portrait of Judge Webster Thayer, who also receives a portion of the blame. His pious pose is little more than a mask for injustice and hypocrisy.

In a lesser-known painting in the series, Shahn reveals an important aspect of the case that is frequently obscured by the legal disputes and the strident rhetoric. *Six Witnesses Who Bought Eels from Vanzetti (Fig. 5-3)* portrays with quiet eloquence the sympathy and regard felt for the prisoners by the working class. The six women cared enough about the welfare of Sacco and Vanzetti to offer testimony on their behalf in the hostile climate of the courtroom. Their dedication also reveals the personal depth of the defendants, whose own political activity was directed toward improving the lot of their fellow workers and their families in a xenophobic atmosphere. Both men were widely recognized in their community as sensitive to the problems of their fellow immigrants. The testimony of the women may be seen, therefore, as a reciprocal gesture of human concern.

At various times in his career, Shahn returned to the theme of the Sacco-Vanzetti case. As late as 1967, he designed a magnificent mural on the subject for Syracuse University. Perhaps the most moving statement of all, however, is

104 The Art of Social Conscience

> IF IT HAD NOT BEEN FOR THESE THING, I MIGHT HAVE LIVE OUT MY LIFE TALKING AT STREET CORNERS TO SCORNING MEN. I MIGHT HAVE DIE, UNMARKED, UNKNOWN A FAILURE. NOW WE ARE NOT A FAILURE. THIS IS OUR CAREER AND OUR TRIUMPH. NEVER IN OUR FULL LIFE COULD WE HOPE TO DO SUCH WORK FOR TOLERANCE, FOR JOOSTICE, FOR MAN'S ONDERSTANDING OF MAN AS NOW WE DO BY ACCIDENT. OUR WORDS-OUR LIVES-OUR PAINS NOTHING! THE TAKING OF OUR LIVES-LIVES OF A GOOD SHOEMAKER AND A POOR FISH PEDDLER-ALL! THAT LAST MOMENT BELONGS TO US- THAT AGONY IS OUR TRIUMPH.

5-4. The Passion of Sacco and Vanzetti. *Ben Shahn.* 1958. *Serigraph. Philadelphia Museum of Art: Purchased from Funds Given by Dr. and Mrs. William Wolgin.*

found in a graphic work of 1958 entitled *The Passion of Sacco and Vanzetti* (Fig. 5-4). The words, visually powerful in their own right, are from a letter by Bartolomeo Vanzetti to his son prior to his execution. Ben Shahn has immortalized this simple statement in a work of art that is universal in its condemnation of injustice.

Shahn followed his *Sacco-Vanzetti* series with a group of paintings about the case of the persecuted labor leader Tom Mooney, who, with Warren Billings, was convicted of a bombing of a "Preparedness Day" parade in San Francisco in 1916. In fact, their conviction had been a frame-up related to the antilabor sentiment in California. Shahn's sympathy for organized labor was apparent. When this series was exhibitted in New York, it was viewed by Diego Rivera, who subsequently invited Shahn to serve as his assistant on the large mural, *Man at the Crossroads,* in Rockefeller Center.

The Depression, meanwhile, was becoming increasingly more severe. Shahn spent several years working as a painter for the Public Works of Art Project and the Farm Security Administration. He also worked for a time as a photographer, and his photography was also socially oriented. During the Depression his primary artistic theme was the plight of the worker caught in circumstances beyond his control.

Scott's Run, West Virginia (Fig. 5-1) provides an extraordinary glimpse of human despair. In a manner that evokes the work of Käthe Kollwitz, Shahn personalizes the consequences of poverty. Here the helplessness of the three men dominates the scene as they ponder their uncertain futures. Shahn reveals the paramount reality of most individual responses in America to the economic disaster of the Depression. Like the men in the picture, millions of Americans regarded their sudden unemployment as a personal moral failure rather than as a result of social and institutional breakdown. This was an important dimension of the malaise of the era, and Shahn captures it with remarkable insight.

Another element to Shahn's artistic portrayal of poverty in America is seen in *Handball (Fig. 5-5)*. This painting is not ordinarily regarded as one of Shahn's more socially significant works, but a closer examination sheds important light

5-5. Handball. Ben Shahn. 1939. *Tempera on paper over composition board. Collection, The Museum of Modern Art, New York. Abby Aldrich Rockefeller Fund.*

106 The Art of Social Conscience

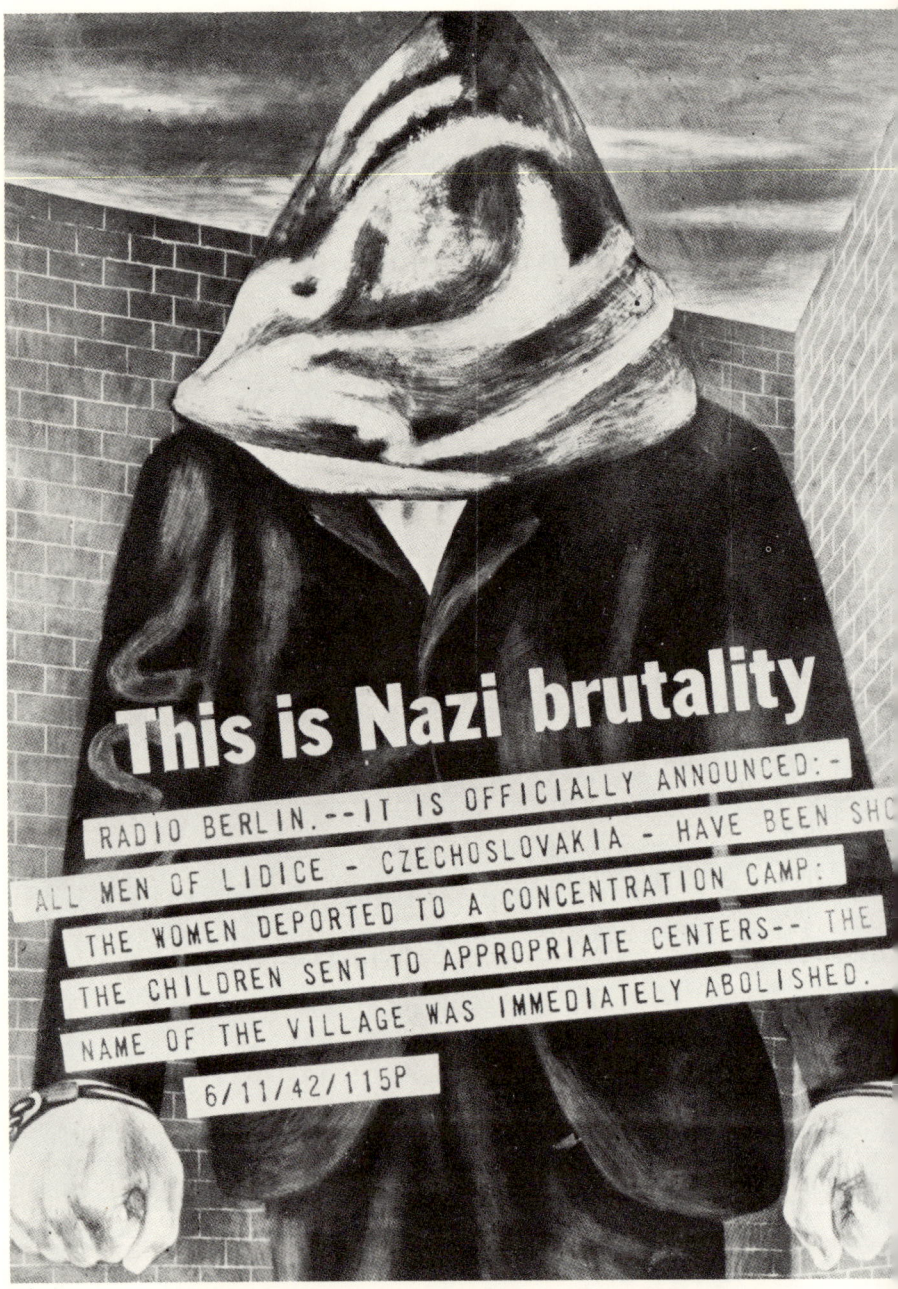

5–6. This is Nazi Brutality. *Ben Shahn. Courtesy Kennedy Galleries, New York /©Estate of Ben Shahn.*

on the painting. The scene of boys playing handball is a common sight in American cities. What is particularly revealing, however, is the glimpse the artist provides of the urban setting. Behind the wall stand the stark tenement buildings that entrap millions of people. The pattern of the harshness of urban life is apparent; the wall in the picture is a metaphor for the barrier to social and economic mobility. This scene was particularly close to the artist, who spent most of his childhood in a Brooklyn slum.

During World War II, Shahn began to develop his talent for graphic art. He continued, of course, with socially oriented paintings. In his position as the director of graphic arts for the CIO, he produced a number of compelling posters. One of the most important, *The Welders,* was especially notable because it portrayed a black and white worker side by side, which was an unpopular, even dangerous position to take at the time.

Shahn was also deeply affected by the tragedy occurring in Europe, and many of his works reflect his personal anguish. One of his most powerful wartime works, which expressed his shock at the Nazi atrocities, is *This is Nazi Brutality* (*Fig. 5-6*). When the Nazi leader of Prague, Reinhard Heydrich, was assassinated in 1942 by members of the Czech Resistance, the Germans retaliated with calculated barbarism. German security police surrounded the small town of Lidice, not far from Prague. In groups of ten, the adult males were murdered by firing squads; the women were removed to concentration camps; the children were taken from their parents; and every building in the village was razed. The hooded, handcuffed victim stands behind a ticker tape, which announces the events. The foreboding sky emphasizes Shahn's outrage at the Nazi act.

In the postwar period Shahn made numerous nonsocial paintings as he moved from social realism to what he described as "personal realism." By this he meant his expression of the moods and qualities of ordinary people in diverse walks of life. He never, however, turned his back on social themes, and, indeed, some of his finest socially conscious art was still to come. In the late 1940s the Centralia, Illinois, mine disaster left a deep impression on the artist, and he commenced work on a number of paintings that expressed the intensity of his feelings. The best example is *Miner's Wives* (*Fig. 5-7*), which portrays a woman who learns that her husband has just been killed in a mining accident. Shahn combines anger and compassion in a magnificent blend of personal and social realism. The wife stands as a symbol of suffering that transcends national boundaries and historical eras. Her eyes peer accusingly, as if to remind the audience that the mining conditions leading to her bereavement have been tragically ignored.

Throughout the late 1940s and early 1950s Shahn continued his personal involvement in left-wing political activity. In 1948 he was active in the presidential campaign of Henry Wallace of the leftist Progressive Party. In the early 1950s he vigorously opposed the increasing oppression of McCarthyism in America. Like so many distinguished writers, teachers, clergymen, artists, and intellectuals, he was summoned before the House Un-American Activities Committee to explain his political ideology. He responded in critical fashion

108   The Art of Social Conscience

5-7. Miners' Wives. Ben Shahn. 1948. Egg tempera on board. Philadelphia Museum of Art: Given by Wright S. Ludington.

both personally and artistically. In general, he satirized these political witch hunts in a series of paintings and drawings.

In 1960–62 Shahn completed a series of paintings and drawings that are as important and powerful as the earlier *Sacco-Vanzetti* series. The more recent series, *The Lucky Dragon,* deals with the moral issues raised by the testing of nuclear weapons. In the postwar era the international tension of Cold War ideology dominated political relationships among the world's super-powers. One of the unfortunate outgrowths of the Cold War was the arms race between the United States and the Soviet Union. Eventually the proliferation of weapons would enable either country to obliterate the other hundreds of times over. The arms race, furthermore, was not without its tragic personal consequences.

On January 22, 1954, a group of Japanese fishermen set out from the port of Yaizu in a boat named "Lucky Dragon." (Ironically, the dragon is a symbol of good fortune in Japan.) The initial fishing success of the crew was limited. Hoping for better luck elsewhere, the boat moved further into the Pacific Ocean. On March 1, as some of the men were asleep and others were preparing for breakfast, a huge incandescence appeared on the horizon and the ship began to shake violently. Soon, radioactive fallout from an American hydrogen-bomb test at Bikini Atoll, some eighty-five miles away, fell upon "Lucky Dragon."

When the boat, which had been outside the restricted area, returned to port, all twenty-three crewmen were hospitalized with symptoms of radiation poisoning. The condition of one crewman, Aikichi Kuboyama, was particularly critical. By May, all the men were sterile. The nation panicked because of the fear that the fish were also contaminated. The Japanese, of course, had sound

5–8. We Did Not Know What Happened to Us. *Ben Shahn. 1960. Tempera. Courtesy of National Collection of Fine Arts, Smithsonian Institution, Washington, D.C.*

reason to fear the consequences of American nuclear adventure. As the months passed, the condition of Kuboyama deteriorated rapidly, and on September 23 he died, the only fatality of the incident.

Ben Shahn saw in this story the terrifying dilemma of humanity in the Atomic Age. He focused on Kuboyama. His series portrays the torment of the victims in powerful human terms at the same time that it raises broader political questions. The full impact of the series is felt only after a consideration of all the paintings and drawings. Several examples, however, highlight the salient themes of the work. *We Did Not Know What Happened to Us (Fig. 5-8)* provides a view of the initial shock and confusion of the boat's crew. The work shows a dramatic change in Shahn's artistic style in its reduced representational character. Clearly, however, there is no change in the force of his social commentary. The radioactive cloud, which is pictured as a flying demon, is symbolic of the living terror experienced by the crew. The monster represents the omnipresent threat of atomic annihilation, and its tentacles reach far beyond the unfortunate crewmen of "Lucky Dragon."

Equally powerful is *The Lucky Dragon (Fig. 5-9)*. In a work reminiscent of the moving statement of Bartolomeo Vanzetti, Shahn again integrates verbal comment into his picture, thus intensifying the ethical questions it poses. The broader character of the painting is not omitted, for the specter of the atomic monster, representing the danger of nuclear annihilation, hovers ominously in the upper-left corner.

Shahn was concerned about the basic questions raised by Kuboyama's death. In a searching commentary on the social responsibilities of science, Shahn issues a strong challenge to scientists in *The Physicist (Fig. 5-10)*. Although thoughtful scientists have long been in the forefront of activities directed toward achieving world peace, far too many of their colleagues have been oblivious to the social implications of their work. Many have deluded themselves into believing that the political uses of their "objective" or "neutral" scientific efforts are not their concern. Shahn indicates the result of that dangerous attitude. The physicist, pointedly concealed in the anonymity of his laboratory garb, holds the results of his labor. Once again, Shahn returns to his allegorical monster as if to issue a warning to the scientific community about the consequences of its work. Shahn was no opponent of scientific research. His own intellectualism convinced him of the high value of the scientific enterprise. At the same time, the painting offers a clear message that no high-minded endeavor can afford immunity against the broader ethical responsibilities of mankind.

The last painting in *The Lucky Dragon* series asks the most important question in its title: *Why? (Fig. 5-11)*. The presence of the strikingly modern gravestone suggests the terrifying questions that remain: Is humanity doomed to destruction, or can man effect changes in the direction of this dangerous course? Will Kuboyama be the only victim? Man has the technological capacity to destroy himself; does he, at the same time, have the social capacity to prevent that destruction?

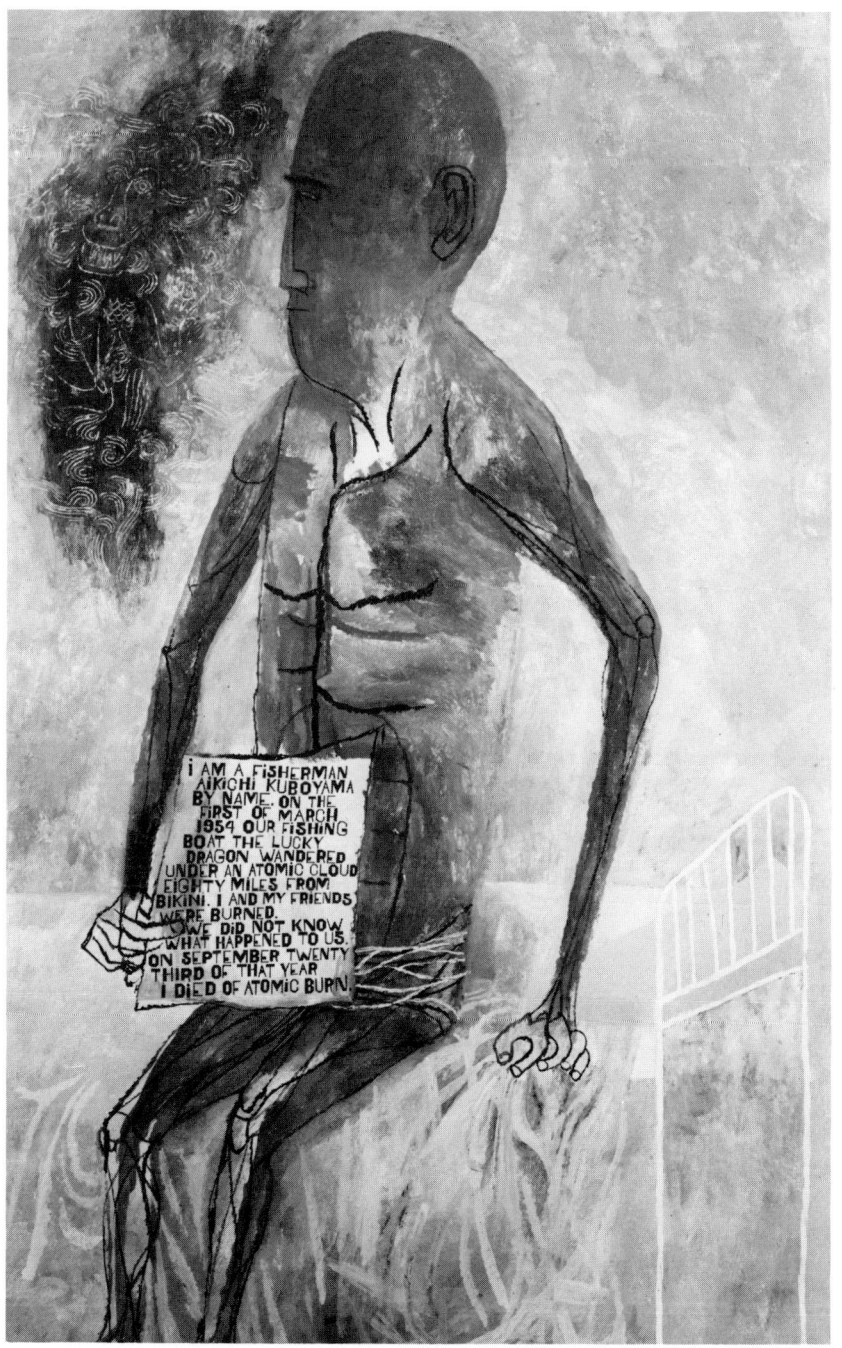

5–9. The Lucky Dragon. *Ben Shahn. 1960. Tempera. Courtesy Kennedy Galleries, New York /* © *Estate of Ben Shahn.*

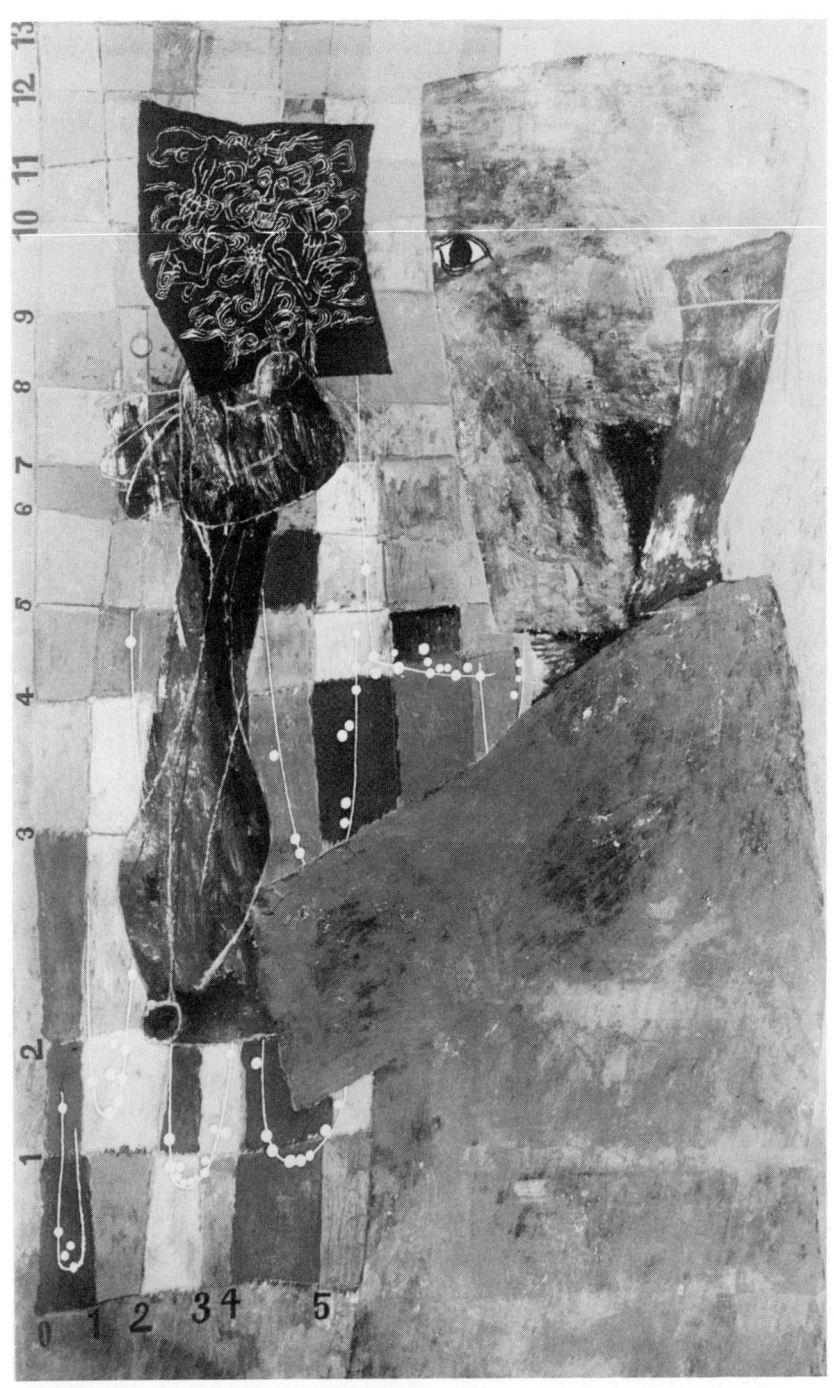

5–10. The Physicist. Ben Shahn. 1961. Tempera. Collection Jack Lawrence, Los Angeles.

5-11. *Why?* Ben Shahn. 1961. Gouache. Collection of Mr. and Mrs. Herbert A. Goldstone, New York.

Through the late 1950s and '60s Shahn continued to create a diversity of work. In 1956 he painted *Goyescas,* the title of which intentionally evokes the memory of the Spanish master. In that watercolor he portrayed a view of Spain under the oppressive yoke of fascism. He pictured a brutal Spanish officer, possibly Franco himself, spreading a cat's cradle over his victims' bodies. In the early 1960s, in conjunction with the thematic concerns of *The Lucky Dragon* series, he executed a powerful poster for the Committee for a Sane Nuclear Policy, which advocated the cessation of hydrogen-bomb testing. In 1964 he opposed the right-wing presidential campaign of Barry Goldwater. In 1965, after civil-rights workers James Chaney, Andrew Goodman, and Michael Schwerner were savagely murdered by racists in Mississippi, Shahn executed a portfolio of memorial prints. Finally, near the end of his life, he used his art to protest American participation in Vietnam. Shahn died in 1969. No greater tribute could be paid to the man who lived so fully and painted so well than the message contained in a painting of 1955 entitled *Credo (Fig. 5-12).* The passionate words of Martin Luther accurately apply to the finest artist America has produced.

Ben Shahn was only one of many major artists who continually integrated a social vision into the content of their art. While many of the others lack the eminence and public recognition of Shahn, the artists who follow are significant

114 The Art of Social Conscience

5–12. Credo. Ben Shahn. 1955. Gouache. Collection Mr. and Mrs. Stanley Marcus, Dallas.

figures in American art. William Gropper, an important contemporary of Shahn's, is a prominent satirist of the 20th century. He was born in 1897 in the teeming ghetto of the Lower East Side of New York City. His contact with the harsh realities of life came early. Both his parents worked in the notorious sweatshops. This background engendered a class consciousness that would be a major characteristic of his art.

His early career as a cartoonist was more significant for its topical relevance than for its contribution to art. His works appeared in numerous periodicals. Many, but not all, appeared in various left-wing journals. Much of his career was spent as the featured cartoonist and pictorial satirist for *The New Masses*, the influential leftist magazine, which in the 1930s attracted literary contributions from many famous American writers such as Ernest Hemingway, John Dos Passos, Theodore Dreiser, and Richard Wright. Although the majority of Gropper's cartoons are ephemeral, some achieve a more universal aspect.

Gropper was a serious painter as well as a cartoonist. He had had rigorous artistic training and he developed a distinctive style. He studied many of the European masters in his quest to develop his own artistic identity, and his paintings and graphic work are, consequently, the products of conscientious, professional craftsmanship. He sought to evoke public response to the glaring ills of society; his themes included the graft and corruption of politics, the lot of

5-13. The Senate. *William Gropper. 1935. Oil on canvas. Collection, The Museum of Modern Art, New York. Gift of A. Conger Goodyear.*

poor farmers and urban workers, and the pomposity and narrow-mindedness of the American middle class. Like Shahn, Gropper has occasionally been dismissed by critics as merely a social propagandist. A deeper consideration of his work, however, reveals a quality of technique that expresses with vigor and enthusiasm social concerns of lasting significance.

Gropper was fascinated by American politics. Over the years he produced a sardonic and critical series of paintings and lithographs depicting Congress. The artist regarded the United States Senate as the best show in the world, which he portrayed in his most famous political satire *The Senate (Fig. 5-13)*. Painted in 1935, it is timeless in its applicability and its critique extends far beyond the nation's capital. The work presents an uncanny view of a self-righteous political windbag speaking to an audience of two bored colleagues in an almost empty chamber. Comparison with Daumier's *The Legislative Belly (Fig. 1-12)* is inevitable; the physical propensities of the main characters in both works are similar in their grotesqueness. Both Daumier and Gropper use satire to suggest that legislators give the welfare of their constituents a lower priority than they give their own personal satisfaction.

The artist reserved a special venom for the industrialist class in America. In *The Tycoon (Fig. 5-14)*, he portrays a callous capitalist with unremitting contempt. Here the influence of the earlier work of George Grosz seems apparent. The cruel expression on the face of the tycoon is the American counterpart to the sordid German speculators who profited at the expense of their fellow citizens. The anticapitalist bias of Gropper has never been expressed with greater power.

The Dictator (Fig. 5-15) carries Gropper's satirical thrust even further. The dominant figure is a paunchy creature who wears in exaggerated quantity the usual trappings of his illegitimate authority. The repulsive qualities of the dictator cannot conceal the human consequences of his rise to power and the policies he pursues. On both sides of the etching are the starving and wretched people whose fate is neglected by oppressive military regimes symbolized by the main character. Once again, the message is far reaching.

Gropper turned to social satire of a general nature at various points in his career. One of his favorite topics was the hypocrisy of the art world. Typical is *Art Patrons (Fig. 5-16)*, which is similar to the work of Daumier in its derisive treatment of people who purchase works of art only because their upward social mobility requires it. The implications are evident; the prices are raised and the standards are lowered, and the philistine tastes prevail. Gropper, in the tradition of all good satirists, uses his art to make a general comment on the asininities of human behavior.

William Gropper has occasionally been described as an American Daumier. Although he will never achieve that stature, the comparison is not without some validity. Like Daumier, he used his talent to ridicule corrupt institutions and point the way toward reform. His range went beyond the satirical and encompassed sympathy and compassion for the downtrodden. In the 1950s he was an

5-14. The Tycoon. *William Gropper. 1954. ACA Galleries, New York.*

118 The Art of Social Conscience

5-15. The Dictator. *William Gropper. 1965. Etching. ACA Galleries, New York.*

5-16. Art Patrons. *William Gropper. Oil on canvas. The St. Louis Art Museum.*

early victim of McCarthyism. As a result, he found it difficult to exhibit and sell his work. Nevertheless, thriving on opposition and living in slightly less perilous times, he has continued his version of the art of social conscience to the present.

Several other prominent American artists have carried on the tradition of socially conscious art. Men such as Reginald Marsh, Moses Soyer, Raphael Soyer, and Philip Evergood illustrated the depth of suffering in the 1930s. One of the major themes depicted during that troubled era was the labor ferment, which had become a domestic issue of great importance. For years, organized labor had been suppressed and hated in America. In the 1930s, however, it was on its way to unprecedented organizational success. Aided by such progressive New Deal legislation as the Wagner Act, unions were recognized by the corporate giants in the American economy. The labor movement was at that time one of the more progressive forces, and unions sought earnestly to achiever justic for American workers. Among the supporters of organized labor were well-known writers, intellectuals, and artists. The cause of labor had indeed become their cause too.

The struggle was not without strife. Violence became the hallmark of labor-management relations. Bloodshed was common, and the police were often employed in the interests of management. Professional strikebreakers, moreover, were frequently used to defeat the organizational efforts of labor unions. On Memorial Day, 1937, in Gary, Indiana, about a thousand workers at Republic Steel Company and their families attended a meeting of the Steelworkers Union, which was then seeking official recognition by the company as the bargaining agent for the employees. A protest march to the plant was organized, but a few

5-17. American Tragedy. *Philip Evergood. 1937. Oil on canvas. Collection of Mrs. Armand Erpf, New York.*

blocks from their destination, the marchers were met by a large police force. Without provocation, the police charged the crowd with tear gas, billy clubs, and, finally with bullets. Ten people were killed.

Philip Evergood, another Social Realist, born in New York City in 1901, responded with a painting on the struggle of the American labor movement. He did extensive research to ascertain the facts of the matter with utmost precision and accuracy. *American Tragedy* (Fig. 5-17) is more than a mere journalistic reconstruction. It is propagandistic in its advocacy of the workers' cause. Like Daumier's *Rue Transonain (see Fig. 1-13)*, however, it is also a condemnation of police misconduct in general. The most prominent feature of the work is the depiction of police brutality, but equally significant is the worker in the center, who endeavors to protect his wife. This can be seen as a symbol of the labor movement's resolve to continue its fight against all odds.

Another significant strain of socially conscious art flourished in the 1930s. The term "Magic Realism" has been applied to several artists whose style combined social realism with the surreal to create a hyper-realism. Magic Realism is an amorphous category that loosely embraces several artists who combined their social vision with extremely bizarre images.

Ivan Albright has created one of the more unusual styles in the history of art. Born in North Harvey, Illinois, in 1897, he exhibited artistic inclinations at an early age. During his service in the army during World War I, Albright was employed to make meticulous medical drawings. This experience influenced his

5-18. Heavy the Oar to Him Who Is Tired, Heavy the Coat, Heavy the Sea. *Ivan Albright. 1928–29. Oil on canvas. Gift of Mr. and Mrs. Earle Ludgin. Courtesy of The Art Institute of Chicago, and also courtesy of Ivan Albright.*

5-19. And God Created Man in His Own Image. *Ivan Albright. 1930–31. Oil on canvas. Property of the artist. Courtesy of The Art Institute of Chicago, and also courtesy of Ivan Albright.*

The American Experience   123

later style, for Albright is notable especially for his vivid, repulsive portrayals of human flesh in various degrees of decomposition. In contrast to Shahn and Gropper, who displayed an active indignation at life's injustices, Albright appears to have resigned himself to the pervasive despair of human living. His perspective is that life is senseless frustration and hardship. His art, however, is fascinating and socially significant, for it reveals both compassion and criticism.

Heavy the Oar to Him Who Is Tired, Heavy the Coat, Heavy the Sea (Fig. 5-18) is typical of the style and content of Albright's work. Here the burdens of life are grandly communicated to the audience. The man has led a difficult, frustrating life. Doubtless he has asked himself many times just why he should continue. Yet he does, and with a resiliency that Albright expresses with persuasive force. The artist's pessimism is qualified with the indication that people can at least survive the burdens of life with a measure of human dignity.

A similar vision can be seen in *And God Created Man in His Own Image (Fig. 5-19)*. Here especially, the sagging flesh of the old man points only to a disturbing reality. The central figure, possibly a derelict, slowly undresses in a seamy hotel room. Thoroughly exhausted, the man is broken by a lifetime of brutal experiences. The ghastly detail of the work emphasizes the squalor of the situation. The foul, ugly body offers a nightmarish view of human life. The work is a classic of antiromantic art. At the same time, however, its content clearly suggests a damning indictment of an indifferent society. The man is far more than an isolated human being who happens to be beyond the pale of respectable social existence. His literal counterparts can be seen even today in hundreds of American cities and in thousands of grimy hotel rooms.

5-20. The Eternal City. *Peter Blume. 1937. Oil on composition board. Collection, The Museum of Modern Art, New York. Mrs. Simon Guggenheim Fund.*

124 The Art of Social Conscience

Peter Blume, another artist identified with the Magic Realists, combines realism with elements of fantasy. Born in Russia in 1906, he came to America as a child. As a young artist traveling to Italy in the early 1930s, Blume was constantly exposed to the depravity of Mussolini's fascist regime. When he returned to the United States, he painted his famous satire *The Eternal City* (Fig. 5-20). By far Blume's most important work, this surreal, biting condemnation of Mussolini is one of the best American examples of political satire in the visual arts.

The viewer is first struck by the vivid green head of the dictator, portrayed as a jack-in-the-box, which emerges from the floor of the Colosseum. This alone would establish the message of the artist; no viewer could avoid the implication that Mussolini is a clown and a buffoon. That, however, is only part of the tale.

More sinister features of Italian fascism are revealed in other parts of the painting. Below the dictator are two of his supporters, one a shady capitalist and the other a common hooligan. On the left, an old woman, injured and poor, sits among the ruins of what was once the glory of Rome. The rubble of the ancient monuments and the image of Christ, cheapened with gaudy jewelry, further suggest the degeneracy of the regime. In the background, in the Roman Forum, Blume portrays mutinous soldiers, a token of the artist's desire for the overthrow of Mussolini. The painting is as complex as its message is obvious. It is the rare example of topical art that has managed to endure. As in the case of Picasso's *Guernica*, *The Eternal City* would be sufficient to establish Blume as an important figure in socially conscious art.

5-21. Coney Island. *Paul Cadmus. 1934. Los Angeles County Museum of Art.*

5-22. *To the Lynching!* *Paul Cadmus. 1935. Pencil and watercolor. Collection of the Whitney Museum of American Art, New York.*

Paul Cadmus, born in New York City in 1904, is perhaps not as well known as the other Magic Realists. His work reveals a fine capacity to infuse the content of his art with topics of unusual relevance in American history. A satirist of a high order, Cadmus has also been responsible for some traditional social protest work. Some of his artistic satire is as merciless as any art ever done in the United States. His most brilliant example is *Coney Island (Fig. 5-21)*, a remarkable work that captures the degenerate aspects of American culture. Portraying the masses at leisure in a proletarian seaside resort, the vision is a brutal view of human nature, as well as a commentary on American values. Cadmus is relentless in his portrayal; he pictures no one for whom any genuine affection could be felt. The slovenly woman on the left, whose breast hangs over her bathing suit as she pours beer on her companion, and the man, center front, reading about Hitler in a pulp magazine as he pinches the child at the right, are caricatures of vulgarity.

Perhaps the American version of George Grosz's *Ecce Homo*, the painting represents the desperate human need for escapism, a need that is particularly aggravated in times of economic distress. Like so many other incisive works of art, *Coney Island* is indicative of the deep disappointment the artist has in his fellow human beings. Cadmus, much like Grosz, communicated his vision in sledgehammer fashion.

A year later Cadmus drew *To the Lynching! (Fig. 5-22)*, which deals with a subject that in 1935 was a popular and grisly spectacle in the United States. For many years it was common to employ vigilante "justice" instead of relying on the slower judicial processes to satisfy the human urge for retribution and violence. In America there have been about five thousand victims of lynch mobs since 1859. Most—but hardly all—occurred in the South and most of the victims were black. Cadmus's drawing evokes the pathological fury of the mob, who must obtain psychic gratification at any cost, including murder. The artist reveals a chilling view of mob psychology, the breakdown of any pretense of individual responsibility, and collective irrationality gone awry. The picture serves as a grim reminder of a sorry chapter in American history.

Although socially conscious art has never been the dominant thrust of American art, its most influential period was the 1930s and early 1940s, when turmoil, social disruption, and persistent injustice gave it a particular impetus. In the 1940s the first American style to have substantial impact on the world of art emerged. Abstract Expressionism, which grew out of the turmoil of the 1930s, dominated the American art world for the next two decades. Jackson Pollock, Franz Kline, Willem De Kooning, Mark Rothko, and Hans Hofmann became some of the most influential artists working in the United States. These artists, who differed substantially in personal style, generally sought to express the intensity of human experiences in abstract nonobjective forms. They used paint in unorthodox ways, attempting to explore new "realities" through immediate sensation and spontaneity. In contrast to socially conscious art, Abstract Expressionism is generally nonrepresentational and does not purport to evaluate topics of political and social controversy.

Despite the historical importance of Abstract Expressionism, there were a few American artists who departed from the mainstream. Some, like the Social Realists of the 1930s, merged social criticism with their artistic pursuits. George Tooker, Jack Levine, and Leonard Baskin are among the finest representatives of this continuing tradition. The content of their work primarily involves a critical view of American life in the second half of the 20th century.

George Tooker, born in Brooklyn in 1920, is a rarity among artists. No one is even remotely similar in artistic style or in the frightening vision of his artistic content. For want of a better designation, he can be included as one of the Magic Realists. He is clearly the most interesting representative of that group. More than any other artist, he portrays the terrifying consequences of human estrangement from a complex world. Tooker's art is a cumulative picture of a society devoid of meaningful human communication. With calculated precision, the artist reveals how modern urban life tramples upon individuality and personality with unrelenting impunity. His paintings are reflections of the dehumanization that has characterized so much of life in an advanced and highly industrialized social order.

The social content of George Tooker's art is more than an abstract commentary. It is, at the same time, extremely personal in its emotional impact. No one who has lived in America — or in any modern society — has failed to experience the realities he portrays. One of the most astute pictures of human isolation is *The Subway* (Fig. 5-23). The wretched figures steal furtive glances at their terrible confinement. They are trapped at every level. Iron bars throughout the station emphasize their physical incarceration, while their own expressions represent the total lack of freedom. What emerges is a picture of man

5-23. The Subway. *George Tooker. 1950. Egg tempera on composition board. Collection of the Whitney Museum of American Art, New York. Juliana Force Purchase.*

condemned to a robotlike existence from which there seems no possible extrication. The artist purposely pictures the characters as if they were in hiding. To complete the tragic vision, Tooker shows three figures at the right of the painting about to enter the revolving door, the symbolic meaning of which is all

5-24. Landscape With Figures. *George Tooker. Tempera. Collection of Mrs. Barbara Lassiter.*

128 The Art of Social Conscience

too obvious. That the characters in the work are versions of themselves only underscores the lack of any personal identity.

Landscape with Figures (Fig. 5-24) adds further horror to the story. In this painting Tooker has created a haunting abstraction of the regimentation of everyday life in schools, factories, universities, armies, and everywhere else in a society where the loss of individuality is encouraged, or even required. Technology has institutionalized the submergence of identity into the collective herd so thoroughly that most people become unconscious collaborators in their own alienation. Indeed, the painting shows a collection of automatons for whom any deviation from the norm would result in acute emotional discomfort. The broader implication is perhaps the grimmest of all: When the human desire for security is reinforced with such appalling social power, the aspiration for a humane society predicated on human autonomy fades into obscurity.

Tooker's treatment of the world of bureaucracy has no parallel. *Government Bureau (Fig. 5-25)* was the direct result of a series of frustrations and maddening personal experiences. Those experiences, repeated daily several million times over, have become one of the dominant facets of life in the last half of the 20th century. The painting is eerie in its truth. The most striking aspect is the total absence of personal responsibility. Nobody behind the pointedly frosted windows of the agency is identified; anonymity has been completely institutionalized. The sallow-faced creatures behind the window are only following instructions and enforcing the rules, and Tooker's expression reinforces one's impression that no one in a bureaucracy is responsible. Significantly, no face is wholly visible.

5-25. Government Bureau. *George Tooker. Metropolitan Museum of Art, New York.*

The ethical culpability of the mindless bureaucratic minions is perfectly apparent. These are the same men and women who, with equal obedience, could have participated in the genocide of Auschwitz and Buchenwald. It is no stretch of the imagination, in fact, to compare them to the faceless French soldiers in Goya's *The Third of May, 1808 (Fig. 1-8)*. In both cases thoughtless acquiescence to authority has resulted in the negation of human life: in one case physically; in the other, spiritually.

Tooker forces the viewer to consider the role of these victims. It is difficult to feel compassion for the passive or mindless. Once again, Tooker's artistic insights are amazingly reflective of actual human experiences. Most people who are confronted by an assault on their identities tend to accept the path of least resistance. Usually, they will conform to any bureaucratic strictures. As in *Landscape with Figures*, Tooker portrays a situation of collaboration with one's own alienation.

Necessarily, a complex society requires a bureaucracy. There is nothing in Tooker's content that suggests a return to romantic primitivism. Instead, he confronts the audience with a terrifying view of bureaucratic excess. Tooker posits a dilemma that is likely to intensify as social forms become even more complex. The force of his art is underscored by the uncertain prospects for reform.

Jack Levine was born in 1915 in Boston, where as a child he was exposed to rampant graft and corruption. He studied at the Boston Museum School and, in the course of his study, was influenced by various European Expressionists. He was an idealistic young man who was distressed by his perceptions of American life, and he resolved to combine his artistic training with his intellectual perceptions. In the course of his career, Levine has accordingly treated themes such as the miscarriage of justice, the greed and insensitivity of the rich, the crookedness of American political life, and specific topical events ranging from Spanish fascism to American policy in Southeast Asia. The artist has, like William Gropper, occasionally been compared to Daumier, but the differences between the two men are probably greater than the similarities. Although their moral and social outrage is much the same, Levine's content is more scornful.

Perhaps it would be more appropriate to compare Levine to George Grosz. The visual distortion Levine uses for artistic emphasis suggests stylistic as well as attitudinal relationships with the German artist. Like Grosz, Levine has created a conscious series of stereotypes that serve as the objects of his scrutiny. His objectives are intentionally rhetorical; he seeks to alert his audience to the dangers he exposes.

One of his earliest paintings and one of his most well known is *The Feast of Pure Reason (Fig. 5-26)*, which combines a bitter tone and an insightful view of power in America. The sardonic title hints at its content. The artist portrays the insidious and cynical combination of political influence and economic power. The Grosz-like tycoon at the right conspires with the self-serving elected official in the center. At the left, ready to enforce any decision, is the policeman,

130 The Art of Social Conscience

5-26. The Feast of Pure Reason. *Jack Levine. 1937. Oil on canvas. Extended loan to The Museum of Modern Art, New York, from the United States WPA Art Program.*

who is presumably well compensated for his services. Although the painting is a reflection of the harsh political vision of a young man of twenty-two, it is uncomfortably close to the truth. Conspiracies are far from unknown in American power politics, although today such arrangements as portrayed by Levine are usually replaced by more sophisticated communities of interest.

Levine has always found the political process in the United States an appropriate object for satirical treatment. *Election Night (Fig. 5-27)* offers an even stronger attack on the American bourgeoisie than on the electoral results that have spawned the celebration. The vacuity of the people, cavorting in contrived camaraderie, dominates the scene and is accentuated rather than concealed by the formality of their dress. Here the artist approaches the savage fury of Grosz, who depicted the Weimar counterparts thirty years before.

Jack Levine has remained an indignant artist throughout the crises of more recent American history. In 1967 he contributed a painting entitled *Invasion (Fig. 5-28)* to the "Protest and Hope" exhibition in New York, which condemned the immorality of the escalation of the war in Vietnam. The bellicose figure of Lyndon Johnson is prominent, as if to emphasize his role as the main architect of the war. The fusion of political protest and technical excellence ensures that *Invasion* will endure as a significant work of art.

5-27. Election Night. *Jack Levine. 1954. Oil on canvas. Collection, The Museum of Modern Art, New York. Gift of Joseph H. Hirshhorn.*

132 The Art of Social Conscience

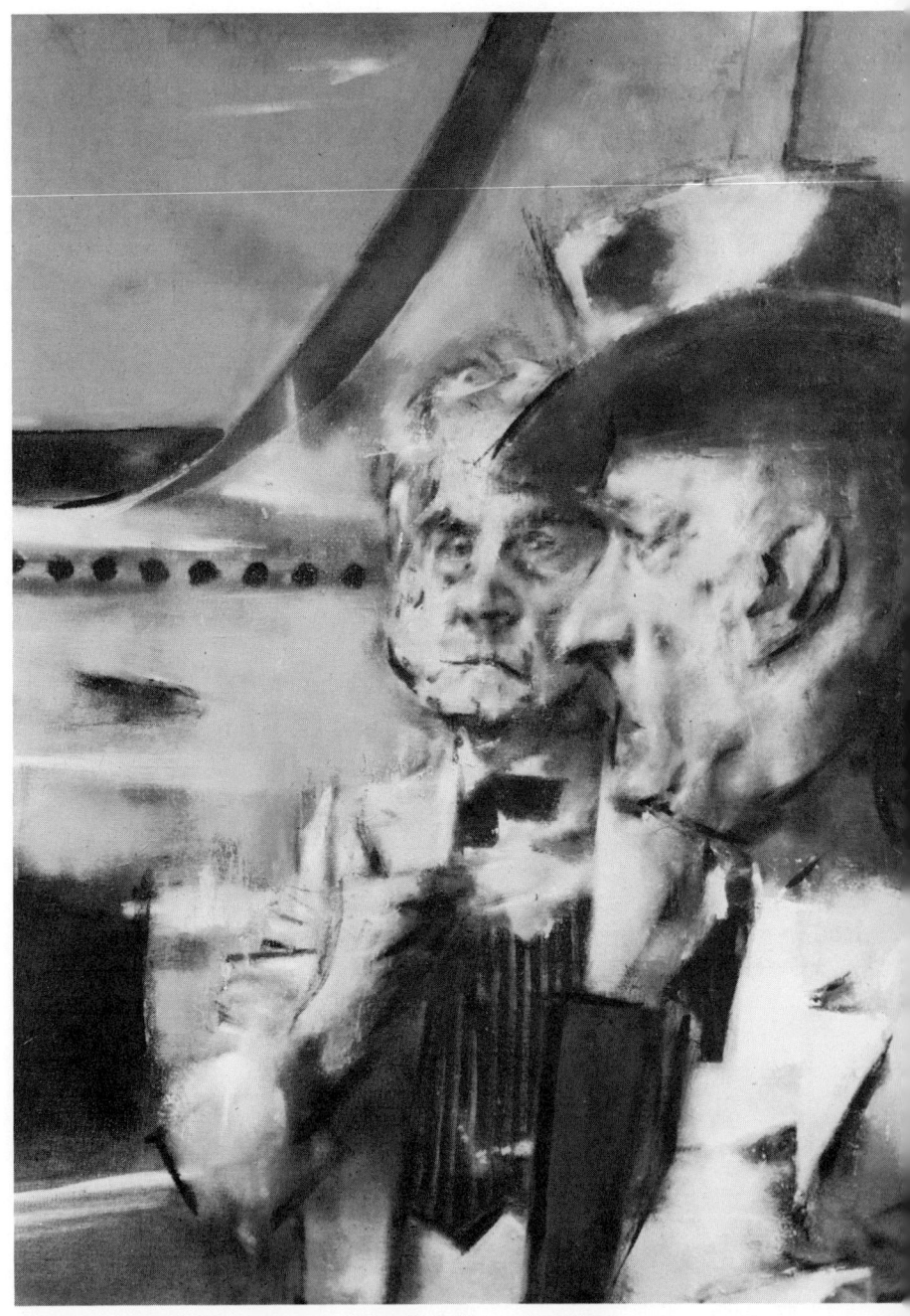

5-28. Invasion. Jack Levine. Courtesy Kennedy Galleries, New York.

The entire career of Leonard Baskin has been devoted to a humanistic personal, social, and ethical philosophy. Like his late friend Ben Shahn, Baskin is a serious intellectual who brings a complex theoretical foundation to his work. He was born in New Brunswick, New Jersey, in 1922, and he is now recognized as a significant figure in contemporary art. His writings reveal a vigorous opposition to the avant-garde in art because of his commitment to figurative content. He has sought to focus on the dilemmas of man in a hostile social environment.

Baskin has confronted the vast complex of life-negating forces that dominate modern existence: war, persecution, personal alienation, the threat of nuclear destruction, ecological catastrophe. His art illustrates the effects of these realities on the lives of human beings. Consequently, his work has a haunting darkness reminiscent of both Kollwitz and Munch. The personal dimension of his work joins with the more familiar social protest and anguish of the earlier Social Realists. The result is a remarkable fusion of the personal and social visions which, in conjunction with a highly distinctive style, makes Baskin one of the outstanding representatives of the art of social conscience.

Baskin's primary reputation rests with his work as a sculptor and as a graphic artist. As a young man, immediately after World War II, he formulated a socialist position, which he sought to incorporate into his sculpture. He found, however, that the results were neither effective nor satisfying. Because he was not content to omit social and political subjects from his work, he turned to graphic art, which he thought was more naturally suited for the presentation of his social ideology. His view was that the print is intrinsically the best medium through which to communicate a message publicly. In his own writings, Baskin acknowledges his debt to the great social printmakers who preceded him: Callot, Goya, Grosz, Rouault, and, perhaps most important, Käthe Kollwitz.

Among his graphics is a series of twelve gigantic works, which the artist describes as the capital achievements of his graphic career. Each is monumental in conception and execution. There are two, however, that are unusually appropriate to the theme of social conscience.

In the early 1950s McCarthyism was rampant throughout American life. The anti-Communist hysteria generated by the Wisconsin senator brought suspicion upon thousands of Americans and inflicted grief and hardship on its victims. Many persons with left-wing pasts lost their jobs, were harassed by public investigative and inquisitorial agencies, and at the same time, suffered the cruel personal persecution of their less politically suspicious neighbors. Although fewer people were arrested and imprisoned than during the Palmer Raids, the McCarthy era remains a blight on recent American history.

Leonard Baskin responded to those hostile times with dramatic indignation. In 1952 he executed a large woodcut entitled *Man of Peace (Fig. 5-29)*. The figure, five feet tall, is literally restrained behind barbed wire, accentuating the political climate of McCarthyism. His facial expression clearly reveals his sorrow and pain. The injured dove further illustrates the pernicious consequences of politi-

134 The Art of Social Conscience

cal persecution. There is, however, a note of hope in the woodcut. In the barbed wire are flowering plants as well as thorns. The plants are far from vibrant, but they remain nevertheless as a possibility of human resiliency and transcendence.

Like Shahn, Baskin is horrified by the possibility of atomic warfare. In 1954 he executed another of his gigantic woodcuts of social conscience. *Hydrogen Man* (*Fig. 5-30*) is stark and apocalyptic in its warning to all humanity. The skin of the figure is decomposing, a dark portent for the future if man is unable to

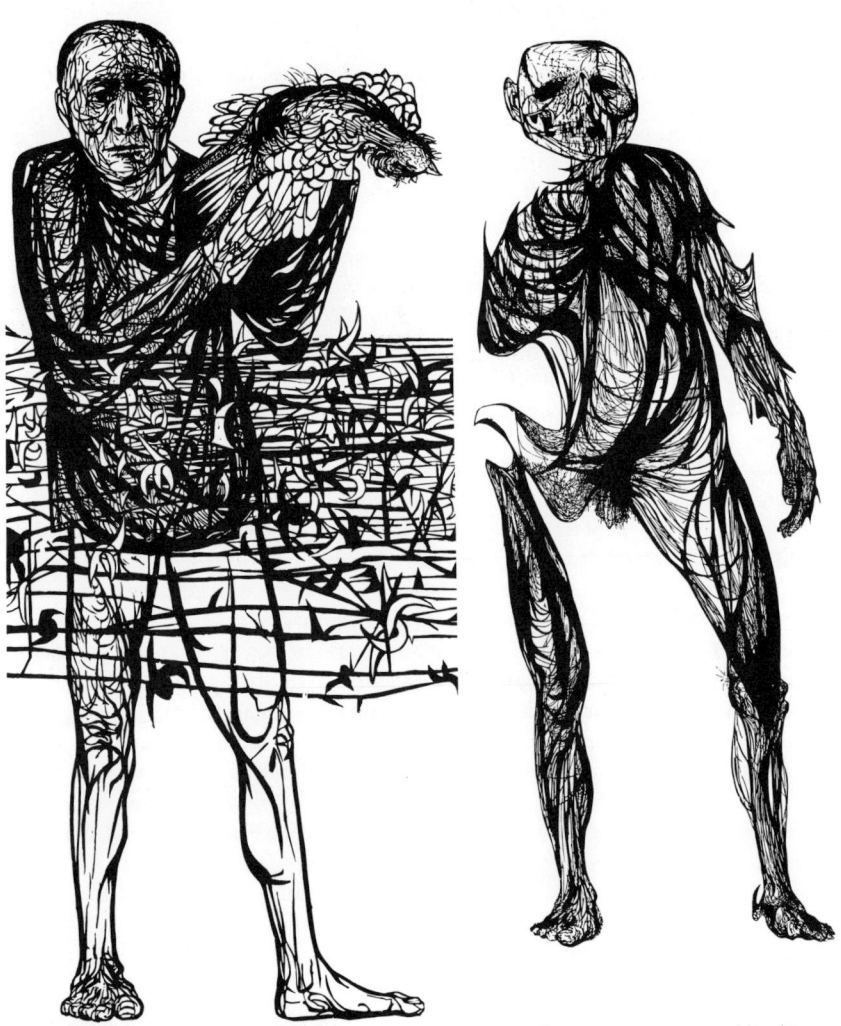

5-29. Man of Peace. *Leonard Baskin. Woodcut. Courtesy of Kennedy Galleries, New York.*

5-30. Hydrogen Man. *Leonard Baskin. Woodcut. Courtesy of Kennedy Galleries, New York.*

The American Experience   135

5-31. Agonized. Leonard Baskin. Woodcut. Courtesy of the Kennedy Galleries, New York.

superimpose rationality on his warlike proclivities. As if to emphasize the persistence of this problem, Baskin has recently turned out additional prints of this woodcut in flaming red.

More recently Baskin has returned to topical themes. He has done a series of drawings that ridicule the arrogant, ignorant sheriffs who stood as the violent symbol of opposition to the struggle for racial justice in America during the 1960s. Like Jack Levine, he contributed a drawing to the New York exhibition "Protest and Hope" as a gesture of protest against the war in Vietnam. Among the most powerful of Baskin's works, however, are those that show the personal consequences of disturbing social realities. Many of his prints and drawings fall into this category. Typical is a 1969 woodcut entitled *Agonized (Fig. 5-31)*. Here the emotional impact of a callous and frightening world is shown with compelling force. The influence of Kollwitz and Munch seems apparent as Baskin seeks to explore the meaning of human existence in the final decades of the 20th century.

In his writing Leonard Baskin has called himself a "moral realist." The condition of man is the totality of his work. His own words best express what he has sought to accomplish:

> The human figure is the image of all men and of one man. It contains all and it can express all. Man has always created the human figure in his own image, and in our time that image is despoiled and debauched. . . . Man has been incapable of love, wanting in charity and despairing of hope. He has

136 The Art of Social Conscience

not molded a life of abundance and peace and he has charred the earth and befouled the heavens more wantonly than ever before. He has made of Arden a landscape of death. In this garden I dwell, and in limning the horror, the degradation and the filth, I hold the cracked mirror up to man. All previous art makes this inevitable.*

In so doing, Baskin adds a major chapter to socially conscious art.

---

*Leonard Baskin, *Baskin: Sculpture, Drawings, and Prints* (New York: Braziller, 1970), p. 15.

6-1. The Leaders and the Masses. *José Clemente Orozco. 1936. University of Guadalajara.*

6 The Mexican Muralists: Rivera, Orozco, and Siqueiros

Mexico has always been a land of outstanding artistic achievement. The flowering of the monumental, magnificent murals of the 1920s and '30s represented a new dimension in the world of art. The major artists in the muralist renaissance—Diego Rivera, José Clemente Orozco, and David Alfaro Siqueiros—achieved universal recognition through works substantially devoted to social and political topics. Each made a major contribution to the history of socially conscious art. As brilliant as these men were, their work is part of a larger artistic tradition.

The origins of public art, which has flourished in Mexico for centuries, are woven into the Indian heritage of Mexican life and society. From prehistoric cave painting to the art of the Aztec, Mayan, and Toltec civilizations, Mexico possesses a rich history of aesthetic accomplishment. This tradition continued even after the Spanish Conquest in the early 16th century, when European influences began to dominate. The feature of the Indian past never perished completely. The Indian style, which sometimes incorporated Christian subject matter, survived in remote Indian villages and churches during the colonial period. Public art, of course, was an important method of communication in a country of limited technological development and widespread illiteracy.

Folk and popular art was a highlight of the Mexican experience throughout its history. One of the most important popular artists was José Posada (1852–1913),

6-2. Hanged Man—A Revolutionary Hanged by the Landlords. *José Guadalupe Posada. 1910–12. Broadside. Reproduced from Posada's Popular Mexican Prints, Selected and edited by Roberto Berdecio and Stanley Appelbaum (New York: Dover Publications, 1972).*

a prolific graphic artist of major influence in Mexico. His work includes an estimated twenty thousand engravings. Many were published as broadsides in various newspapers and were widely distributed throughout the country. Their themes encompassed all aspects of life: politics, natural calamities, scandal, crime, Mexican history, popular heroes, and many related themes. Important in his own right, Posada is especially significant here for two intricately related reasons.

Much of Posada's work constitutes a notable contribution to the history of socially engaged art. Many of his engravings were highly satirical and critical of the existing social order. His opposition to the dictatorship of Porfirio Diaz was frequently expressed in his art. He was also sympathetic to the revolutionary tendencies emerging in Mexico toward the end of his life. *Hanged Man—A Revolutionary Hanged by the Landlords* (Fig. 6-2) is illustrative of his socially conscious work. In this engraving the artist portrays the morbid consequences of revolutionary political activity. Those who seek to alter the structure of society through revolution must be prepared to die for their cause. Posada adds a note of bitterness as he reveals responsibility for the execution; the artist's sympathy for the rebellion against oppression is made with perfect clarity.

Equally important was Posada's influence on later generations of artists who transformed the character of socially conscious art by fusing folk and popular art with a subversive and radical political content. In the 20th century this emerged as the major artistic development in Mexico. Both Orozco and Rivera repeatedly acknowledged their professional debt to Posada. Orozco wrote in his autobiography that Posada's work was the catalyst for his own imagination, while Rivera compared Posada to Goya and Callot. While the final critical judgment of Posada may be slightly more modest, the impact of the artist's influence is obvious.

The Mexican Revolution of 1910–17 set the stage for the renaissance of mural art. After the revolutionary gains were consolidated, Rivera, Siqueiros, and Orozco, as well as several other artists, began a series of remarkable pictorial narratives and commentaries on public buildings throughout the land. Their subjects included national history, conflict and oppression, and the aspirations of the Mexican people. Consequently, in the major cities in Mexico, especially the capital and Guadalajara, truly great art is available to everyone.

A serious acquaintance with Mexican mural art is impossible without some background on Mexican history—especially because historical topics are a fundamental part of the content of that art. The muralists continually refer to specific historical events and personages in their work. More than most examples of socially conscious art, the works that follow often have a historical focal point as their critical perspective.

The Spanish Conquest, and the subsequent subjugation of the indigenous population, is a recurring theme of the Mexican muralists. On April 21, 1519, Hernan Cortés and some five hundred Spaniards landed on the shore where the city of Veracruz now stands. The Aztec nation, which had been dominant before

140 The Art of Social Conscience

the invasion, was vanquished within two years. Cortés and his men captured, tortured, and finally murdered Montezuma, the Aztec leader, and then embarked on the systematic destruction of virtually every aspect of Aztec religious and cultural life. After a short time, little was left of the Aztec civilization. Catholicism and the Spanish language were imposed by force. Resistance was met by terror and violence.

Spain began to harvest the natural resources of its new colonial prize. Gold and silver were mined, new cities were built, and businesses were established. Western civilization, with all its benefits and burdens, spread in the aftermath of the conquest. Tyranny and oppression became the rule. Indians were forced to work in the mines and elsewhere under conditions of wretched maltreatment and physical brutality. Attempts at rebellion were immediately crushed. The native population was essentially held in a state of serfdom while political and economic power remained in the hands of a small elite.

The Church was an active force in the processes of colonial domination. Priests instructed the native Mexicans in Spanish, taught the catechism, and thus facilitated the transformation of Indian culture into the new order. They approached their work with zealous righteousness, and the Church acquired control over the Indian masses in a relatively short time. What followed was a period of feudal landholding, which contained the majority of the population in a state of physical and emotional servitude. The Church, the large landholders, and the bureaucracy controlled life in Mexico for the next three centuries. By the early 19th century Mexico was a society with two clearly defined social classes: Spaniards who held most of the property and wealth and the other ninety percent of the population who were servants and laborers for this class.

In 1810 a priest named Miguel Hidalgo, seeking to end three centuries of servitude, proclaimed independence for New Spain (as Mexico had been called since the conquest of Cortés). Hidalgo instituted a peasant revolt, but within a year he was defeated and quickly executed. His name became the symbol of the Mexican aspiration for freedom and independence. Over a century later, José Clemente Orozco immortalized the symbol in a large portrait of the rebel priest in the mural he painted at the Government Palace in Guadalajara *(Fig. 6-3)*. Part of a larger work, the detail of Hidalgo is not a literal depiction of the man. His presence dominates a scene of revolutionary strife as a powerful and energetic force for liberty. Orozco created a universal image in the fiery Hidalgo of the aspiration for human liberation from colonial domination everywhere.

In 1813 the mestizo priest José Morelos issued a declaration of independence, but two years later he was captured and executed. Not until 1821 did Mexico finally achieve independence, as a consequence of complicated internal political developments in Spain rather than a result of a military victory of an army of independence in Mexico.

Mexican independence set the stage for a century of political intrigue, turbulence, wars, occupations, coups d'etat, and executions, all following one

6-3. Hidalgo. *José Clemente Orozco. 1937. Palace of Government, Guadalajara.*

another in rapid succession. The most constant feature of political life was the battle between conservatives and liberals. The conservatives relied on the Church and the army as the foundation for the new nation. The liberals, on the other hand, were far more secular in orientation and sought important reforms in landholding.

The conflict eruped in civil war in 1857. The liberal government under Benito Juárez had promulgated a program of reform, which included separation of church and state and the nationalization of large portions of ecclesiastical property. By 1858 there were two governments in Mexico; the conservatives were established in Mexico City, while the liberals, under Juárez, held the city of Veracruz. In 1860 the liberals triumphed and reform laws were instituted throughout the country. Juárez, a major figure in Mexican history, was to be frequently and sympathetically portrayed years later in the art of the Mexican muralists.

Juárez suspended the payment of debts owed to European governments and nationals because of the precarious financial position of the Mexican government, caused primarily by the massive expenditure of funds for the civil war. In 1863 French troops occupied Mexico City and Archduke Maximilian of Austria was installed as emperor. The liberal forces of Juárez resisted, while Mexican conservatives, initially happy with Maximilian, became disillusioned with his comparatively liberal policies. In 1867, however, Maximilian was ousted and subsequently executed. Juárez restored order and served as president until his death in 1872. In 1876 his successor was overthrown by Porfirio Diaz, who ruled as dictator for over thirty years.

Under the Diaz dictatorship, political order was established and industry was developed with the help of American capital. Diaz favored the upper classes, and his regime permitted and encouraged the widespread exploitation of workers and peasants. Meanwhile, education was neglected and most of the population was powerless in the political decisions which intimately affected their lives. Incipient attempts at reform were resisted vigorously by Diaz. The dictator's infatuation with foreign capitalists worked to the economic and emotional detriment of the small but emerging middle class. The brutality of the regime continued. By the first decade of the 1900s, however, seeds of revolution were evident. Downtrodden workers and agrarian peasants became increasingly discontent and the middle class also became restive.

In 1910 a political campaign headed by Francisco Madero sought to defeat Diaz. By 1911, after Madero had been arrested and sent into exile, guerrilla bands under various leaders were active in several parts of the country. Two of these leaders, Pancho Villa and Emiliano Zapata, were to play a significant part in the downfull of Diaz. Both would later appear as subjects in the work of some of the Mexican muralists.

After Diaz resigned in May 1911, Madero returned as president, but it became quickly apparent that he did not intend to add a social dimension to his political revolution. In 1913 he was overthrown by Victoriano Huerta and executed. By then the nation was reduced to a state of complete political confusion. Huerta, Carranza, Obregón, Villa, and Zapata held various regions of the country and fought savagely among themselves.

Emiliano Zapata opposed all the governments that succeeded the Diaz dictatorship, and he sought more basic reforms. A militant who used violence whenever necessary, Zapata and his bands of followers burned the buildings on the haciendas, murdered the owners, and distributed the land to the peasants. His army then assisted in cultivating the land for the benefit of the peasantry. The movement was a genuine effort at agrarian reform: The Zapatistas sought land rather than political domination. The beneficiaries of the movement were the peasants. Agrarian reform, identified with Zapata, became the most important symbol of the Mexican Revolution. Although he was later shot by a political rival, Zapata provided a firm social dimension to the Revolution.

Bloody military conflicts dominated the scene for many years. Although a revolutionary constitution was established in 1917, it was several years before any real measure of political stability was restored. The impact of the Revolution, however, fundamentally changed the character of Mexican life. The establishment in 1920 of the government of General Alvaro Obregón created the conditions for the flowering of the mural art that would propel Mexico to the forefront of world art.

Obregón was no radical. His desire was to transform an agrarian society into a modern capitalist order. Land distributions were made and education, so long neglected, was now encouraged. Obregón's intelligent, energetic minister of education, José Vasconcelos, stimulated the cultural life of the nation by turning the walls of public buildings over to artists like Rivera, Orozco, and Siqueiros, who were actually placed on the payroll of the Ministry of Education. Almost at once, the painters proceeded to use their art to criticize. Throughout the 1920s and '30s, mural topics included scathing attacks on the Church, the downfall of capitalism, reactions to the recent revolutionary strife, and, on occasion, proclamations of faith in socialism. The latter theme was expressed by painters who pictured such world revolutionary figures as Marx and Lenin and such symbols as hammers and sickles. The spectacle was amazing: artists in the employ of the government using the walls of government buildings to criticize that government and the larger social order. Socialist content, fused in part with an ancient mural style, found expression in an emerging capitalist nation. Most of the prominent mural painters had formed the radical Syndicate of Mexican Revolutionary Painters, Sculptors, and Engravers, a trade union for artists that also served to consolidate the radicalism of its members. Siqueiros and Rivera were the major figures in the movement, although Orozco was also heavily involved in its activities. Both Rivera and Siqueiros had by then become militant Communists. Organizational policies, accordingly, usually reflected that influence.

The three major figures of Mexican muralist art in the 20th century differed in political belief, personal temperament, and artistic style. At various stages in their careers, they bitterly opposed one another. All, nevertheless, were social artists in the finest tradition. All three injected their social ideology and critical vision directly into the content of their art. Their differences, however, were equally significant. Rivera, although fervently involved in left-wing politics, was never a systematic political theorist, and he was only marginally familiar with the writings of Karl Marx. At times almost a romantic visionary, he valued the colorful world of the ancient Indian civilizations as much as he advocated a socialist transformation of Mexican society. That he consistently believed in the socialist ideal and used his art to support that belief, however, cannot be denied.

Orozco was much different in temperament. He was an intensely private person who felt constricted by the ideological dogmas of the left-wing organizations. While he always remained sympathetic, he was far more pessimistic and skeptical than the majority of people more formally aligned with those groups. His commitment to the poor and oppressed is clearly indicated by the content of his art. At the same time, however, he turned his satirical brush on those persons with equal fervor. Siqueiros was the most politically active of the three. A long-time functionary of the Communist Party, he made political dedication the paramount focus of his life. Art, like everything else, was subordinated to that main objective. Remarkably, his artistic accomplishments did not suffer severely from his hierarchy of values.

Diego Rivera (1886–1957) was the most renowned figure in the Mexican mural tradition. His artistic inclinations emerged when he was still a young boy. He enrolled in formal art studies in Mexico City, where he learned to paint in the tradition of the Spanish academic artists. For several years thereafter, in Paris, he painted in the Cubist style innovated by Picasso, Braque, and Gris, and studied other major European masters of modern art. In 1920 he met Siqueiros in Paris. Their conversations involved both politics and art, and together they sought ways to transform art to make it available to the masses.

When Rivera returned to Mexico, Vasconcelos offered him the walls of the National Preparatory School for the creation of a mural, a large-scale allegorical work entitled *Creation*. Shortly thereafter, Rivera undertook a long and extensive project in the Ministry of Education. The series of frescoes here, devoted substantially to political and social themes, marked the emergence of Diego Rivera as a socially conscious muralist.

Depicting the life of the ruling class in stark contrast to the poverty of the masses, Rivera also used his art to prophesize the nature of society after the transformation of capitalism into a socialist order. The panel, *The Night of the Poor (Fig. 6–4a)*, shows the cramped and miserable conditions of the Mexican poor. The people huddle together stoically as they endure the collective tragedy of proletarian existence. Unlike the rich, whose lives are full of decadence and self-indulgence, the poor have only their aspirations for an end to their hardship. In the companion panel, *The Night of the Rich (Fig. 6–4b)*, Rivera expresses his disdain for the rich. His work in the Ministry of Education is thus an early example of class-advocacy artistic expression.

Rivera undertook further projects during the mid-1920s, and a few years later he traveled to the United States. Living and working in San Francisco, Detroit, and New York in 1931-34, he created murals of lasting artistic and social value in each city. His easel paintings, drawings, and graphic art also were usually devoted to social and political subject matter.

In 1932, at the Art Institue of Detroit, Rivera painted a mural interpreting the Machine Age and the impact of technology on social life. His most famous work, however, was done in New York City. In 1933 Rivera was invited, after lengthy negotiations, to execute a mural at Rockefeller Center. The theme was the ponderous-sounding *Man at the Crossroads Looking with Hope and High Vision to the Choosing of a New and Better Future*. The irony of a Communist artist working under the commission of the paramount symbol of capitalism gave rise to an extraordinary controversy. Rivera had conceived a radical mural replete with images of Communist ideology, including a portrait of Lenin among the groups or workers and technicians in charge of the New World. The Rockefellers demanded that Lenin's image be removed from the work, but Rivera refused. Eventually the Rockefellers ordered the mural destroyed. Later, in Mexico City, Rivera reproduced the same mural with minor modifications.

Rivera remained in New York to paint a series of murals at the New Workers' School, portraying, from a Marxist perspective, the American historical experience from the colonial period through the beginnings of the Depression and the New Deal. The general theme is the class struggle and the exploitation of labor by the capitalists. The result is simplistic and intellectually limited, but the effort is nevertheless a major example of politically committed art.

Particularly interesting is the panel entitled *The New Freedom* (Fig. 6-5), a dramatic but unsubtle view of labor in chains in the United States: Workers are literally handcuffed to their machines under the watchful eye of the factory owner. Several notable figures in the history of 20th-century American persecution are also prominent. At the right, Tom Mooney glances out of his cell, while underneath him Sacco and Vanzetti are being electrocuted. Above them are the nine Scottsboro boys, another major cause in the history of the American Left. At the top right, a policeman whips a worker before the imprisoned Statue of Liberty. In short, the picture is a brutal protrait of American life. Clearly, Rivera's Communist ideology lends itself to artistic exaggeration. The parade of horrors he depicts is a reductive view of America. Its vision may heighten political indignation, but it also discourages intellectual precision. Ultimately a failure because of its overexaggeration, the panel nevertheless contains more than a grain of truth. The essence of socially conscious art is the communication of a message. Here, that message is grossly overdone.

Shortly after his return to Mexico in 1934, Rivera resumed work in the National Palace in Mexico City on a gigantic mural portraying the epic history of the Mexican nation. Here again, Rivera employs his own brand of Marxist dialectics to express a panoramic view of the struggles of the Mexican people. This monumental work reflects the continued turbulence of Mexican political, economic, and cultural life from the Conquest to the present. Salient events in the

6-4a. Night of the Poor. *Diego Rivera. 1923–28. Secretariat of Public Education, Mexico City.*

6-4b. Night of the Rich. *Diego Rivera. 1923–28. Secretariat of Public Education, Mexico City.*

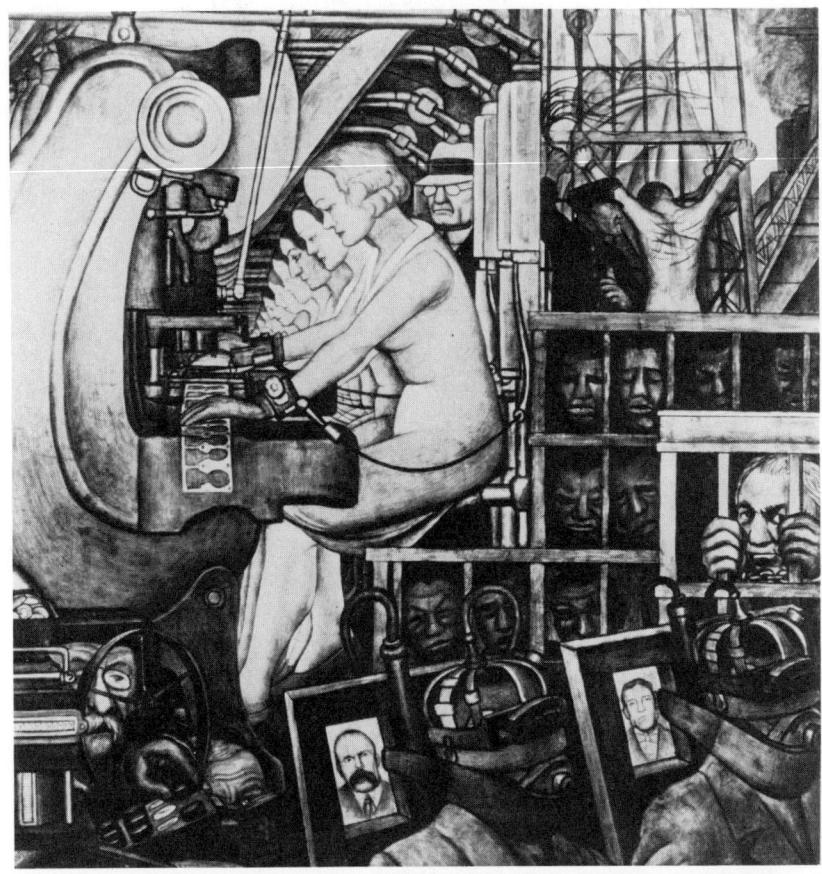

6-5. The New Freedom. *Diego Rivera. 1933. The New Worker's School, New York.*

nation's history are given powerful emphasis, and major historical personages such as Hidalgo, Juárez, and Zapata are prominently portrayed. Not historically accurate, the mural is nevertheless magnificent in conception and execution. Its immense size and the spectacular color are almost overwhelming, and only a personal, total confrontation with the work can lead to a comprehensive understanding of its content. Rivera is a master of a style of mural art that fuses historical subjects together in one work without divisions into panels or frames. Necessarily, any detail must be presented out of context.

A fine example is found in the central arch of the stairway at the National Palace *(Fig. 6–6)*. At the apex the words "Tierra y Libertad" (Land and Liberty)—the historical aspirations of the Mexican people—emphasize Rivera's passionate commitment to those ideals. Holding one end of the banner is Emiliano Zapata, with whom the slogan is so closely identified, and holding the other end is a worker, symbolizing the common interests of peasants and

6-6. Land and Liberty. *Diego Rivera. 1929–35. National Palace, Mexico City.*

150 The Art of Social Conscience

6-7. Mexico Tomorrow. *Diego Rivera. 1929-35. National Palace, Mexico City.*

workers in forging a new, humane order in Mexican life. Below them is the figure of Miguel Hidalgo, the hero of independence. At the bottom of the detail, Rivera depicts the invincible armor of the Spanish conquerors and the relatively defenseless Indians they fought. The detail, like the mural as a whole, is rich in complex historical allegory. Rivera's primary intention was to show the dialectical character of Mexican history as it works its way up to the progressive synthesis of a classless society. The work is thus a forceful blend of the panorama of the past and the hopes of the future.

Those hopes are given concrete form in the detail entitled *Mexico Tomorrow* (*Fig. 6-7*) at the left wall of the National Palace. At the center Karl Marx holds a Spanish translation of the opening lines of *The Communist Manifesto* and points the way to the social order of the future. At the extreme right of this detail, directly to the right of the "Huelga" (Strike) banner, the artist portrays the hanging of two rebels, one an *agrarista** and the other a Communist. Directly to the left of the two horses at the lower right corner, three more *agraristas* are about to be shot. Their fearless, resolute expressions show a determination to continue the struggle despite the consequences. Their impending deaths reveal the viciousness of those who hold the peasantry in absolute servitude. At the left center,

*The designation given to agrarian rebels who refused to be exploited by dominant landowners.

6-8. The Landing at Vera Cruz. *Diego Rivera. 1929–35. National Palace, Mexico City.*

almost directly below the outstretched finger of Marx, is a cleric who is more occupied with his amorous pursuits than with the spiritual salvation of his flock. Rivera thus joins the distinguished company of other artists who, over the centuries, have depicted the recurring hypocrisy of the clergy.

A theme that is given special emphasis at the National Palace involves the terrible suffering of the indigenous population during the Spanish Conquest. In a detail known as *The Landing at Vera Cruz (Fig. 6–8),* Rivera powerfully depicts the brutality of Cortés men as they tortured, maimed, and killed the captured Indians. The branding of the Indian at the bottom of the panel is only the most prominent of the barbarous acts; others in the detail are equally repulsive. Here Rivera's Marxist ideology has little to do with the more universal message that emerges: Such conduct is intolerable as a matter of basic humanity.

The mural at the National Palace was the crowning achievement of Rivera's artistic treatment of the history of his native land. Many of the themes developed here were amplified in other works. The mural in the Palace of Cortés in Cuernavaca, for example, as colorful and as historically complex as that in the National Palace, forcefully reiterates the theme of the Indians persecuted by Cortés and his mercenaries.

Rivera continued his political and artistic activities throughout the 1930s and '40s, and, more often than not, he was able to combine them. His career was not without its problems, however. From 1935 to 1943 he was out of favor and was unable to obtain public walls for mural work, so he turned to easel painting, watercolors, graphics, and drawing. To compound his problems, his political life was also turbulent. He quarreled with the Communist Party and in 1936 associated himself with Leon Trotsky, then the arch-enemy of the official Communist world. The vicissitudes of his personal affairs added even further to his troubles.

Rivera eventually returned to left-wing political acceptability and to work as a muralist. In 1947 he evoked another major controversy by including the words "God does not exist" in a massive work at the Del Prado Hotel. A strong protest ensued, and Orozco and Siqueiros, not at the time on good terms with Rivera, rallied to his defense. Eventually, however, Rivera removed the offending phrase.

Major projects of the 1950s were murals at the Lerma waterworks, which supplied water to the capital, and at the Theater of the Insurgents in Mexico City. Both murals contain topics of substantial social significance. In the former Rivera again criticized the upper classes and supported the struggles of the workers. In the latter he portrayed with great sympathy the heroes of Mexican revolutionary ideals. Near the end of his life Rivera was involved in a movement to oppose the testing of nuclear weapons. He died at the age of seventy in 1957, after a life of political ferment, artistic eminence, and personal turbulence. Diego Rivera did more to portray the epic story of his countrymen than any of his contemporaries. His monumental murals remain landmarks of socially conscious art.

The most complex of the Mexican muralist painters, José Clemente Orozco is not as well known internationally as Rivera. The contrast between them is striking. Rivera used his art to create a hopeful social paradise in conformity with his vision of a better world. For all his criticism of the old order, his primary object was more to herald and celebrate the coming of the new order. Rivera's art, at times naive, is replete with a romantic glorification of workers and peasants. Orozco had a far greater sense of realism. No less committed to the creation of a more just system of society, he rarely saw social life in a simplistic context. He used his art to destroy illusions and to portray the violence and conflict that are universal features of social existence.

Orozco's themes are less grandiose than Rivera's, but no less socially conscious. He dwelt on the grimmer aspects of life in order to understand them more fully, and so that he might oppose them more intelligently. Frequently appalled by what he observed during the course of his life, he was temperamentally unable to lose his art either in escapist triviality or in ideologically motivated distortions of truth. For Orozco, life was a deadly serious business, full of treachery, chaos, and misery. The content of his art reveals at every level a profoundly impressive dedication to the truth as he perceived it.

Orozco was born in the state of Jalisco. As a child in Mexico City, he frequently passed the shop where José Posada worked on his popular engravings.

He was fascinated by the process and was thus introduced to the world of art. He completed studies in architecture and agriculture and also managed to obtain training in art. During an experiment at school, he lost his right hand and the partial vision in one of his eyes. As a student, he was also active politically at the time of the revolutionary ferment in Mexico.

In 1917 Orozco visited the United States. As he crossed the border to Laredo, Texas, U.S. Customs officials seized and destroyed many of his drawings on the grounds that they were lewd and immoral. For several years Orozco lived and worked in San Francisco and New York. By 1922, however, conditions in Mexico were ripe for the muralist renaissance, and like Rivera and Siqueiros, Orozco participated in the project at the National Preparatory School in the Capital. He focused on the Mexican revolutionary struggle and the panorama of fire and death that characterized that era.

Trenchant social criticism was a significant feature of his work at the school. Typical is the panel known as *Law and Justice* (Fig. 6-9), in which Orozco turns his satirical talents to the legal institutions of society. At least as sardonic in its content as Daumier's memorable treatment, Orozco's panel portrays law and justice cavorting in an intoxicated embrace. Their smirks mock the ideals they

6-9. Law and Justice. *José Clemente Orozco. 1921–24. National Preparatory School, Mexico City.*

are ostensibly established to serve. Instead, their frivolity only shows that behind the facade of justice stands a more defective reality. Here, then, is yet another artistic reminder of the enormous gap between social ideals and social realities. Several other panels in Orozco's mural at the National Preparatory School accomplish the same objective. Among his other satirical targets are bourgeois society and even the foolishness of the workers.

Far less epic in his portrayal than Rivera, Orozco concentrates instead on the tragic human realities. In a detail known as *Soldier's Widow* (now, unfortunately, in a state of severe deterioration), Orozco transcends the military and political features of the Mexican Revolution to show a more universal reality. One of thousands of war widows, the woman must now face the hardships of life alone. Like Käthe Kollwitz and Georges Rouault, Orozco has penetrated to the core of personal suffering. It is a frightening and memorable vision.

In 1927 Orozco returned to the United States, where he was to accomplish some of his most magnificent mural work. At Pomona College in California he executed a monumental mural entitled *Prometheus,* portraying the eternal role of

6-10. Latin America. *José Clemente Orozco. 1933. Courtesy of the Trustees of Dartmouth College. Hanover, N.H.*

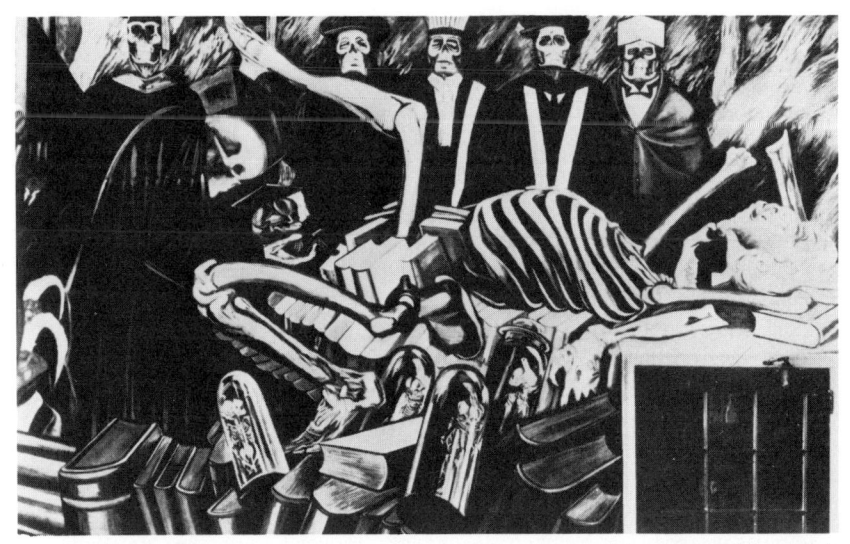

6-11. Stillborn Education. *José Clemente Orozco. 1933. Courtesy of the Trustees of Dartmouth College, Hanover, N.H.*

the rebel and the burdens he must bear. In 1930–31, in addition to numerous easel paintings and lithographs, Orozco painted several panels at the New School for Social Research in New York City, in which he projected his vision of the forces that have shaped human society. Gandhi and Lenin are prominent in the work, and imperialism is soundly denounced. Orozco's purpose in general was to use his art to encourage a world of peace without exploitation and racial discrimination.

The following year the artist executed what is probably his most impressive work in the United States. He was offered a commission at Dartmouth College in New Hampshire, where he was provided with complete freedom and a decent salary. His project there combined biting satire of U.S. social, economic, and educational life with a more general attack on imperialism. The latter theme receives its fullest expression in a panel entitled *Latin America (Fig. 6–10),* in which he represents the agrarian revolutionary Zapata as the central symbol of Latin America, thus identifying himself again with the progressive objectives of the Mexican Revolution.

More significantly, those objectives are brutally subverted by the power of U.S. imperialism. An American general about to stab Zapata in the back is supported by a gangster and a banker, whom Orozco finds virtually indistinguishable. Although exaggerated, this picture strikes close to the actualities of U.S. relations with its Latin American neighbors. The record of economic exploitation by U.S. corporations is as clear as it is distasteful, and the record of U.S. military intervention in Latin American affairs adds another level of support to Orozco's artistic allegations. American adventures in Guatemala,

Cuba, the Dominican Republic, and Chile in the 1950s, '60s, and '70s suggest, sadly, the timeless character of Orozco's critique.

The work at Dartmouth also includes a perceptive satire on the sterility of higher education and academic research. *Stillborn Education (Fig. 6-11)* is a disconcertingly truthful account of the paucity of creative intellectual work in the modern university. Orozco depicts the people who dominate university life as incompetent skeletal midwives who assist in the birth of a miniature replica of themselves. Amid the afterbirth of ponderous but intellectually dubious tomes and surrounded by the coffin-encased bones of those who never came to full academic tenure, the high priests of academia debase the integrity of their calling.

The irony of his attack is that it appears on the wall of an Ivy League university. Like the presence of Daumier's caustic lithographs in lawyers' offices, the physical presence of Orozco's satire in the academy may discourage a careful consideration of its critical content. Such a result would be unfortunate. Orozco was a perceptive observer of the affairs of mankind. His experiences convinced him that much of the work which appears as "scholarship" advances personal careers far more than it advances human knowledge. He sought to express that insight in a powerful and serious work of art. That work demands an equally serious response.

Orozco resumed his mural work in Mexico in 1934. In a few years he was called to his home state of Jalisco, where he created the most brilliant murals of his career. His first project was at the University of Guadalajara, where he portrayed man as worker, educator, rebel, and thinker. As a whole, the content of his art at the university is far gloomier than that of his notable contemporaries. An example is his unromantic treatment of the masses. In a segment entitled *The Leaders and the Masses (Fig. 6-1)*, Orozco portrays people as blindly and stupidly following a group of unscrupulous and venal leaders. The effect is an unsavory vision of the proclivities of the working class venerated so consumately by Diego Rivera. Orozco, however, could not capitulate to ideological demands or to personal self-delusion. Instead, his art penetrates the more basic truths about the human condition. His continued approval of movements for progressive social transformation never interfered with his need to express the truth in his work, a view that sometimes set him dramatically apart from his colleagues in the muralist movement.

His next project was to paint the walls of the staircase at the Palace of Government in Guadalajara. Here the portrait of Hidalgo is the focal point of the mural. Other themes in this building included many of the familiar objects of satirical attack. Orozco shows the Church in an insidious alliance with the military as they combined to destroy human hope and impede social progress.

In Guadalajara the artist finished his crowning achievement, a powerful, intense mural, at the Hospicio Cabañas, a home for orphaned children. Here, in a panoramic view of mankind, Orozco sought to present man in a comprehensive and realistic perspective, revealing his kindness and generosity as well as his

6-12. The Indian Supplicant. *José Clemente Orozco. 1938–39. Hospicio Cabañes, Guadalajara.*

6-13. By the Prison Gate. *David Alfaro Siqueiros. 1930. Oil on canvas. Collection San Francisco Museum of Art. Gift of Mrs. Charlotte Mack.*

cruelty and foolishness. The cumulative view, however, is far from pleasant. Orozco's view of the majority of his fellow human beings is gloomy indeed, and he seems obsessed in his repeated expressions of that attitude.

Another and more controversial theme at the Hospicio was the pictorial treatment of the Spanish Conquest. Unlike many other Mexican artists, Orozco portrays the Indian cultures as barbarous and uncivilized. While he offers no excuse for the savagery of Cortés and his men, he regards the European influences in a positive light. In a dramatic panel *(Fig. 6–12)* Orozco depicts a harsh Franciscan monk standing over an Indian supplicant. The cross is forged in the shape of a sword in order to show the manner in which Christianity was introduced into the New World. At the same time, however, the Spanish conquerors imposed the tools of their language. The letters of the alphabet that appear in this panel suggest that there was also a beneficial dimension to the Spanish presence. In illustrating the mixed blessings of the Conquest, Orozco tried to unite a desire for human justice with an intellectual perception of his subject.

His last significant mural work is found on the walls of the Mexican Supreme Court building. Orozco used the citadel of the law to attack that institution with merciless fury. Taking the classic figure of Justice as a point of departure, he distorted her into a cynical charlatan who degrades the principles she is supposed to uphold. The work is a splendid fusion of ethical opposition to injustice with intellectual perception. This was the framework in which Orozco worked until his death in 1949.

A reasonable assessment of José Clemente Orozco places him at the top of the Mexican muralists. Deeply humanitarian yet deeply skeptical, he managed throughout his career to avoid the extreme pitfalls of both postures. His art was never so gloomy that it lost an ability to express sincerely felt compassion for the downtrodden and oppressed. It also never suffered from the kind of political or moral tunnel vision that sacrifices truth on behalf of a "higher" cause. To combine realistic perception, moral commitment, and artistic grandeur is a rare and valuable accomplishment. In so doing, Orozco became one of the giants of modern art.

David Alfaro Siqueiros (1896–1974), the most sophisticated political ideologist among the three great 20th-century Mexican mural painters, was well aware of the theoretical doctrines of the revolutionary programs he espoused. Much more involved in the political conflicts of Mexico (and elsewhere) than his colleagues, Siqueiros combined revolutionary political activity with the development of socially conscious art of quality and stature.

Siqueiros was raised in an atmosphere of social liberalism, which contributed to the early awakening of his revolutionary inclinations and his lifelong penchant for direct political action. In 1911 he was enrolled at the Academy of San Carlos, where he was involved in a celebrated student strike. After being apprehended for his excessive zeal and violence during that affair, he was incarcerated for a brief period. Several other prison terms would follow throughout his career.

Siqueiros was a soldier during the Revolution. In 1918, however, he served another term in prison for military indiscipline. Shortly after his release, he went to Europe, where he met Diego Rivera and painted several works that fall into the category of the art of social conscience. One of his themes, understandably, was the sufferings of prison life. A painting entitled *By the Prison Gate (Fig. 6-13)* is typical of the powerful way Siqueiros captures the depths of human feelings—a feature that is the consistent hallmark of his art. In this picture the artist portrays a little girl waiting forlornly outside a prison. Her father probably is imprisoned and she wonders when he will come home. Not understanding why he is there, she knows only that she is deprived of his love and protection. The artist shows the impact of prison on the innocent victims, a perspective usually neglected by judicial authorities as they regularly consign men and women to prisons throughout the world. In a broader thematic sense, Siqueiros joins an artistic tradition that includes artists such as Goya and Rouault.

On his return from Europe, Siqueiros headed the Syndicate of Mexican Revolutionary Painters, Sculptors, and Engravers, and like his colleagues Orozco and Rivera, he contributed murals to the National Preparatory School—works that contain elements of the socially conscious content that would emerge later. For the next several years, Siqueiros was vigorously involved in union activities in Mexico and attended political congresses in the United States, South America, and the Soviet Union. In 1929 he participated in a large demonstration of workers that developed into a violent confrontation with the authorities. In the aftermath Siqueiros was arrested and sentenced to his third term of imprisonment. During his incarceration, he resumed his work. On his release, again active in radical politics, he was expelled from Mexico, and for a time he lived and worked in Los Angeles and New York. In Argentina, where he lectured on mural painting, he also spoke publicly against the military government and was again briefly imprisoned.

On his return to Mexico, Siqueiros engaged in a series of polemical attacks on Diego Rivera, another manifestation of left-wing intramural squabbling, conducted with greater ferocity than is usually displayed against its natural right-wing opponents. A typical painting of that period is *Proletarian Victim (Fig. 6-14)*, which again expressed the personal impact of social oppression. The title also underscores the overt class-conscious character of his art. The impact of the message, however, is somewhat muted by the bluntly unsubtle nature of the work. Like Rivera's, Siqueiros's art was on occasion prone to overexaggeration.

His continued period of painting was interrupted by the Spanish Civil War. Siqueiros left at once to fight on behalf of the Loyalist cause. His exposure to active combat and his observations of the suffering in that conflict led him to produce his most famous single painting, *Echo of a Scream (Fig. 6-15)*, which transcends the Spanish Civil War as it depicts the eternal grief of the innocent victims. Significantly, Siqueiros uses children as his symbol for those whose lives have been irreparably shattered by the ravages of war.

6-14. Proletarian Victim. *David Alfaro Siqueiros. 1933. Duco on burlap. Collection, The Museum of Modern Art, New York. Gift of the Estate of George Gershwin.*

6-15. Echo of a Scream. *David Alfaro Siqueiros. 1937. Duco on wood. Collection, The Museum of Modern Art, New York. Gift of Edward M. M. Warburg.*

Returning to Mexico in 1939, he subordinated art to politics because he was involved in Communist Party activities. As a Stalinist, he was vigorously opposed to Trotsky, who had found refuge in Mexico after having been persecuted throughout Europe by Stalinist agents, and in 1940 Siqueiros participated in an attempted assassination of Trotsky. Again arrested, he was released on the condition that he leave Mexico. He went to Chile, where he painted murals depicting heroes of Latin American independence movements. After further travels and work elsewhere in Latin America, he returned to Mexico in 1944.

6-16. New Democracy. David Alfaro Siqueiros. 1944–45. Palace of Fine Arts, Mexico City.

In 1945 he resumed his socially conscious mural art. Before the attempt on Trotsky's life, he had painted a mural in collaboration with other artists at the building of the Mexican Union of Electricians, a massive artistic polemic against capitalism. Now, several years later, at the Palace of Fine Arts in Mexico City, he painted an allegorical presentation of the struggle for a new world. The central panel, *New Democracy (Fig. 6–16)*, shows a woman surging forward in an attempt to shatter the bonds of oppression and exploitation. At her left is the fallen body of Fascism, injured in the recent war, but far from dead. In her right hand she carries a torch of freedom, symbolic of the new order. Like Rivera, Siqueiros emphasizes a vision of the future. *New Democracy* is powerfully expressive, and its symbol is a persuasive presentation of the message the artist intended.

6-17. Diaz The Dictator. David Alfaro Siqueiros. 1957. Chapultepec Castle, Mexico City.

164 The Art of Social Conscience

Siqueiros's later murals were variations on the clash between capitalism and socialism. Essentially he portrayed the rebellious proletariat, who are destined to change the character of social life. From 1956 to 1960, however, he turned directly to the theme of the Mexican Revolution for the first time. In a work at the Chapultapec Castle, he deals effectively with the character of the Diaz dictatorship. A major detail of the work *(Fig. 6-17)* shows the dictator and his supporters, the big landowners and the intellectual sycophants who served as his advisors. The dictator is sitting with his feet upon the Mexican Constitution, as if to show his contempt for the ideals it represents. Meanwhile, he and his entourage are entertained by several dancing women. The implication is that Diaz and his supporters have time for frivolity while the Mexican masses suffer horror at their hands. The detail presents a harshly accurate glimpse of the Diaz regime and reveals the artist's partisan stance. Again, the impact of socially conscious art is heightened by the critical perspective it seeks to engender.

Work on the mural was interrupted in 1960 when Siqueiros, who had become executive secretary of the Communist Party, was arrested for complicity in encouraging subversive street violence. He was imprisoned for four years while intellectuals and others throughout the world protested and mounted a campaign on his behalf. When he was released, he resumed work with his customary enthusiasm. His major project was at the Siqueiros Auditorium. A notable feature of this work is a sympathetic portrait of his colleagues Rivera and Orozco, with whom, after years of sometimes bitter differences and conflicts, the aging revolutionary-artist perhaps sought a reconciliation in an artistic gesture of solidarity.

Sometimes limited by a doctrinaire political vision, Siqueiros nevertheless emerges as a major figure in modern art. More than most painters now and in the past, he was able to capture the pain and suffering of mankind. His portrayals of weeping women and crying children are eternally human and reflect the artist's passionate desire to remove the conditions that have caused their despair. His death in January 1974 closed the chapter on one of the great movements in modern art.

Beyond the individual contributions of Rivera, Orozco, and Siqueiros to the art of social conscience, the renaissance of public mural painting itself adds to the highest ideals of that art. Millions of people daily may view with ease some of the greatest art in the Western Hemisphere.

7-1. Outstretched Arms. *Bedřich Fritta. Sketch.*

7 Concentration Camp Art

The internationally recognized socially conscious artists have used their talents to express dissatisfaction with political and social life. Above all, they empathized with the victims of social injustice and political oppression. Many were passionately involved in political affairs. With the notable exceptions of Daumier, Courbet, and especially Siqueiros, they were not imprisoned for their political activities, and they rarely suffered as much as the people they portrayed artistically. An important contribution to socially engaged art, however, has sometimes been made by the victims themselves. One of the more remarkable examples of this arose during the early 1940s, amid one of the most barbarous episodes in history.

The psychology of creativity is complex and sometimes bewildering. The most adverse conditions sometimes evoke extraordinary intellectual or artistic responses. The art produced in confinement, under conditions of the most extreme brutality and extermination in Nazi concentration camps, is part of the tradition of socially conscious art. Produced for the most part by men and women—and boys and girls—who did not survive their incarceration by the Nazis, their works endure as a testament to the resiliency of the human spirit.

Whether the work produced by these artists is good or even great art is largely irrelevant. An evaluation of their work based solely on formal aesthetic criteria would be inappropriate. Concentration camp art was produced furtively and under the threat of severe penalties, including death. The pictures were drawn

166   The Art of Social Conscience

under the most wretched conditions by people who were not widely known as artists. Some, in fact, did not become artists until their imprisonment. Artistic expression became the only possible way to reveal the horror of their lives. Here, particularly, the content of art is important in that it records the torture, the starvation, and the suffering endured by millions of people. These artists used whatever tools and materials were available. The works that have survived had to be concealed in order to avoid detection.

The history of the destruction of European Jewry has been comprehensively documented. As a result of an official, calculated, and systematic policy of extermination, over 6,000,000 Jews were murdered, mostly from 1941 to 1945. Under the racial mythology of the Third Reich, the Nazi apparatus moved from legal restrictions against Jews in Germany and the occupied countries to a series of extermination camps throughout the Continent. Known grotesquely as "The Final Solution," this policy was conceived and executed by Heinrich Himmler and his subordinates. The major names are known to virtually everyone: Auschwitz, Buchenwald, Dachau. There were many other camps throughout Germany and Eastern Europe that carried out the relentless process of annihilation. Life in these camps was hell on earth. The documentary evidence and the accounts of the survivors paint a picture as incredible as it is horrifying. That the nation which purported to be the most civilized in Europe was responsible for the most barbarous period of 20th-century history raises questions that may never be satisfactorily answered.

The art produced by concentration camp prisoners is a valuable and significant historical source. It enables the observer to obtain a vivid sense of the day-to-day horror to which the victims were subjected. Their art records the ubiquitous acts of sadism, the gratuitous violence, and, equally important, the state of mind of the victims. Concentration camp art serves as a warning to those who would oppress their fellow man, and it also stands as a remarkable human achievement.

Artworks were undoubtedly created in all the camps during the Nazi era, but the primary available source of concentration camp art is from the camp known as Theresienstadt in northwestern Czechoslovakia, not far from Prague. Hundreds of artworks from there are publicly available in the archives of the State Jewish Museum in Prague. There have also been exhibitions of the art from Theresienstadt on the grounds of the former concentration camp itself, in the town of Terezin. In 1969 an important and excellent book entitled *The Artists of Terezin* was published by American novelist Gerald Green, which contains a well-selected sample of over one hundred reproductions. Theresienstadt is the frequently used German name for the concentration camp in the town originally founded by Emperor Joseph II and named for his mother, Maria Theresa. The town had served as a military fortress and later housed a prison for political inmates. The town of Terezin will long be remembered, however, as the site of one of the most insidious concentration camps in the Nazi apparatus.

What distinguished Theresienstadt from the other camps throughout Europe was the cruel fraud which the Nazis attempted to perpetrate by virtue of its existence. The camp was represented as a model and humane relocation center, a special ghetto designed for the Jews of Europe. It was established to create an illusory showplace for Jews so that foreigners could be satisfied with the purportedly decent treatment of the residents.

The Nazis reported that Theresienstadt was created as a center for the elderly and privileged Jews. It was supposed to be a place where self-government would be established and where normality would prevail. In fact, many of the trappings of normality *were* present. Shops, cafes, synagogues, a system of currency and postage were all given prominent public emphasis, and there were fewer SS guards. Many of the deportees actually believed the German lies, particularly when they had heard rumors about the life in Buchenwald or Bergen-Belsen. The Nazis, however, planned Theresienstadt as an instrument of their cynical policy. The fate of the residents had been well planned.

For all its facade, Theresienstadt was a collection point for transportation east to Auschwitz, where the gas chambers and ovens carried out Nazi policy with morbid efficiency. The presence of Theresienstadt was designed specifically to facilitate "The Final Solution," and statistics reveal the grim reality. During its infamous existence, Theresienstadt had a total of 140,000 inmates at one time or another, including 76,000 Jews from Czechoslovakia, 42,000 from Germany, 15,000 from Austria, and 6,500 from other European nations. The average population was about 40,000, but at times it was much higher. Although most prisoners were Jews, there were also a few Communists, other political prisoners, and members of the resistance movements from many European countries.

Theresienstadt was not a place of systematic extermination. Its primary purpose was to serve as a way station in support of that grisly objective. Yet thousands also died in Theresienstadt, mostly of starvation, exhaustion, and disease, but also from beatings, individual executions, and suicides. Approximately 87,000 prisoners were transported to other camps, primarily Auschwitz. The total death toll was about 112,000 men, women, and children.

The first deportations to Theresienstadt began in 1941. Jews from Prague were forced to assemble for processing and transportation to their "model ghetto." Meanwhile, their possessions were stolen by members of the SS. Conditions in the camp were appalling: The quarters were crowded and supplies were minimal; rules were imposed and violations were punished severely; beatings were frequent; and anyone who had believed the Nazi myth of a model ghetto was quickly disillusioned.

As time passed, conditions worsened. Food was horrendous and many died from malnutrition. New brutalities were constantly initiated. Hangings were ordered for even petty violations of the regulations. More ominously, transports to Auschwitz began, adding further terror to the inmates' lives. The Germans, however, continued the "model ghetto" myth. More stores were opened and cafes were established. Prisoners were encouraged to participate in a cultural

168 The Art of Social Conscience

life as if nothing in their lives had changed. In fact, an active cultural life did flourish despite the horrible context of life in a concentration camp. Lectures were organized, theater performances presented, and numerous operas and other musical events performed. The Nazis permitted this activity only because it was consistent with their public pronouncements on the character of life in Theresienstadt.

The colossal fraud perpetrated by the Germans was successful for a shockingly long time. In June 1944, a commission from the Danish Red Cross visited the camp. In preparation, the Nazis created the biggest show of all. Barracks were painted, concerts were organized, worthless currency was issued, and children's play facilities were established. Injured and infirm prisoners were quickly dispatched to Auschwitz. The realities were carefully hidden. The Danish inspectors were satisfied and later submitted a laudatory report to the International Red Cross detailing the humane treatment of the Jewish "residents" at Theresienstadt. The art of the camp artists would eloquently dispute that report.

These artists, who worked clandestinely, revealed the totality of conditions in the camp as well as the hunger and misery of the inhabitants. The authorities were aware of these artistic endeavors and sought to apprehend the artists. In time many were seized, questioned by such Nazi luminaries as Adolf Eichmann, tortured, and shipped to other camps and almost certain death.

The primary artists of Theresienstadt were Otto Ungar, Leo Haas, Karel Fleischmann, Bedřich Fritta, and Alfred Kantor. Only Haas and Kantor survived their Nazi imprisonment. These men were different in personality and

7-2. Potemkin-Style Shops. *Bedřich Fritta. Painting.*

Concentration Camp Art **169**

background, but each used his artistic talent to record his perceptive and damning observations. Each, in different ways, has made an important contribution to the art of social conscience in the 20th century.

Bedřich Fritta had been a politically conscious commercial artist in Prague before his deportation to Theresienstadt. His use of art to record and protest the vile character of concentration camp existence was therefore a natural expression for him. When it was discovered that he was responsible for an artistic condemnation of the Nazi fraud, he was severely beaten and transported to Auschwitz, where he died a week after his arrival.

Fritta's art reveals the monumental hoax of Theresienstadt. In a painting entitled *Potemkin-Style Shops (Fig. 7-2),* he illustrates the shops designed by the Nazis to deceive the outside world. Fritta reveals the fragility of that deception; the shops are mere facades and nothing more. The reality of death and misery is partially obscured by the facade, but it is clear to all who care to penetrate the surface. Official observers from the outside, apparently, were content to do otherwise.

In another work Fritta provides a grimly realistic view of the wretched and foul conditions in Theresienstadt. *In the Attic (Fig. 7-3)* is a nightmarish scene of the sick and the elderly. Huddled together in cold, crowded quarters, they reveal in their expressions their overwhelming despair. Such was the fate of the people sent to the "model ghetto." Again, a work of art, as much as any document or statistic, indicates the inhumanity of terror and oppression.

A sketch *(Fig. 7-1)* made by Fritta is the most moving and disturbing of all his artistic efforts. The outstretched arms of the figure as he sinks inexorably into

7-3. In the Attic. *Bedřich Fritta.*

170 The Art of Social Conscience

hopelessness and death provide a vision of human tragedy that transcends even Theresienstadt and Auschwitz. The forceful eloquence of the work elevates it to the highest level of socially conscious art.

Leo Haas had also developed a political consciousness before he arrived in the concentration camp. His art reveals a bitter and sarcastic view of life in Theresienstadt. More than any of the others, his artistic content is characterized by a critical denunciation of the atrocities he witnessed. He also used his art to express and communicate a powerful compassion for the victims of the Nazi terror. When his work was discovered by the authorities, he, too, was shipped to Auschwitz. Fortunately, his artistic talents were needed by the Germans and he was sent to yet another concentration camp, where he managed to survive until the liberation.

His sketch entitled *Camp Commander (Fig. 7-4)* is an example of the satirical thrust of his concentration camp art. The swagger of the Nazi commander is intentionally portrayed in sharp contrast to the prisoners crowded behind the wall. The drawing is understandably and effectively bitter in tone. It is, moreover, an example of the use of art as political resistance, a weapon in the apparently never-ending fight against the tyrannical conditions that make resistance necessary.

7-4. Camp Commander. *Leo Haas. Sketch.*

7-5. Transport to the East. *Leo Haas.*

Another dimension of Haas's art is seen in *Transport to the East* (Fig. 7-5), which portrays a group of stamped and numbered victims on their way to almost certain extermination. This, of course, was the raison d'être for Theresienstadt. No one is spared; men, women, and children march off to be slaughtered. Their expressions reveal, at this stage of their incarceration, that they have no illusions about their fate. Although this work is a bitter denunciation of "the final solution," it is not lacking in compassion.

Otto Ungar, a shy, modest man, had been a teacher in a Jewish secondary school in Brno, the capital city of Moravia, and one of the subjects he taught was art. In many respects he is the most tragic of the Theresienstadt artists. He too was beaten when the Nazi authorities discovered his work. In his case, however, the normal sadism of the concentration camp guards achieved new levels of viciousness. Knowing that he was an artist, the guards crushed his hand with clubs. Two of his fingers had to be amputated. Like Fritta and Haas, he was sent to Auschwitz. There, through an inexplicable miracle, he did not die. Instead, he was sent on one of the infamous death marches from one concentration camp to another. He eventually ended up in Buchenwald, not far from the German city of Weimar. He held on to life until the liberation, but he died a few months later, a belated victim of Nazi persecution.

172 The Art of Social Conscience

7-6. Portrait of an Old Woman. *Otto Ungar.*

Ungar's work entitled *Portrait of an Old Woman (Fig. 7-6)* depicts the personal realities of imprisonment in a concentration camp. The artist shows a profound sympathy for the woman, revealing the sadness that dominates her life. That portrayal is a matter of great importance. It is shockingly easy, when 6,000,000 have perished, to forget the individuals who were the victims of Nazi racial lunacy. Ungar's portrait serves as a reminder that there are human sorrows and sufferings, which can only be obscured by mountains of grim statistical data.

Dr. Karl Fleischmann was a physician who painted as a hobby. At Theresienstadt he ministered to the needs of other prisoners—a full-time job and more, since disease was a persistent problem in the concentration camp and the death rate was substantially more than one hundred per day. Still, Fleischmann found time to draw and paint, and his works survive as a monument to the determination of some human beings to triumph over conditions of unmitigated barbarism. In October 1944, he was included in one of the final transports to Auschwitz and was sent immediately to the gas chambers upon his arrival.

Fleischmann's painting *First Night of New Arrivals (Fig. 7-7)* is an especially poignant work. The newly arrived German Jews in Theresienstadt had believed the lies of the Nazis and had hoped to reside in a model ghetto for elderly Jews. Their arrival put an immediate end to those wishes. As they entered the camp, they were stripped of clothing and valuables, given a humiliating personal search, and thrown into vermin-ridden quarters not even fit for animals. Here, then, are the consequences of instant disillusionment, effectively communicated by the artist through the facial expressions of the subjects. The painting is at once

7-7. First Night of New Arrivals. *Karel Fleischmann. Painting.*

174 The Art of Social Conscience

a condemnation of Nazi duplicity and a comment on the perpetual human capacity for self-delusion.

Alfred Kantor was a young man in Prague at the time of his deportation to Theresienstadt. After two years there he was sent to Auschwitz. Five months later he was shipped to a forced-labor camp near Dresden. He was fortunate to survive. Upon his release, he was determined to record his experiences as an inmate in Nazi concentration camps. In the two-month period after his liberation, he created a book of 127 drawings, which were published in book form in English under the title *The Book of Alfred Kantor*. It is a remarkable effort which captures accurately the character of life under such dreadful conditions. Although the style is immature, the art is particularly interesting because it seeks to re-create the salient events of daily camp existence. Its indictment lies primarily in its realistic depiction of actual occurrences. It thus makes the atrocities of the Nazi authorities speak for themselves.

Virtually all of Kantor's drawings provide insights into the terrifying conditions which millions endured, but his most powerful works are those which depict his stay in Auschwitz. His illustration of the latrine room there *(Fig. 7-8)* reveals the total lack of privacy, as well as the intolerable lack of sanitation. The sign, "Cleanliness is your health," can only be described as an obscene joke on the part of the Nazi captors. For them, physical discomfort and deprivation were not enough. Repeatedly, they sought opportunities to subject the prisoners to added emotional torment. The picture of the latrines is indicative of what people faced in Auschwitz. It is an effective artistic accusation in the forceful simplicity of its description.

Kantor's drawing of Dr. Joseph Mengele *(Fig. 7-9)* is the most disconcerting of his works. Mengele was a monstrous example of the sadists and psychopaths who rose from obscurity to positions of high authority during the Nazi period. As a physician, he was responsible for the medical experimentation at Auschwitz, which was barbarous beyond description. He also took delight in personally selecting people upon arrival for immediate death in the gas chambers or for work details, which would result in only slightly prolonged life. Kantor's portrait of the brutal doctor compels the viewer to contemplate the larger issues. The observer must wonder what makes a Dr. Mengele and how a political system arose which brought him to such prominence.

One cannot deal with concentration camp art without at least brief mention of the child artists at Theresienstadt. Children's art is usually and justifiably excluded from serious consideration in the world of art criticism. The extraordinary historical circumstances at Theresienstadt, however, justify a modest exception. To view the artistic efforts of the children imprisoned in a concentration camp is a wrenchingly painful experience. More than anything, it registers in the viewer a sense of the ultimate depravity of the Nazis.

There were 15,000 children under the age of fifteen incarcerated at one time or another. Only about one hundred survived. Most were shipped to their deaths in Auschwitz. They left a legacy of artistic work which ranges from the hopeful

Concentration Camp Art 175

7-8. Latrine. *Alfred Kantor. From The Book of Alfred Kantor (New York: McGraw-Hill Book Company, 1971). Used with permission of McGraw-Hill and Alfred Kantor.*

176 The Art of Social Conscience

7-9. Dr. Mengele. *Alfred Kantor.* From *The Book of Alfred Kantor.* (New York: McGraw-Hill Book Company, 1971). Used with permission of McGraw-Hill and Alfred Kantor.

Concentration Camp Art 177

pictures of children everywhere to the most perceptive observations of concentration camp life. The latter work was done by children who knew well that they were doomed. The children in Theresienstadt were organized by teachers into various artistic activities. Watercolors, pencil and crayon drawings, and collages were made out of whatever materials were available.

The State Jewish Museum in Prague has four thousand examples of the art produced in Theresienstadt by the child artists. Tragically, many of the examples are conscious pictures of SS guards, executions, and burials. A poignant example of such work is a detail of a pencil drawing done on cardboard by Josef Novak (*Fig. 7-10*), who was deported to Theresienstadt in 1942 and sixteen of

7-10. Pencil Drawing. *Joseph Novak. 1943. From I Never Saw Another Butterfly, edited by H. Volavkova (New York: McGraw-Hill Book Company, 1964). Used with permission.*

178   The Art of Social Conscience

whose works have been preserved. This drawing was done in 1943, a year before his death in Auschwitz at the age of twelve. Here he presents a vision of the starkness that pervaded the concentration camp. The grayness of the lead pencil adds to the grim view of the cramped dwellings in which he and the other children were forced to reside. Since one of his other works of art in the archives is a picture of an execution, it is reasonable to assume that his portrayal of the bleak dormitory at Theresienstadt is a thoroughly intentional view of personal sorrow. This and similar work must be sadly included as a chapter in the long history of socially conscious art.

Regrettably, the works of the artists of Theresienstadt are not the only examples of concentration camp art of the 20th century. Although the Nazi experence cannot be matched for cruelty or sadism, a disgraceful incident in American history during World War II gave rise to artistic efforts which reflect and condemn a series of political policies and widespread social discrimination.

In 1942 the United States government, already at war with Japan, ordered what was euphemistically called the "relocation" of 110,000 American residents of Japanese ancestry. Of these numbers, 70,000 were U.S. citizens who were removed from their homes and jobs in the Pacific Coast states of California, Oregon, and Washington. This resulted by virtue of a proclamation by President Franklin D. Roosevelt that granted authority to the U.S. military to designate geographic areas from which people of Japanese ancestry could be excluded. Pursuant to that authority, these people were taken to remote camps scattered throughout the western and southern United States.

These measures met with the enthusiastic approval of millions of Americans, including many prominent figures in public office. They also evoked the vigorous opposition of civil libertarians and others who were shocked and horrified by a procedure that seemed cruel, arbitrary, and unconstitutional. The legal issues were resolved by the United States Supreme Court. In a decision that can only be described as a masterpiece of sophistry, the Court ruled that the exclusion was legal because it was within the war power of the Constitution for the military to conclude that the presence of the Japanese-Americans constituted a present or potential danger to American security. The rationale of *Korematsu v. United States* was transparently designed to deflect public attention from the concession of the Court to political expediency.

The internment of 110,000 people cannot be viewed in legal terms alone. The basic issue is the propriety and morality of transporting thousands of citizens and residents from their homes without any evidence of wrongdoing. The underlying social and historical realities serve to explain the deportation more satisfactorily than do the strained arguments of the Supreme Court. There had long been a history of anti-Oriental sentiment on the West Coast. The Japanese in particular had borne the brunt of this racist influence and overt discrimination. Many Japanese immigrants had succeeded in traditional American enterprises. They had prospered as they established profitable businesses and agricultural ventures. The resentment caused by their success only exacerbated the racist attitudes that had already existed. World War II and the Japanese bombing of Pearl Harbor provided a convenient pretext to move from racist sentiment to concrete racist action. Important sources of public opinion, notably the Hearst newspapers, seized the opportunity to create pressure to force the Japanese-Americans out of their homes and businesses.

With the formal orders of exclusion, the Japanese were forced to liquidate their holdings in haste. Consequently, they suffered incalculable financial losses, selling at times for ten percent or less of the actual value of their property. Those who purchased property at those figures received the windfalls of racial discrimination. Some property was also seized by the government. Years later the internees received compensation estimated at only a small fraction of the property's value.

The Japanese-Americans were ordered to appear at various centers in preparation for transportation to the concentration camps. Those camps, stark and barren, were surrounded by barbed wire and armed guards. Many were bitterly cold in the winter and insufferably hot in the summer. Minimum standards of comfort were absent and sanitation was less than acceptable. The deprivations and brutalities of the Nazi experience were never matched, of course, but even this comparison cannot justify so deplorable an episode in American history.

The inmates of these camps suffered far more than physical discomfort. The emotional burden of confinement and the suspicion of potential traitorous conduct left incalculable scars. The irony of the distinguished military service of many Japanese-American young men only added to these emotional burdens. The spirit of artistic activity, however, lightened at least a few of these burdens. Amid the dismal existence of regimentation, traditional Japanese crafts such as flower arrangement, calligraphy, and wood carvings abounded. In addition, there were paintings and drawings that detailed the ugly realities of the "relocation." Many of these latter works serve as powerful accusations of the policies and social forces that led to the establishment of concentration camps on American soil.

The works of several artists constitute an addition to the art of social conscience. The most important is Miné Okubo, whose artistic range goes far beyond her experiences as an inmate in an internal concentration camp. Born in 1912 in Riverside, California, into a family of remarkable artistic talent, she received her formal training at the University of California at Berkeley. Travels in Europe also contributed to her artistic development. When she returned to California, she observed Diego Rivera working in San Francisco. Rivera's powerful influence was to affect both style and content of her art.

In 1942 Okubo was evacuated because of her ancestry. She and her brother were initially taken to the Tanforan Race Track in San Bruno, where they remained for six months. While incarcerated, she executed a series of charcoal drawings about the evacuation. These haunting works, which record the hopelessness and dejection of the evacuees, reveal the sense of gloom that pervaded

7-11. Moving In. *Miné Okubo.* From the Oakland Museum catalogue *Miné Okubo: An American Experience.*

the Japanese-American community. They also picture the somber realities of life under confinement.

A typically forceful example is *Moving In* (Fig. 7–11), which portrays three adults and a child carrying the burdens of their terrible situation. Pain and betrayal are apparent on their sorrowful faces. Particularly prominent is the weighty box carried by the central figure, symbolic of the troubles that have been imposed upon his life. The child, vaguely aware that the security of his existence has been torn apart, seeks the protection of his mother. The barracks and mountains in the background are sad portents of what is to come. Like so many other examples of socially conscious art, the work fuses a psychological and social reality into a powerful commentary.

Okubo also created a series of paintings about the evacuation. In one month at San Bruno, she completed fifty works which dealt with similar themes. Carefully and skillfully, she revealed the intensity of the emotional state of the imprisoned people. In a particularly moving example entitled *Dust Storm* (Fig. 7–12), she conveys a sense of the shame which so many of the internees felt. In this work the characters recoil as much from the shock of being uprooted as they do from the temporary presence of a storm. Rivera's influence is apparent. Okubo obliges the viewer to imagine what it would be like to be forcefully removed from one's community, job, and friends. The power of that effect serves as the most significant condemnation of the policies that imprisoned the West Coast Japanese-Americans.

Concentration Camp Art 181

Okubo was finally assigned to the Central Relocation Camp in Topaz, Utah. During her stay there, she was associated with a literary magazine known as *Trek*, which included numerous examples of her art. She illustrated many of the magazine covers, and many of these record the difficult nature of life in the camp. They are keenly perceptive observations and serve as an interesting counterpart to her imprisoned fellow artists in Theresienstadt. One of the most impressive facets of her work at Topaz was her portrayal of the communal features of the imprisoned persons, who try to maintain both human dignity and psychological stability under such adverse circumstances.

A poignant example of Okubo's work for *Trek* is on the December 1942 cover of the magazine *(Fig. 7–13)*. The supposedly happy spirit of Christmas is belied by the troubled expressions of the incarcerated family. Okubo uses contrast effectively in a work that highlights the basic inhumanity of the relocation orders.

Similarly powerful is her *Trek* cover of June 1943 *(Fig. 7–14)*. Here, the artist portrays four adults and a child in one washroom—people without privacy, trying to stay clean and neat. One man shaves while another washes his clothing. A woman carries a bucket while another scrubs her child. Again, the content of the work stimulates its audience to contemplate the loss of the personal privacy it takes so much for granted—a deprivation that is the inevitable consequence of imprisonment.

7-12. Dust Storm. Miné Okubo. Pastel. From the Oakland Museum catalogue *Miné Okubo: An American Experience.*

182 The Art of Social Conscience

7-13. Trek cover, December 1942. Miné Okubo. From the Oakland Museum catalogue Miné Okubo: An American Experience.

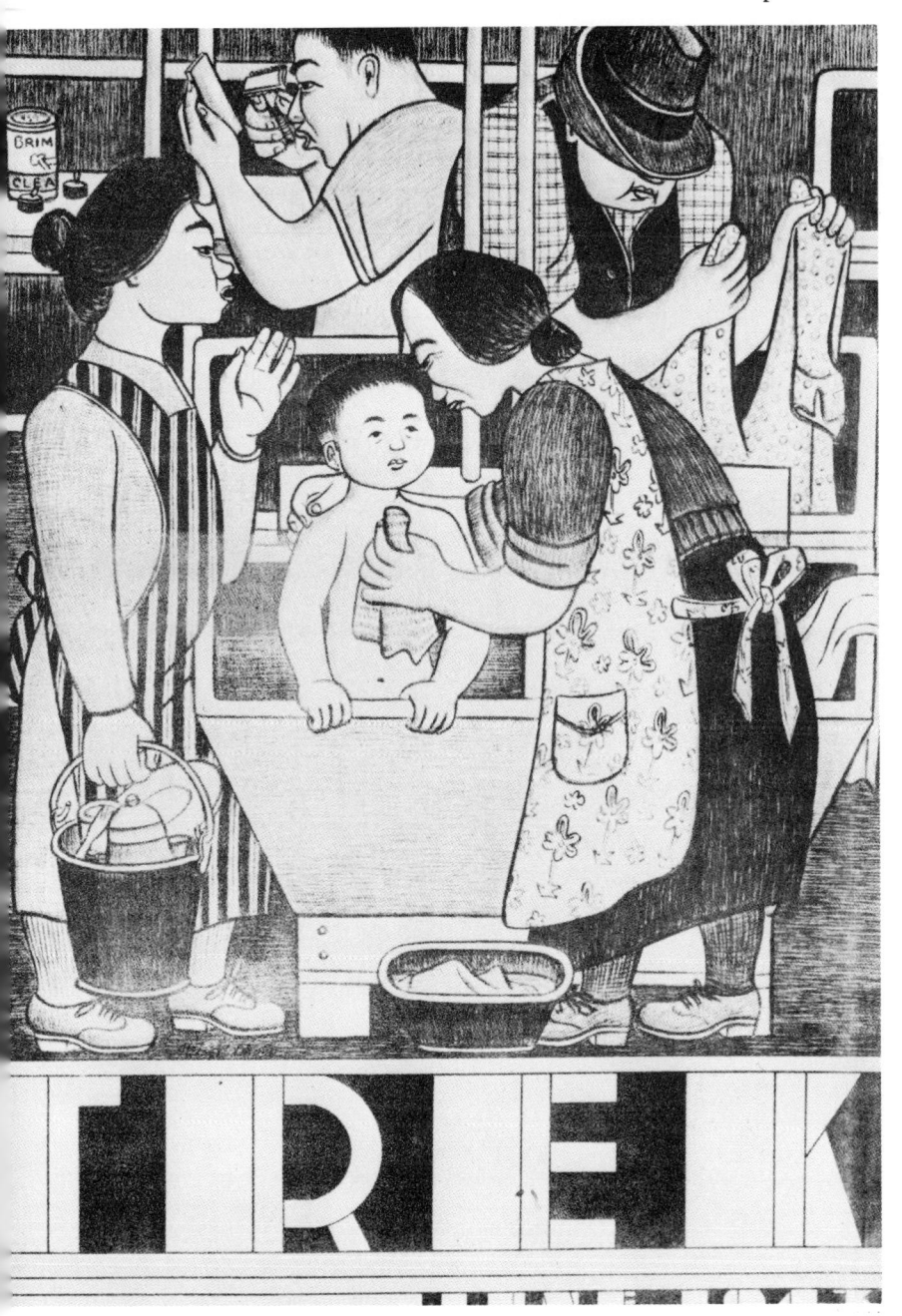

Concentration Camp Art 183

7-14. Trek cover, June 1943. *Miné Okubo. From the Oakland Museum catalogue Miné Okubo: An American Experience.*

184 The Art of Social Conscience

Miné Okubo was released from Topaz in 1944. After the war her drawings of life in an American concentration camp were published in a book entitled *Citizen 13660*, the number assigned to her in 1942. Since that time she has worked actively as an artist and has dealt with numerous subjects in various styles. Her exhibitions have appeared in cities throughout the United States.

The artistic accomplishments of Miné Okubo and her counterparts across the Atlantic contribute to the art of social conscience. Their works criticize and condemn the oppressive institutions and conditions that created concentration camps, and they express sympathy and compassion for the tragic victims. Most of all, however, they bear witness to perhaps the worst period of the historically brutal 20th century.

8-1. Vance, a Trapper Boy, 15 Years Old, Has Trapped for Several Years in a West Virginia Coal Mine. *Lewis Hine. International Museum of Photography at George Eastman House, Rochester, N.Y.*

8 Photography and Social Content: Hine, Capa, Bourke-White, and Lange

Photography as a fine art has long been established. For almost a century and a half, the camera has made impressive contributions to the visual arts. The early 19th century saw the emergence of a photographic technique that encouraged its sophisticated practitioners to employ the medium artistically. Exhibitions were held as early as 1851 in London, Paris, and New York.

During that century, some of the finest examples of photography became publicly prominent. The Frenchman Paul Nadar was the first major portraitist, whose subjects included such luminaries as Sarah Bernhardt and Théophile Gautier. The American Mathew Brady covered the Civil War in a series of remarkable photographs, including scenes of the Battle of Bull Run and the destruction of Richmond. Louis Daguerre and Eadweard Muybridge are photographic counterparts to the major figures of 19th-century painting and graphics.

Not until the 20th century, however, did photographic art come into major prominence. Throughout the world, art museums have held photographic exhibitions as a regular feature of their public programs. A voluminous literature on the art of photography has appeared, especially in recent years. Alfred

185

186 The Art of Social Conscience

Stiegletz, Henri Cartier-Bresson, Ansel Adams, and Diane Arbus are as widely acclaimed in their medium as Marc Chagall, Alexander Calder, and Le Corbusier are in theirs. With this increasing popularity, it appears likely that photography will remain an important medium in the visual arts.

Photography, like the other arts, both expresses and explains, and it can give form to thoughts, feelings, and emotions of enormous complexity. It requires creative elements beyond the physics of light and optics; a sensitivity for communicative expression is necessary to achieve enduring artistic value. The photographer selects his subject matter and emphasizes a theme. To do that well requires the same kind of imagination and perception as in painting and printmaking. The range of photography is as wide as that of any visual art: It includes both representational and abstract work. Boundaries for subject matter are limited only by the imagination of the artist.

The history of photography has contained many themes and topics, one of which, naturally, has been a critical vision of social and political life. Most of this work has involved the use of photography as a social document. The medium lends itself to accurate reportage. The documentary photographer, however, seeks more than mere description, and in his choice of emphasis he can highlight those realities he chooses to abstract from their broader environmental context. In a sense, all documentary photography has social content, but the work of the men and women discussed here has generally had more specific social and ethical intentions. These photographers sought to persuade their audiences of the moral urgency of their subject matter. Their work constitutes the clearest and most dramatic examples of socially conscious art as it has been perceived throughout this book. The photographic dimension of the art of social conscience is vigorous and impressive as it highlights many of the inadequacies of social existence. Like its counterparts in painting and graphic art, it uses creative power to expose the harsh realities of life. Some of the photographs express deep compassion for the suffering and downtrodden, while others express vehement denunciation of the people, policies, or institutions responsible for human suffering. Perhaps most important, the photographs encourage the viewer to think about the social problems presented and to speculate about ways in which improvements might be effected.

It is appropriate to begin with one of the major early figures in American photography. The work of Lewis Hine serves as the foundation for much of the engaged photography that followed. His career, dedicated entirely to the social vision, stimulated the imagination and conscience of most of the photographers who would later document the pathos of Depression life. Hine was a social crusader who used his camera to expose the brutal character of American industrial life in the early decades of the 20th century. Born in Wisconsin in 1874, he recorded, over a period of thirty years, the terrible sufferings of anonymous people in a variety of circumstances on two continents. His work was varied and a number of socially significant themes emerged. The most dramatic work, however, is found in the early part of his career. His treatment of the personal consequences of industrialization in America remains universal and unrivaled in its impact. Hine was an early muckraker in that he attempted to bring human problems to the public's attention. That desire was united with an equally fervent quest for social reconstruction.

By the turn of the century, America had become a teeming place, rapidly urbanized by unprecedented industrialization. Although that process was to bring eventual prosperity, it was accompanied by squalor, crowded living conditions, inner-city strife, and massive personal despair. All too frequently, the hopes engendered by industrialization failed to materialize. Alienation, chaos, and economic misery dominated the lives of millions. Hine captured that ambience with magnificence in his photograph *Row of Tenements* (Fig. 8-2), which portrays the nature of urban life in the early part of the century. Life in the tenement is cramped, there is no privacy, vermin abound, and the struggle for survival is intensified daily. The ultimate purpose of this photograph is consciously didactic: Hine's purpose was to capture these intolerable conditions so that his audience would be so offended they would seek to change them.

The influx of European immigrants added further problems to the already crowded conditions in the large cities of the Eastern seaboard. Thousands of people, from virtually every European country, disembarked at Ellis Island. Each faced an uncertain future in the new land and each hoped for a measure of economic prosperity and freedom from political or religious persecution. Hine took a series of memorable photographs of this wave of immigration. His picture of an Italian family *(Fig. 8-3)* is a fine example, revealing the apprehension of the mother and her children as they are tagged and made ready for processing.

8-2. Row of Tenements. *Lewis Hine. Courtesy University of Maryland Library, College Park, Md.*

Hine's compassion for his subjects is perfectly evident. This deep concern for humanity is the hallmark of his work.

The early decades of the 20th century gave rise also to a period of scandalous child labor, a subject that became the most powerful and significant of all the photographic art of Lewis Hine. In 1900 there were about 1,750,000 children between the ages of ten and fifteen "gainfully employed" in the United States. Boys and girls alike labored in grimy factories, dangerous mines, and miserable agricultural fields, sometimes for fifty cents a day or less, and frequently in shifts of ten or twelve hours, or more. Accidents and injuries were commonplace, and even fatalities were not uncommon. Children who worked in the mines developed consumption and other respiratory diseases. Few precautions were taken to prevent such consequences.

There were some state laws against child labor but, more often than not, they were ineffective and fraught with loopholes, which encouraged cynical and widespread evasion. It was not until 1916 that Congress responded with legislation designed to combat this glaring evil. After the legislation was passed, the Supreme Court, in its all-too-frequent function as an institution to serve dominant and powerful economic interests, nullified the law, ruling that it was beyond the constitutional authority of federal legislation. As a result, child labor continued through the prosperity of the 1920s and was not ended for good until the early days of the New Deal.

It is valuable, of course, to verbally chronicle the horrible patterns of child labor in America, but it is even more effective to capture those evils in a photograph. The latter shows graphically, beyond the point of dispute and controversy, just how sordid the situation was. Hine had come to New York in 1901, where he observed numerous disgraceful examples. His reaction was one of moral outrage at the conditions that would keep illiterate children in servitude. He knew, of course, that child labor was ultimately inefficient, but this was not the moral foundation for his photographic commentary. Rather, it was the compelling premise that child labor was intrinsically evil.

Hine traveled throughout the country in order to record the tragedy of this social evil. He never neglected the individual as he condemned the broader social and economic forces. Each child, and the specific nature of his work, is carefully identified. Once again, socially conscious art achieves a fusion of social and personal reality. The gruesome pattern emerges in the photograph captioned *Leo, 48 Inches High, 8 Years Old, Picks Up Bobbins at 15¢ a Day. Fayetteville, Tennessee. November, 1910 (Fig. 8–4)*. The picture shows a case which was far from extreme. The viewer cannot fail to comprehend the full horror and immorality of the situation. Sympathy and accusation alike emerge from the photograph and serve as an important historical source for an understanding of that period.

Another apppalling glimpse of this tragedy is found in the photograph captioned, *Vance, a Trapper Boy, 15 Years Old, Has Trapped for Several Years in a West Virginia Coal Mine (Fig. 8–1)*. Hine reveals an adolescent required to do work barely fit for an adult. Here the personalization underscores the horror. The ex-

8-3. Italian Family with Their Bundled Belongings, Waiting for Instructions. *Lewis Hine. International Museum of Photography at George Eastman House, Rochester, N.Y.*

190 The Art of Social Conscience

8-4. Leo, 48 Inches High, 8 Years Old, Picks up Bobbins at 15¢ a Day. Lewis Hine. 1910. Courtesy University of Maryland Library, College Park, Md.

pression of the child reflects that he has been beaten by life. Robotlike, he goes to work, performs his duties, and goes home, only to repeat the process the following day. No prospect for an autonomous or fulfilling life is possible. Here, then, Hine reveals with savage force the human consequences of industrial advancement.

Hine continually sought to protest the inequities of social and economic life. He photographed slums, the grinding poverty of the elderly, and the problems of racial minorities. Following World War I he toured Europe and recorded the lives of people in the wake of that devastating event. His themes included begging, starvation, and the plight of the refugee, all of which provide an eloquent statement of human compassion. Typical is the photograph captioned *A Street Beggar, Belgrade, Serbia (Fig. 8–5)*. The message of the work is timeless as it records, and protests against, the conditions that caused this woman's degraded state. Hine's perspective is clear beyond doubt: this situation must not be tolerated by civilized human beings.

On his return to the United States, Hine portrayed workers at construction sites and other scenes in both urban and rural America, but his later photographs lacked the forceful magnificence of his earlier ones. When he died in 1940, he was largely neglected as an artist. Only recently, as poverty has grown as a subject of social concern has his work been rediscovered. Even now, however, this pio-

8-5. A Street Beggar, Belgrade, Serbia. *Lewis Hine.*

192 The Art of Social Conscience

8-6. Death of a Spanish Loyalist. Robert Capa. 1936. Courtesy of Magnum Photos, Inc., New York.

neering figure in American photographic history is not widely known outside the arts. It is time for that to change, for as Ben Shahn noted, "Hine was one of the Great."

In his comparatively short career, Robert Capa established himself as probably the finest war photographer of all time. Born Andrei Friedmann in Hungary in 1913, he moved to Paris, where he began to experiment with a camera. In 1935 he assumed the name Robert Capa. His career as a serious photographer began during the Spanish Civil War. Traveling to Spain as a photojournalist, Capa was deeply moved by his experiences with ordinary people who were affected by political forces beyond their control. His natural empathy for human suffering emerged in Spain as the hallmark of his work. Out of the Spanish conflict came many powerful photographs that captured that tragic affair. These landmark works of socially conscious art portray the brutality and pain common to all war, but the civil war in Spain was exacerbated by the more advanced technology of the 20th century.

Capa journeyed to Spain with his wife, Gerda, in 1936. Together, they covered the war and produced a book entitled *Death in the Making*. (Gerda never lived to see the final product, however, for she was crushed to death by a tank during a military retreat.) Capa emphasized the implacable realities of war. The harshest reality, of course, was death, and Capa's work is a record of that ultimate fact. Shortly after his arrival in Spain, he took his most famous photograph, *Death of a Spanish Loyalist (Fig. 18–6)*, which has become a classic in the history of photography. The subject is a Spanish Loyalist soldier at the instant of his death. The tragic majesty of the photograph is self-evident, and its significance is manifest on several levels. While its ultimate meaning is a powerful universal statement on war, it can and should be viewed within the political context of the civil war in Spain. The picture reveals the agony of that land as it was torn asunder. More significantly, the death of a Loyalist soldier signals the impending end of the Spanish Republic and the bitter defeat of the idealistic men who fought and died for its cause. On a more timeless level, the work is a vision of the consequences of all war. As Picasso was able to do in *Guernica,* Capa combines the specific and the eternal.

The other Spanish war photographs are equally dramatic if somewhat less famous. Capa's work shows the tired and exhausted soldiers fighting for the Republic. His pictures reveal with compassionate perception the weary struggle that would shortly end in defeat. His most powerful and disturbing work pertains to the effects of the war on the civilian population. The victims of the town of Guernica were not the only innocent people to die. Capa shows the ubiquitous horror the Spanish people faced from 1936 to 1939. No clearer example can be found than the picture of civilians during an air raid in Bilbao (*Fig. 8–7*). No one was really safe in Spain, and death and destruction struck often from the skies. The women and children as the prominent subjects symbolize the innocence of the victims. The fear and anguish of the people are obvious and the observer can only wonder how long such terrifying memories will last in the minds of the survivors.

8-7. Air Raid in Bilbao, Spain, 1937. *Robert Capa. 1937. Courtesy of Magnum Photos, Inc., New York.*

194 The Art of Social Conscience

8-8. Portrait of a Small Child. Robert Capa. Courtesy of Magnum Photos, Inc., New York.

8-9. The Last Day Some of the Best Ones Die. *Robert Capa. Leipzig, Germany, May 7, 1945. Courtesy of Magnum Photos, Inc., New York.*

A portrait of a small child caught amid war and violence *(Fig. 8-8)* summarizes Capa's efforts in Spain. The little girl could be from any country ravaged by any war. The sad eyes of the child show the suffering she has endured beyond her years. Even more poignantly, the photograph suggests that that suffering is far from over. The work is reminiscent of the haunting graphics of Käthe Kollwitz in its powerful depiction of the human consequences of social disruption.

Although the war in Spain ended in 1939, Capa's career was just beginning. In 1938 he went to China, where he recorded the fighting between the Chinese and the Japanese invaders. Again, he witnessed tragedy. The results of his work added to the already prodigious art of wartime brutality. His next assignment was World War II. Capa covered the war in England, in North Africa, in Italy, in France, and finally in Germany. He covered the D-Day invasion, the Allied liberation of Paris, the retreat of the German army, and the plight of uprooted civilians throughout the Continent. His most moving picture of the war, taken in its final moments, is a portrait of the last soldier to die *(Fig. 8-9)*. Here the ultimate meaning of war is revealed. The soldier lies dead, a young man with a bullet hole between his eyes. The soldier is not identified, appropriately here, because he represents the fifty million people who perished during World War II. A pool of blood dominates the picture, telling the realistic story of the impact of war in general.

The events of the postwar era kept Capa employed as a war correspondent for the rest of his life. In 1948 he went to Israel, where he photographed the struggle to create a nation in the face of the massive attack of invading Arab armies. In 1954 he went to Indochina, where the insurgent forces of Ho Chi Minh were fighting against French colonial domination. His photographic artistry there was equally powerful. He recorded the ubiquitous tragedy of the people of Southeast Asia—the death and sufferings of the civilian population, which is even more disconcerting in light of events in Vietnam in the 1960s and '70s. The photograph captioned *Cemetery in Nam Dinh (Fig. 8-10)* is an uncanny preview of what was to dominate Vietnamese life for the next two decades. Here is a view of personal sorrow that has been repeated thousands of times. Capa, in capturing the grief of the mother with her child, has focused attention on one of the central tragedies of 20th-century history.

On May 25, 1954, Robert Capa was killed when he stepped on a mine. He was an early casualty of the war in Vietnam. He died as he was recording even further horrors with his camera. The photographer detested war, yet he was determined to use his talents to reveal its pervasive stupidity. His work is characterized by a sense of overwhelming compassion. He cared deeply for the victims of war, and the artistic results of that concern stand as yet one more reminder of war's futility. It is naive, of course, to think that his work will have any serious political effect. Neither did Goya's *Disasters of War*. But as long as artists continue to use their talents to elevate the conscience of mankind, change at least remains possible.

8-10. Cemetary in Nam Dinh. *Robert Capa. Indochina, May 1954. Courtesy of Magnum Photos, Inc., New York.*

198 The Art of Social Conscience

Photojournalism has always lent itself well to social criticism and protest. The finest photojournalism, like that of Robert Capa, achieves a more universal perspective that elevates it to a high artistic plane. Its critical and searching thrust, moreover, makes it a significant part of the art of social conscience. In America, there has been an impressive tradition of that kind of photojournalism.

8-11. Young Farm Boy Using Newspapers on Wall. *Margaret Bourke-White.*

8-12. Chain Gang and Burly Police Captain. *Margaret Bourke-White.*

200 The Art of Social Conscience

One of the best examples is the photography of Margaret Bourke-White, who was born in New York City in 1906. Her range of topics was considerable, and during her long and productive career she achieved a number of photographic "firsts." She covered both the domestic and the international scene for over thirty years, recording wars, political conflicts, revolutions, and hundreds of subsidiary and related events. A major current of her work was photography as social criticism.

In the 1930s she toured the southern United States with novelist Erskine Caldwell, to whom she was later married. The photographs she made during this trip were to become landmarks of socially conscious art. She sought out the most destitute areas of the South, where she captured the plight of the sharecroppers—people who had worked desperately hard for an entire lifetime and could show virtually nothing for it. Her work stands as a powerful indictment of an almost feudal economic arrangement that was inhuman in its consequences.

Bourke-White also used her camera to portray the insufferable conditions of poverty in which thousands of persons, both black and white, were forced to live. Her photograph of a young farm boy in Louisiana *(Fig. 8-11)* is a masterpiece of protest art. The boy's family was forced to use newspapers to insulate their living quarters. The little boy stands with his dog, looking forlornly at a fate he cannot possibly comprehend. The artist's message is simply that no one should have to endure such grotesque poverty.

One of Bourke-White's most notable works from that trip illustrated the character of the system of criminal justice in the South. She discovered what can only be described as the classic example of the brutality of the chain-gang system. Her photograph *(Fig. 8-12)* shows the inmates, chained together like beasts, dressed in stripes to increase the humiliation of their imprisonment. The most powerful element of this picture is the burly police captain, barking orders and clutching the omnipresent symbol of his authority. The stark reality of the situation speaks for itself in a powerful commentary on human injustice.

Margaret Bourke-White also covered World War II as a photocorrespondent. During that assignment, she had many adventures as she accompanied pilots on aerial combat missions. Like Capa's, her works are vivid on the grim nature of war. Her most extraordinary photograph, however, taken shortly before the end of the war, was not of a combat situation. She had traveled with the Third Army commanded by General George S. Patton. When they reached the concentration camp at Buchenwald, Patton was so incensed that he ordered his military police to gather the neighboring Germans to see the camp personally. Inevitably, the refrain "we never knew" was sounded with monotony. Bourke-White photographed the mounds of corpses, the skeletal remains in the furnaces, and the pieces of skin used for ornamentation by the perverted personnel of Buchenwald. Most important, she photographed the survivors *(Fig. 8-13)*, barely alive and riddled with disease. Her picture is a monument of tragic social protest art.

In 1960, *Life* Magazine sent Bourke-White to do a photo-essay on the Union of

8-13. Survivors of Buchenwald. *Margaret Bourke-White.*

South Africa. The most glaring feature of life in that land is the system of racial oppression known as apartheid. An inseparable facet of that racism is the pattern of economic exploitation. The mining of gold, in turn, is a major element of that exploitation. During her stay, Bourke-White observed and recorded the human effects of racial discrimination. Insisting on observing the actualities of work in the gold mines, she spent half a day in the depths of the mines and saw the daily life of the black workers who were required to work for eight hours beneath the earth's surface. Since the white supervisors were the first to emerge from the depths, many of the black workers were underground for as long as eleven hours; the extra hours were without compensation. Bourke-White's moving photo-

8-14. South African Miners. *Margaret Bourke-White*.

Photography and Social Content 203

graph of two of these miners *(Fig. 8-14)* captures their unending hardship. Their faces reflect the more general oppression they endure under apartheid in South Africa. Daily they must live with special passes, total subjugation legal discrimination, and grinding material deprivation. The photograph combines compassion for the miners with condemnation of South African social injustice.

Margaret Bourke-White continued her photographic artistry until her death in 1971 from Parkinson's disease. Her work constitutes an important chapter in the history of photography and a substantial one in the photography of social conscience.

Dorothea Lange's contributions to socially conscious photography are comparable in stature to those of the finest socially conscious painters and graphic artists. One of the giants of her medium, Lange responded to the turbulence of the times in which she lived and worked. Her combination of excellent artistic

8-15. White Angel Breadline. *Dorothea Lange. The Oakland Museum.*

form and sensitive and perceptive content established her as a seminal influence in modern documentary photography.

Lange's career spanned more than thirty years. Born in 1895 in Hoboken, New Jersey, she became a photographer as a young woman. By 1918, after having received some formal training in the craft, she embarked on a series of travels with a friend. The trip ended abruptly in San Francisco when their funds were exhausted, and she proceeded to open a commercial photography studio in that city. In time, however, she began to explore the world outside the studio with her camera. She had always had interest in people and felt within herself a commitment to them. The events of the times, furthermore, made those interests inevitably concrete.

That the decade of the 1930s was a period of despair for millions has already been noted. Social protest painters recorded on canvas the public and private agony caused by economic forces beyond the control and understanding of most Americans. Lange used her camera to perform the same function. In 1933 the first of her famous photographs appeared. Taken in San Francisco, *White Angel Breadline (Fig. 8-15)* portrays an old, grizzled man contemplating the material emptiness of his life. Bitterness blends with despair as he turns his back, perhaps in shame, to the others awaiting a handout. Rarely has the effect of poverty on people been so movingly recorded.

Lange's work came to the attention of Professor Paul Taylor of the Economics Department at the University of California. Impressed by the quality and social importance of her photographs, he invited her to join him in a project he was undertaking on the problems of migrant labor. She and Professor Taylor later married and established an outstanding collaborative team which would last for her lifetime.

Lange continued her documentary photography throughout the 1930s, working for several years for the Farm Security Administration, along with other luminaries of photography. Her most powerful work chronicled the human tragedy of superfluous Americans moving westward from Oklahoma and Arkansas. These people were considered pariahs, the American counterparts to the Indian untouchables. The photography of Dorothea Lange ennobled them by capturing their humanity. In 1936 she produced one of her finest works, *Migrant Mother (Fig. 8-16)*, an aching portrayal of the emotional burdens of social disruption and economic insecurity. The unforgettable look of distress on the face of the mother summarizes the plight of the dispossessed. The artist's deep compassion reminds one of Käthe Kollwitz. Innumerable other works of Lange achieve a similar heartrending reaction.

In 1938–39 Lange and Taylor collaborated on a book entitled *An American Exodus,* which was published in 1940. She provided the photographs and he wrote the text. This collaboration treated many of the same themes Lange had recorded earlier. The book is a remarkable accomplishment that can be viewed as a complement to John Steinbeck's *The Grapes of Wrath.* It is an invaluable document for anyone who wants to understand the spirit of the times.

8-16. Migrant Mother. *Dorothea Lange. The Oakland Museum.*

206 The Art of Social Conscience

The photographs are uniformly superb. Each captures a tragic dimension of the social catastrophe of the 1930s. Typically profound is a picture of life in a migrant labor camp in Tulare County, California *(Fig. 8-17)*. These were the conditions to which thousands of people were reduced. For a dollar a week the migrant vagabonds could camp, set up a tent, and use the water and electrical facilities, but they were cramped and miserable places, with an omnipresent

8-17. Life in a Migrant Labor Camp. *Dorothea Lange. The Library of Congress, Washington, D.C.*

8-18. Oklahoma Child with Cotton Sack Ready to Go into Field with Parents at 7:00 A.M. *Dorothea Lange. The Library of Congress, Washington, D.C.*

ambience of gloom. Men, women, and children would wait to pick fruit in the fields, often earning only enough to purchase gasoline so that they could move on to the next camp and the next fields.

Migrant work was hard and the pay was minimal. No one was immune from its harshness. Lange captures this reality in another forceful, moving photograph. One of the pictures from *An American Exodus* shows a child leaving with her parents to work in the fields *(Fig. 8–18)*. The poignancy of the photograph is overwhelming. That a child must suffer so cruelly is a savage commentary on society in general. The sympathy of the artist combines with the broader social protest of the picture's content.

By the 1940s Dorothea Lange had achieved recognition as an American photographer and artist. In 1942 she worked for the War Relocation Authority. Her job was to photograph the internment of the West Coast Japanese-Americans. The results of that work later formed the nucleus of the book and exhibition entitled *Executive Order 9066*. Her pictures were taken with obvious personal sincerity and yet with understandable dissatisfaction. A cumulative view of these photographs reveals the disgraceful treatment accorded the internees and the personal hardship they endured. Lange's photographs, like the paintings and drawings of Mine Okubo, record the shame that *should* be felt by the architects of the policy and the millions who lent their active or passive support.

Dorothea Lange's photographs of people leave a lasting impression. Children

208 The Art of Social Conscience

8-19. Grandfather and Grandchildren Awaiting Evacuation Bus. *Dorothea Lange. National Archives, Washington, D.C.*

no less than adults were treated officiously during the evacuation. A memorable picture shows a grandfather and his children waiting for the bus to take them away from their homes *(Fig. 8-19)*. Tagged and checked against the master list of daily departees, the old man strives to maintain an air of dignity in the face of such adversity. Lange captures that posture with impressive clarity. Her photograph is sound evidence that not everyone who is subject to politically imposed dehumanization must therefore sacrifice his own humanity.

8-20. Manzanar Relocation Center. *Dorothea Lange. National Archives, Washington, D.C.*

For many of the Japanese-Americans, the destination was the Manzanar Relocation Center. Lange has rendered an image of that camp that reveals its oppressive bleakness *(Fig. 8–20)*. A hot duststorm accentuates the stark character of the facilities that housed thousands of people for three long years. The central position of the American flag adds a bitter note of irony to the presence of a concentration camp in the middle of the desert.

The end of the war shifted the acute social conscience of Dorothea Lange to other topics. For several years she was ill and remained at her home in Berkeley.

8-21. The Defendant, Alameda County Courthouse, Oakland. *Dorothea Lange. The Oakland Museum.*

210 The Art of Social Conscience

In the 1950s, however, she resumed her artistic activity with enthusiasm, conceiving and executing several projects in the United States and elsewhere. In 1955 she returned to themes of immediate social significance. In the series *The Public Defender*, she examined major aspects of criminal law and administration. Her setting was the Alameda County Courthouse in Oakland and her perspective was of the agony of a defendant caught in a frightening process of criminal prosecution. Although she implies no apology for criminal conduct, her vision involves a view of law that emphasizes the reaction of the accused to his plight.

Typical is the photograph entitled *The Defendant (Fig. 8–21)*, in which Lange portrays a person charged with a crime as he sits in the courtroom, head in hands in a dramatic reaction of apprehension and bewilderment. The viewer can only speculate about his shattered life as he contemplates time in prison, separated from job and family and friends. No excuse need be given for his crime in order to sympathize with his feelings. Lange's photograph is reminiscent of Goya, Daumier, and Rouault in the compassionate treatment of human beings involved with the law.

Throughout the 1950s and '60s, her work was exhibited nationally and internationally. She traveled extensively and took photographs in such disparate lands as Ireland, Korea, Egypt, and Venezuela. In 1964 a recurrent illness was diagnosed as cancer, and in October 1965, she died in Berkeley. Dorothea Lange was to photography what Ben Shahn was to painting and what Käthe Kollwitz was to engraving and lithography. Above all, her career helped to solidify photography as an extraordinarily effective medium for social commentary in art.

9-1. Angulo 18. Juan Genoves. 1967. Acrylic on canvas. Courtesy of the Art Institute of Chicago.

9 New Directions in Socially Conscious Art

The previous chapters have surveyed a major and recurring theme in the history of art. The painters, graphic artists, and photographers heretofore presented have treated subjects of profound political and social significance in their works. Expressions of social conscience remain a viable and impressive force in modern art. Immune for the most part from the vicissitudes of stylistic fashion, the modern representatives of socially conscious art continue to use their abilities to comment on both the topical and timeless problems of social life.

Working in various media, many modern socially engaged artists continue to explore sectarian interests, or seek to direct their art to vastly different audiences. The purpose of this chapter is to explore briefly some recent tendencies that have broadened and expanded the art of social conscience. What follows, then, is an eclectic collection that may stimulate further interest and investigation. Some of the artists are international figures whose works are unquestionably of lasting quality. Others are lesser known or even anonymous artists whose works may be more transient. The content of each effort, however, reflects vital social issues. Consequently, each deserves consideration without regard to the final critical judgment of artistic merit.

There are several contemporary painters whose art is socially significant but whose styles or themes are unique or otherwise beyond the scope of previous chapters. One is the Spanish artist Juan Genovés, born in Valencia in 1930. His works have no counterpart in modern art. He combines a powerfully stark style with a chilling vision of individual and mass annihilation. Using somber tones of black and gray, he paints scenes of faceless and nameless people trying vainly to escape a variety of gruesome fates—men and women awaiting execution, individuals being exterminated by unknown assassins, and masses of panic-stricken people fleeing from ambiguous forces of destruction.

One of his most effective paintings, *Angulo 18 (Fig. 9-1)*, painted in 1967, portrays a running mob in the view of the cross hairs of a gun sight. The scene is deliberately vague. Genovés offers no specific explanation for the attack. There is no particularized location and no discernible event. The generality of the painting, however, is the source of its greatest impact. In avoiding a protest of any given war or atrocity, the artist is able to focus the attention of his audience on the isolation and political impotence that dominate modern life. His social commentary, therefore, is all the more terrifying because of its universality. His powerless victims are abstractions of millions of people throughout the world. Their plight is really the story of much of the social life of mankind, especially in the 20th century. The artistic brilliance of Genovés is a fitting tribute to a world which in thirty years has seen the horrors of Auschwitz, Hiroshima, and Vietnam.

The oppression of blacks, particularly in the United States, has generated a series of strong artistic reactions. Many of the works of serious and sensitive black artists have added important new dimensions to socially conscious art. Perhaps the premier artist in this tradition is Jacob Lawrence. His art reflects a genuine commitment to both the Afro-American experience and to the broader social concerns of mankind. Born in 1917 in Atlantic City, New Jersey, Lawrence is often regarded as a younger member of the Social Realists. Although he received formal artistic training, his primary inspiration came from Brueghel, Kollwitz, Rivera, and Orozco.

The major characteristics of Lawrence's work is his use of picture narratives in series form, in the manner of Hogarth, Kollwitz, and Shahn. His groups of paintings chronicle and interpret the historical struggles of blacks. His early series deal with the key figures of liberation movements, including Toussaint L'Ouverture, Frederick Douglass, and Harriet Tubman. Subsequent works depict contemporary history and the hardships of social life in the urban North. In each series Lawrence promotes a sense of urgency about using art for political

New Directions in Socially Conscious Art   213

9-2. Panel 55 from the *Migration Series. Jacob Lawrence. The Phillips Collection, Washington, D.C.*

and social instruction. In this sense there is a natural relationship to the Depression artists of the 1930s.

One of Lawrence's powerful series is *Migration*, begun in 1940. Ambitious in conception, it is a comprehensive account of the movement of blacks from the rural South to the urban centers of the North during World War I. Its sixty paintings are replete with hope and social criticism as they portray the human consequences of massive demographic change. Lawrence exposes both the economic injustice and violence of life in the South and the difficulties of urban adjustment in the North. The excitement and joy of thousands turned quickly to grief and despair as blacks were cramped into squalid urban tenements. In Panel 55 of the *Migration* series *(Fig. 9–2)*, the artist reveals the depths of tragedy experienced by the migrants in the early part of the 20th century. As a result of their crowded and unhealthy conditions, many who journeyed northward contracted tuberculosis and died. In the painting Lawrence depicts three figures bearing the coffin of a recent victim. The simple burial box symbolizes the hardship of existence, while the flowers on top allow for hope for future change. A visual counterpart to the Afro-American blues experience, the painting is an early example of the excellence that has characterized Lawrence's entire career.

214 The Art of Social Conscience

No more perceptive treatment of the sad condition of American blacks can be found than in the works of Charles White. As a boy in the jungles of Chicago, he witnessed firsthand the wretched conditions of economic deprivation and social discrimination that his people faced daily. He knew, too, the personal consequences of being despised and insulted because of the color of his skin.

As in the case of many other artists, White's talents and inclinations were apparent at an early age. After years of frustration—trying to develop his art at the same time he had to eke out a financial existence—he finally received formal training at the Art Institute of Chicago. In time his reputation as an artist grew, and he became recognized as one of the finest black artists in the country. In succeeding years, he has had an immense range of experiences, including associations with well-known persons in the arts, extended travels, and numerous university teaching positions in art.

As an artist, White has focused on the conditions and experiences of blacks in America. His works display a consistent humanism, which empathizes with the victims of racism. Most of his works are drawings and lithographs, although he has maintained an interest in painting. In 1966 he created a series of charcoal drawings entitled *J'Accuse*. The individual pictures are eloquent statements of the human burdens of oppression. A moving example is *J'Accuse No. 8 (Fig. 9–3)*, which portrays a woman carrying a large load of foodstuffs on her back. The load is symbolic, of course, for the black woman in America has often had to be a tower of strength. This is especially true because black males have been ruthlessly emasculated both economically and emotionally. White's drawing is an

9-3. J'Accuse No. 8. *Charles White. 1966. Charcoal. Collection of Mr. Lawrence Roberts, Courtesy of Heritage Gallery, Los Angeles, Calif.*

9-4. *My Land. Jerry Reed. Courtesy Contemporary Crafts, Inc., Los Angeles, Calif.*

216 The Art of Social Conscience

9-5. Madonna from Madison Avenue. *Rosemary Lafollette. Mixed media. Collection of the artist.*

appreciative summation of the resolve of millions of black women to endure in the face of massive hardship throughout centuries.

In the early 1960s the drive of black Americans for equal opportunity became the paramount domestic issue in American life. The student sit-ins to end segregated facilities in the South heralded a civil rights movement that shook the value foundation of the white population. The movement spread rapidly to every part of the country. Nonviolence was met by violence, and hundreds of protestors were injured or killed, while thousands of others were arrested and jailed. As the decade ended, the civil rights movement became more militant and cries of "black power" began to replace the more moderate slogans of earlier years.

A concurrent and related development was the renaissance of young, socially committed black artists. Many of the men and women have been active participants in what they recognize as the struggle of their people. Many have found that their art is inseparable from their political involvements. Frequently, they view their artistic products as important consciousness-awakening influences in the black communities in America. Overt social criticism has been a major theme of black art in recent years. Many paintings and graphic works have been savagely critical of the pattern of American racism. Some artists have intentionally avoided subtlety in content in order to focus attention on the glaring racial inequities that have existed throughout American history.

Other black artists have sought to use their talents to help forge a new identity for their race. They have occasionally looked to Africa as a source of personal and communal pride. An example is a painting entitled *My Land (Fig. 9-4)* by a young artist named Jerry Reed. In it a guerrilla fighter with a rifle is shown imposed over the entire African continent. The intent is unmistakable. The artist seeks to convince his viewers that violence is a necessary path to their own liberation and that their struggle is inseparably bound with that of their brother revolutionaries in Africa. What is important is not the substantive validity of those views but the use of art to generate self-respect in being black. This and hundreds of similar paintings have had the effect of breaking down the socially conditioned patterns of passivity that have internally brutalized millions of black Americans.

In the early years of the 1970s, other liberation movements have appeared throughout the world. As part of their various efforts to obtain power and social recognition, artistic activity has been an influential element of their struggles. In the United States, recent years have seen a proliferation of artistic works that depict the problems and aspirations of such groups as prison inmates and Chicanos. Feminism has also had an emergent artistic dimension. Women artists have explored the conditions of their oppression and expressed their hopes for more fulfilling personal and occupational roles. An example is a collage by Rosemary Lafollette entitled *Madonna from Madison Avenue (Fig. 9-5)*. Using materials from women's magazines, the artist has shown how the mass media have conditioned the lives and expectations of millions of women. At virtually every stage of her childhood, a girl is trained to believe that she should be glamorous in order to attract a husband. The top part of the collage is a deliberate caricature of that ideal. The garish features of the woman's face reflect the stupidity of the commonly accepted definition of female aspirations. Even more significantly, it is an acidulous commentary on what men regard as feminine beauty. The bottom part of the collage completes the picture. Here a baby is presented in order to highlight the childbearing role of women. This, too, is part of the Madison Avenue-inspired mythology. It has influenced millions of women to assume that only through bearing and raising children can they find ultimate feminine fulfillment. In short, the work calls attention to the still-present social influences that are so destructive to the personal development and autonomy of both men and women.

Throughout the history of art, the poster has been particularly adaptable to the presentation of partisan positions on various causes and controversies. A poster is a complex and interesting combination of a work of art and a notice to the public. Usually intended for reproduction in large quantities, it tends to be hurried in its execution because of the immediacy of the cause. The poster often combines a verbal message with visual stimuli designed to attract a wide audience. In the past, most posters have been directed to specific commercial objectives. At the same time, posters of social protest and political revolution have also been prominent. The overwhelming majority of these efforts have been transient and without durable artistic value. Others, however, have combined passionate advocacy with unusual artistic quality. In the 20th century major and diverse artists such as Käthe Kollwitz, Joan Miró, Pablo Picasso, and Alexander Calder have used the poster medium to offer social commentary in art.

In the past decade poster art throughout the world has become a vital artistic force on behalf of vaious social causes. Posters from Cuba, France, and the United States in particular have added an important dimension to socially conscious art. Aggressive and direct, examples from all three countries have called attention to some of the most important problems of recent political history. The Cuban experience is especially significant because impressive artistic form has given shape to radical social content. Unlike authorities in most other Communist countries, those in Cuba have permitted and encouraged a certain flexibility in artistic innovation and experimentation. One of the major centers for poster activity in Cuba is the government-sponsored Organization of Solidarity with Asia, Africa, and Latin America. This agency is an effective propaganda entity for the creation of posters that treat with great favor the various movements for national liberation on the three continents. Their most famous example is *Day of the Heroic Guerrilla (Fig. 9–6)*. The most striking feature of the poster is the central figure of Che Guevara, the hero of the international guerrilla movement. Since his capture and death in Bolivia in 1967, Guevara has

New Directions in Socially Conscious Art 219

9-6. Day of the Heroic Guerrilla. *Poster issued by the Organization of Solidarity with Asia, Africa, and Latin America.*

9-7. Gendarme. *Student poster. Paris, 1968.*

become an almost romantic symbol for thousands of persons in scattered parts of the world, particularly in Third World countries. In this work, his image is shown reverberating throughout the South American continent as if to indicate the revolutionary future of that region. The color combination adds a pleasant aesthetic element to the work. Talented artists were employed to create Cuban posters which convey political sentiments in an attractive formal context.

In May 1968, Parisian students occupied the Sorbonne as part of a nationwide strike that almost toppled the government of President De Gaulle. During the turmoil of the rebellion, many students were vigorously active in producing posters on behalf of their struggle. Hundreds of designs were created and thousands of copies were distributed and affixed to walls throughout the university area. Posters were produced hourly in response to the latest political developments. Student commentary was frequently witty and occasionally bitter. The posters served to convey a sense of solidarity and to protest the institutions of bourgeois society. Much of the work was accomplished collectively in what was called a "people's workshop," a model, the participants hoped, for future industrial organization in France.

Because most of these posters were produced quickly for immediate objectives, they lacked the timelessness of the more enduring examples of poster art. They did, however, accomplish many of their immediate objectives. Almost always simple in design and rough in execution, they convey a powerful sense of urgency. An impressive example protests the brutality of the French police in the streets of Paris (*Fig. 9–7*). The pose of the gendarme, shown with his shield and ominous-looking club, suggests that he is about to brutalize one or more of the student rebels. In fact, the poster is a fairly accurate reflection of what actually happened in Paris during the spring of 1968. Bloodshed was commonplace in the Latin Quarter, and observers reported scores of instances of excessive police violence. Captured students who were cut off from their fellows were savagely beaten. The poster applies with immediate force to that troubled situation, but its broader message far transcends the abortive rebellion in France.

The activist decade of the 1960s in America generated thousands of posters for various causes and movements. From the struggle for civil rights to the war in Vietnam to the corruption of the Nixon administration, American students and others have responded with a plethora of critical pictorial reactions. Like those of their contemporaries in France, most have had a topical urgency, which precludes their inclusion in any survey of more durable poster art. The major stimulus was the specter of American military involvement in Southeast Asia. The war generated hundreds of protest posters. Each escalation of the war by Lyndon Johnson and later by Richard Nixon gave impetus to scores of posters. During the extension of the war to Cambodia in May 1970, thousands of American students mobilized in a flurry of antiwar activity. That mobilization itself was responsible for a truly massive output of protest posters throughout the land.

222 The Art of Social Conscience

9-8. End Bad Breath. *Seymour Chwast. Courtesy of Seymour Chwast and Push Pin Studios, Inc., New York.*

New Directions in Socially Conscious Art   223

Some of the posters are simple in design and general in theme, while others are more complex on both levels. An interesting example is *End Bad Breath* (Fig. 9–8). Created by Seymour Chwast, the poster shows a mad Uncle Sam spewing forth a deadly halitosis. The uncomplicated structure of the work in no way impedes the effectiveness of its message. The poster combines seriousness of purpose with a bitter wit.

A medium related to the poster is the political or social cartoon. Even more than the poster, however, the daily or weekly cartoon suffers from the effects of immediacy and superficiality. Rarely in the history of the medium does an individual cartoon manage to transcend its subject and become a work of art. Nevertheless, there are honorable exceptions, most notably those of Honoré Daumier a century ago in France. In the United States, there is a tradition of critical cartooning that stands on the periphery of the art of social conscience. Among its major figures are Thomas Nast in the 19th century and Herblock in the 20th. In the 1960s a young cartoonist named Ron Cobb appeared on the American scene. His efforts are savage commentaries on the inequities and asininities of American society. Profoundly concerned with injustice, he has created a series of devastating cartoons that comment with disconcerting insight on contemporary life in America. A powerful example depicts the morbid

9-9.   Leatherneck. Ron Cobb. 1966. Permission of the artist.

224 The Art of Social Conscience

9-10. Peace. Beniamino Bufano. San Francisco International Airport.

New Directions in Socially Conscious Art 225

consequences of the widespread public infatuation with war toys *(Fig. 9-9)*. The child is bayoneted by the working model of a United States Marine. The gruesome exaggeration notwithstanding, Cobb's point is serious indeed. Long-term exposure to war toys encourages the acceptance of war as a natural and inevitable social process. Perhaps even more disturbingly, it inures people to the suffering and destruction that always accompany armed conflict. That result, surely, is cumulatively more insidious than the instant exaggeration of the cartoon.

Sculpture is a medium which has not ordinarily been directed to socially conscious objectives as they have been defined throughout this book. Leonard Baskin, a socially oriented artist internationally recognized for his sculpture, abandoned that medium for direct political commentary. The most important modern developments in sculpture, moreover, tend to be highly abstract in form and content. There are, however, significant modern examples of socially engaged sculpture. The noted San Francisco artist Beniamino Bufano frequently created sculptural monuments to peace—finely executed efforts that are impressive works of art. A notable example stands at the entrance to the San Francisco International Airport. Entitled *Peace (Fig. 9-10)*, the work is constructed of steel, granite, and mosaic. Once again, it is a noble expression of a long-unfulfilled human aspiration.

9-11. Execution. *George Segal. Sculpture. The Vancouver Art Gallery, Vancouver, B.C.*

226 The Art of Social Conscience

Two prominent American artists have recently created sculpture that falls within the parameters of socially significant art. George Segal creates life-size plaster casts of human figures in elaborate, realistic settings. Associated by some critics with the Pop Art movement in the United States, Segal has used his work to concentrate on the human condition. His assemblages reflect an obvious concern with people's feelings and emotions, especially loneliness, a theme which constantly appears in his work. In 1967 Segal contributed a major work to the "Protest and Hope" exhibition in New York. *Execution (Fig. 9–11)* is a powerful and shockingly realistic portrayal of four victims of a war-related killing. It has no immediate, concrete reference point, but instead is a more generalized comment on man's eternal capacity for violence and destruction.

Closely related to Segal is Edward Kienholz. His works, too, are elaborate assemblages that expand the boundaries of sculpture. More important here, Kienholz uses his creations to express trenchant criticism of major features of contemporary American society. One of his most forceful works is *The State Hospital (Fig. 9–12, detail),* which portrays the victim of a callous and insensitive society. The assemblage is a room in a mental asylum in which a patient, strapped to his bed, is isolated with only the brutal image of himself for companionship. To underscore the horror of the situation, Kienholz fashions the

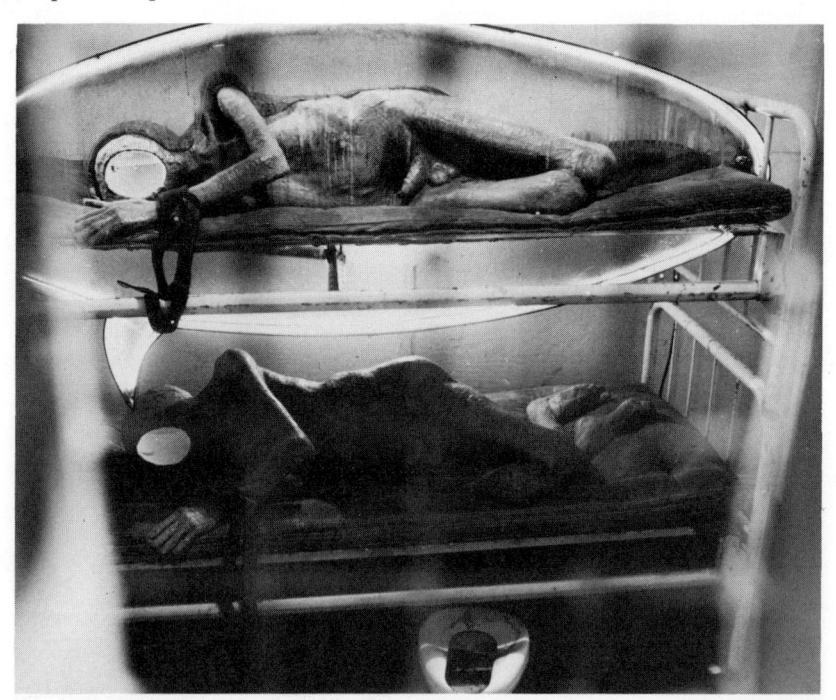

9-12. The State Hospital. *Edward Kienholz. Sculpture. Moderna Museet, Stockholm. Courtesy of the artist.*

9-13. Smorgi-Bob, the Cook. *Robert Arneson. 1971. Earthenware. Collection San Francisco Museum of Art.*

patient's head into a fish bowl. The impact of this sculptural vision goes far beyond the squalid realities of institutional maltreatment of mental patients. Those features reflect a more basic social malaise.

Ceramic art is an intriguing medium for social commentary, yet work in clay, deeply rooted in the history of art, has rarely been adapted to a critical vision of society. Of the countless ceramic works currently available, only a mere handful were devised with the express intent of communicating any message at all. Aesthetic, functional, or abstract forms comprise the vast majority of ceramic products. At the same time, however, some recent American examples have made a modest contribution to the art of social conscience. A contemporary development in ceramics has been labeled "funk art." The category is far from precise and there are no definitive guidelines that assign a given ceramic work to that designation. Nevertheless, one strain of "funk" contains direct or easily implied criticisms of certain elements of American society.

Robert Arneson is a notable American ceramist whose works are ordinarily considered examples of funk art. Some of his products, verging on the absurd, are genuine and impressive examples of comic art. Others, however, reveal a keen understanding of American life. An outstanding example is a work in porcelain entitled *Smorgi-Bob, the Cook (Fig. 9-13),* in which the artist portrays himself before an enormous table of food. A sensuous delight, this regal repast is destined to be a source of pleasant memories for the lucky participants. These people, however, are indulging in the gluttony that has become common among the recently affluent of American suburbia. Post-World War II prosperity has generated an accompanying and massive dedication to self-indulgent pursuits. Arneson has captured a major strain of American middle-class existence in this work. He leaves it to the observer to draw the appropriate and damning inferences.

The reader who has thoughtfully considered the content of the art throughout this book can hardly avoid the conclusion that past and present societies have had monumental failings, which have caused grievous anguish to many millions of human beings. The world has always been imperfect and no one seriously expects that evils such as injustice, war, starvation, and persecution will disappear overnight. The artists of social conscience have not been naive visionaries who simplistically assumed that their protest or socially critical art would somehow transform human society into a higher ethical plane. Their most impressive contribution to that ideal is simply that they refused to be parties to social misconduct and political oppression. An ethical person may lack the power to prevent the ubiquitous parade of social horrors; nothing, however, can compel him to be guilty of complicity in them.

Succeeding generations will face new and equally complex social issues. New styles of art will emerge and new artistic giants will add important chapters to the history of art. No one, surely, can predict the future directions of the artistic enterprise. What is certain is that there will continue to be sensitive men and women who will combine their mastery of artistic technique with a passionate commitment to social criticism and change. The honorable tradition of socially conscious art will end only when the quality of human existence has been made truly humane. History suggests that the art of social conscience will therefore endure in the future.

Bibliography

Chapter 1: Art and Social Conscience

Adhémar, Jean. *Honoré Daumier.* Paris: Tisné, 1954.
Antal, Frederick. *Hogarth and His Place in European Art.* London: Routledge & Kegan Paul, 1962.
Baxendall, Lee. *Marxism and Aesthetics: An Annotated Bibliography.* New York: Humanities, 1969.
Bechtel, Edion de Turck. *Jacques Callot.* New York: Braziller, 1955.
Berger, John. *Ways of Seeing.* London: British Broadcasting Corporation and Penguin, 1973.
Boon, K. G. *Rembrandt: The Complete Etchings.* New York: Abrams, 1963.
Burke, Joseph, and Colin Caldwell. *Hogarth: The Complete Engravings.* New York: Abrams, 1968.
Cain, Julian. *Daumier—Lawyers and Justice.* Boston: Boston Book and Art, 1970.
Chipp, Herschel B. *Theories of Modern Art.* Berkeley, Calif.: University of California Press, 1968.
Delteil, Loys. *Honoré Daumier.* 10 vols. Paris: [The Author], 1925-29.
Egbert, Donald D. *Social Radicalism and the Arts.* New York: Knopf, 1970.
Ferrari, Enrique L. *Goya: The Complete Etchings, Aquatints and Lithographs.* New York: Abrams, 1962.
Fischer, Ernst. *The Necessity of Art.* Harmondsworth and Baltimore, Md.: Penguin, 1963.
Foote, Timothy. *The World of Brueghel.* New York: Time-Life Books, 1968.
Getlein, Frank, and Dorothy Getlein. *The Bite of the Print.* New York: Potter, 1963.
Grossman, F. *Pieter Brueghel: Complete Edition of the Paintings.* London: Phaidon, 1973.
Harris, Bruce, and Seena Harris. *Honoré Daumier: Selected Works.* New York: Crown, 1969.

Hauser, Arnold. *The Social History of Art.* Vols. 1–4. New York: Vintage Books, 1957–58.
Klingender, F. D. *Goya and the Democratic Tradition.* New York: Schocken, 1968.
Lang, Berel, and Forrest Williams. *Marxism and Art: Writings in Aesthetics and Criticism.* New York: McKay, 1972.
Larkin, Oliver W. *Daumier: Man of His Time.* Boston: Beacon, 1966.
Paulson, Ronald. *Hogarth: His Life, Art, and Times,* 2 vols. New Haven, Conn.: Yale University Press, 1971.
Scharf, Aaron. *Art and Politics in France.* Bletchley: Open University Press, 1972.
Schickel, Richard. *The World of Goya.* New York: Time-Life Books, 1968.
Selz, Peter. *German Expressionist Painting.* Berkeley, Calif.: University of California Press, 1957.
Shahn, Ben. *The Shape of Content.* Cambridge, Mass.: Harvard University Press, 1957.
Shikes, Ralph E. *The Indignant Eye.* Boston: Beacon, 1969.
Thomas, Hugh. *Goya: The Third of May: 1808.* New York: Viking, 1972.
Vincent, Howard P. *Daumier and His World.* Evanston, Ill.: Northwestern University Press, 1968

Chapter 2: Expressionism and Social Content

Courthion, Pierre. *Georges Rouault.* New York: Abrams, 1962.
Heller, Reinhold. *Munch: The Scream.* New York: Viking, 1972.
Hodin, J. P. *Edvard Munch.* New York: Praeger, 1972.
Jewell, Edward A. *Georges Rouault.* New York: Hyperion, 1945.
Maritain, Jacques. *Georges Rouault.* New York: Abrams, 1954.
Messer, Thomas M. *Edvard Munch.* New York: Abrams, 1967.
Rouault, Georges. *Miserere.* Boston: Boston Book and Art Shop, 1963.
Schiefler, Gustav. *Edvard Munch: Das graphische Werk, 1906–1926.* Berlin: Euphorion, 1928.
Timm, Werner. *The Graphic Art of Edvard Munch.* Greenwich, Conn.: New York Graphic Society, 1969.

Chapter 3: The Pivotal Role of German Social Art

Grosz, George. *A Little Yes and a Big No.* New York: Dial, 1946.
———. *Ecce Homo.* New York: Brussel & Brussel, 1965.
———. *Love Above All, and Other Drawings.* New York: Dover, 1971.
Heise, C. G. *Käthe Kollwitz: Einunzwanzig Zeichnungen der Späten Jahre.* Berlin: Gebruder Mann, 1948.
Herzfelde, Wieland. *John Heartfield.* Dresden: Verlag der Kunst, 1962.
Hess, Hans. *George Grosz.* New York: Macmillan, 1974.
John Heartfield 1891–1968: Photomontages. Exhibition catalogue. Paris: ARC Musée d'Art Moderne de la Ville de Paris, 1974.

Klein, Mina C., and H. Arthur Klein. *Kathe Kollwitz: Life in Art.* New York: Schocken, 1975.
Lewis, Beth I. *George Grosz: Art and Politics in the Weimar Republic.* Madison, Wisconsin: University of Wisconsin Press, 1971.
Nagel, Otto. *Käthe Kollwitz.* Dresden: Verlag der Kunst, 1963.
Zigrosser, Carl (ed.). *Prints and Drawings of Käthe Kollwitz.* New York: Dover, 1969.

Chapter 4: Social Dimensions in the Art of Picasso

Arnheim, Rudolf. *The Genesis of a Painting: Picasso's Guernica.* Berkeley, Calif.: University of California Press, 1962.
Berger, John. *Success and Failure of Picasso.* Harmondsworth and Baltimore, Md.: Penguin, 1965.
Blunt, Anthony. *Picasso's Guernica.* New York: Oxford University Press, 1969.
Chevalier, Denys. *Picasso: The Blue and Rose Periods.* New York: Crown, 1969.
Penrose, Roland. *Picasso: His Life and Work.* New York: Harper and Row, 1973.

Chapter 5: The American Experience

American Painting 1910–1970. New York: Time-Life Books, 1970.
Baigell, Matthew. *The American Scene.* New York: Praeger, 1974.
Baskin, Leonard. *Baskin: Sculpture, Drawings and Prints.* New York: Braziller, 1970.
———. *The Graphic Work 1950–1970.* New York: Far Gallery, 1970.
Baur, John. *Philip Evergood.* New York: Praeger, 1960.
Bush, Martin H. *Ben Shahn: The Passion of Sacco and Vanzetti.* Syracuse, N.Y.: Syracuse University Press, 1968.
Freundlich, August L. *William Gropper: Retrospective.* Los Angeles: Ward Ritchie Press, 1968.
Garber, Thomas. *George Tooker.* Exhibition catalogue. San Francisco: The Fine Arts Museums of San Francisco, 1974.
Getlein, Frank. *Jack Levine.* New York: Abrams, 1966.
Hudson, Richard, and Ben Shahn. *Kuboyama and the Saga of the Lucky Dragon.* New York: Yoseloff, 1965.
Ivan Albright. Exhibition catalogue. Chicago: Art Institute of Chicago, 1964.
Johnson, Una E. *Paul Cadmus: Prints and Drawings.* Brooklyn, N.Y.: Brooklyn Museum, 1968.
Larkin, Oliver. *Art and Life in America.* New York: Holt, Rinehart & Winston, 1960.
———. *Twenty Years of Evergood.* New York: Simon and Schuster, 1946.
Miller, Dorothy C., and Alfred H. Barr (eds.). *American Realists and Magic Realists.* New York: Museum of Modern Art, 1943.
Prescott, Kenneth W. *The Complete Graphic Works of Ben Shahn.* New York: Quadrangle, 1973.

Rodman, Selden. *Portrait of the Artist as an American: Ben Shahn: A Biography with Pictures.* New York: Harper, 1951.
Rose, Barbara. *American Art Since 1900: A Critical History.* New York: Praeger 1975.
Shahn, Bernarda B. *Ben Shahn.* New York: Abrams, 1972.
Shapiro, David (ed.). *Social Realism: Art as Weapon.* New York: Ungar, 1973.
Soby, James Thrall. *Ben Shahn: His Graphic Art.* New York: Braziller, 1957.
———. *Ben Shahn: Paintings.* New York: Braziller, 1963.

Chapter 6: The Mexican Muralists

Berdecio, Roberto, and Stanley Appelbaum. *Posada's Popular Mexican Prints.* New York: Dover, 1972.
Cardoza y Aragon, Luis. *José Clemente Orozco.* Buenos Aires: Losada, 1944.
Charlot, Jean. *The Mexican Mural Renaissance, 1920-25.* New Haven, Conn.: Yale University Press, 1963.
Echavarria, Salvador. *Orozco: Hospicio Cabañas.* Mexico, 1973.
Fernandez, Justino. *El Arte Moderno en México.* Mexico: Antigua Libraría Lobredo, 1937.
José Guadalupe Posada: Ilustrador de la Vida Mexicana. Mexico: Fondo Editorial de la Plástica Mexicana, 1963.
Micheli, Mario de. *Siqueiros.* New York: Abrams, 1968.
Orozco, José Clemente. *José Clemente Orozco: An Autobiography.* Austin, Tex.: University of Texas Press, 1962.
Plenn, Virginia, and Jaime Plenn. *Guide to Modern Mexican Murals.* Mexico: Ediciones Tolteca, 1963.
Reed, Alma. *Orozco.* New York: Oxford University Press, 1956.
Rivera, Diego. *My Art, My Life.* New York: Citadel, 1960.
———. *Portrait of America.* New York: Covici, Friede, 1934.
Rodriguez, Antonio. *A History of Mexican Mural Painting.* New York: Putnam, 1969.
———. *Siqueiros.* Mexico: Fondo de Cultura Economica, 1974.
Suarez, Orlando. *Inventario del Muralismo Mexicano.* Mexico: UNAM, 1972.
Tibol, Raquel. *Siqueiros: Vida y Obra.* Mexico: Colección Metropolitana, 1973.
Wolfe, Bertram D. *Diego Rivera.* New York: Knopf, 1939.
———. *The Fabulous Life of Diego Rivera.* New York: Stein & Day, 1969.

Chapter 7: Concentration Camp Art

Bosworth, Allan R. *America's Concentration Camps.* New York: Bantam, 1968.
Children's Drawings and Poems—Terezin, 1942-44. New York: McGraw-Hill, [1960?].
Eaton, Allen H. *Beauty Behind Barbed Wire.* New York: Harper, 1952.
Green, Gerald. *The Artists of Terezin.* New York: Hawthorn, 1969.
Hilberg, Raul. *The Destruction of the European Jews.* Chicago: Quadrangle, 1961.

Kantor, Alfred. *The Book of Alfred Kantor*. New York: McGraw-Hill, 1971.
Miné Okubo: An American Experience. Exhibition catalogue. Oakland, Calif.: Oakland Museum, 1972.
Okubo, Miné. *Citizen 13660*. New York: Columbia University Press, 1946.
Volavkova, Hana. *A Story of the Jewish Museum in Prague*. Prague: Artia, 1968.

Chapter 8: Photography and Social Content

Bourke-White, Margaret. *Portrait of Myself*. New York: Simon and Schuster, 1963.
Caldwell, Erskine, and Margaret Bourke-White. *You Have Seen Their Faces*. New York, Viking, 1937.
Callahan, Sean (ed.). *Photographs of Margaret Bourke-White*. Greenwich, Conn.: New York Graphic Society, 1972.
Capa, Robert. *Images of War*. New York: Grossman, 1964.
Conrat, Maisie, and Richard Conrat. *Executive Order 9066*. Cambridge, Mass.: MIT Press, 1972.
Documentary Photography. New York: Time-Life Books, 1972.
Elliot, George (ed.). *Dorothea Lange*. New York: Museum of Modern Art, 1966.
Gutman, Judith M. *Lewis W. Hine and the American Social Conscience*. New York: Walker, 1967.
Hood, Robert E. *12 At War: Great Photographers Under Fire*. New York: Putnam, 1967.
Lange, Dorothea, and Paul S. Taylor. *An American Exodus*. New York: Reynal & Hitchcock, 1939.
Lewis Hine. New York: Grossman, 1974.
Newhall, Beaumont. *The History of Photography from 1839 to the Present Day*. New York: Museum of Modern Art, 1949.
Robert Capa. New York: Grossman, 1974.
Steichen, Edward (ed.). *The Bitter Years, 1935–1941*. New York: Museum of Modern Art, 1962.
Stryker, Roy Emerson, and Nancy Wood. *In This Proud Land: America 1935–1943 as seen in the FSA Photographs*. Greenwich, Conn.: New York Graphic Society 1973.
Tucker, Anne (ed.). *The Woman's Eye*. New York: Knopf, 1975.

Chapter 9: New Directions in Socially Conscious Art

Atelier Populaire: Posters from the Revolution, Paris, May 1968. Indianapolis, Ind.: Bobbs-Merrill, 1969.
Atkinson, J. Edward (ed.). *Black Dimensions in Contemporary American Art*. New York: New American Library, 1971.
Baynes, Ken. *War*. Boston: Boston Book and Art, 1970.
Brown, Milton. *Jacob Lawrence*. Exhibition catalogue. New York: Whitney Museum of American Art, 1974.

234 Bibliography

Cobb, Ron. *My Fellow Americans.* Los Angeles: Sawyer, 1970.
———. *Raw Sewage.* Los Angeles: Sawyer, 1970.
Horowitz, Benjamin. *Images of Dignity: The Drawings of Charles White.* Los Angeles: Ward Ritchie, 1967.
Kienholz, Edward. *11 + 11 Tableaux.* Exhibition catalogue. Stockholm: Moderna Museet, 1970.
Kunzel, David. *American Posters of Protest, 1966–1970.* Exhibition catalogue. New York: New School Art Center, 1971.
Lewis, Samella S., and Ruth G. Waddy (eds.). *Black Artists on Art.* 2 vols. Los Angeles: Contemporary Crafts, 1969.
Rickards, Maurice. *Posters of Protest and Revolution.* New York: Walker, 1970.
Schwartz, Barry. *The New Humanism: Art in a Time of Change.* New York: Praeger, 1974.
Seitz, William. *Segal.* New York: Abrams, 1972.
Selz, Peter. *Funk.* Exhibition catalogue. Berkeley, Calif.: University Art Museum, 1967.
Stermer, Dugald (ed.). *The Art of Revolution.* Introduction by Susan Sontag. New York: McGraw-Hill, 1970.
Wilkening, H., and Sonia Brown. *Bufano.* Berkeley, Calif.:Howell-North, 1972.
Yanker, Gary. *Prop Art.* Greenwich, Conn.: New York Graphic Society, 1972.

Acknowledgments

For well over two years, I have looked forward to the joyous occasion of acknowledging the many persons who have contributed to *The Art of Social Conscience*. The origins of the book lie in the countless fruitful discussions with friends and colleagues over the years. It is impossible to acknowledge fully the intellectual influence of Professor James E. Harmon, my finest teacher during my undergraduate years. His critical insights into politics and into life in general, his sense of humor, and his high regard for verbal lucidity have served as ideals for me for over 16 years. My association with Richard Swearingen has been similarly invaluable. His historical insights and his enormous erudition stimulated me to examine art in its broadest social context. More than any other art historian, Antje de Wilde helped me to focus my conversational interests in a systematic way. In no small way, her brilliant knowledge of art, her commitment to the intellectual enterprise, and her political consciousness served as the primary influence in the decision to write this book. Extensive conversations with her and Hans van Marle constantly helped me to clarify my own ideas. Professor Herschel Chipp of the University of California provided additional encouragement and significant specific assistance throughout the project. Gerald Fleming of the University of Surrey contributed his awesome intellect and his constant encouragement. The general influence of Ken Salter pervades the text. Vic Lieberman deserves special thanks for his suggestion that class preparation notes could, in time, be transformed into a book. My parents, Peter and Selma Von Blum, set the stage for this effort years ago by generating an enduring family political consciousness.

My first seminar in art and social content enabled me to test my ideas on a uniquely outstanding group of undergraduate students. In significant ways, the following persons share in whatever contribution this book may make: John Trochet, Walter Toki, Barbara McAuley, Jim Buehler, Karen Bondy, Laurie Alexander, Joyce Johnston, Debbie Honigman, Rebecca Margolese, Teri Cohn,

236 Acknowledgments

Jon Meltzer, Robbie Lieberman, Jane Silverman, Steve Green, Jo Anne Malone, Gail Gosney, Steve McNamara, Fran Lindner, and Roanne Olonoff.

Several people were extraordinarily helpful during the initial research and writing stage of the project. Keith Thoreen contributed both the resources of the University of California slide collection and his own considerable insights into political and social art. Gino Frosini graciously allowed me to use the visual and verbal resources of his Berkeley gallery, Dow and Frosini. The staff members of numerous libraries provided enormous technical assistance and personal encouragement. I am particularly indebted to the staff of the libraries of the University of California at Berkeley, the Whitney Museum of American Art, the Museum of Modern Art, the Worcester Art Museum, and Stanford University. Bruce McAuley, Ben Kaplan, Judy Kaplan, Steve Rood, Bonnie Baskin, and Joy Feinberg all offered valuable insights and suggestions. It is impossible to neglect the stimulation of Senator Sam Ervin and his Congressional colleagues. Their vigor, eloquence, and persistence in exposing the Watergate criminals furnished me with the adrenalin and excitement necessary for the arduous task of completing the manuscript.

During the revision stage, Professor Peter Selz offered perceptive commentary on the history of socially conscious art. My contact with him has been one of the most pleasant and intellectually stimulating relationships in the years I have taught at Berkeley. I am grateful for the assistance of Irene Sawyer, whose outstanding knowledge of Afro-American art has been especially helpful to me in this work. Throughout the aggravating period of obtaining reproductions, several people exhibited the kind of personal sensitivity that enabled me to weather the Kafkaesque frustrations of this process. Special mention must be made of Bernarda Shahn, Susan Bradford, Peter Grosz, Lillian Brenwasser, and the staff of the Kennedy Galleries in New York, and the staff of the A.C.A. Gallery in New York. I also appreciate the cooperative and gracious help of several artists whose works appear in this book. A revealingly sympathetic letter from George Tooker during the worst period of the permissions hassles did wonders for my morale.

Many individuals provided outstanding technical, clerical and editorial assistance. Ron Wanglin did a magnificent job as a research assistant, and he has my eternal gratitude for typing the first draft of the manuscript. Juanita Martinez and Melitta Beeson have helped with the voluminous correspondence at every stage. William Petzel has furnished photographic expertise of the highest order. Finally, Cherene Holland has performed the Herculean task of editing the entire manuscript. She has my grateful appreciation.

In any project such as this, a few persons contribute so profoundly that no acknowledgment could possibly be adequate. Professor Alain Renoir, founder and former chairman of the Division of Interdisciplinary and General Studies at the University of California at Berkeley, created an academic environment supportive of this kind of intellectual work. He provided extraordinary personal encouragement for my continuing efforts to transcend the orthodoxy of contemporary academic scholarship. His continued personal support and his tireless commitment to civilized values have made my association with him a highlight both of my academic career and of my life in general. Dick Deering, perhaps the most erudite person I have known, eagerly shared his wealth of knowledge with me throughout the writing of this book. He was an invaluable and constant source of information, editorial assistance, and personal friendship. Stewart Wax deserves my deepest gratitude for his truly massive efforts. Undoubtedly, he saved me from overwhelming despair through his impressive organizational talents in the tedious process of obtaining permissions. His real contributions, however, go far beyond that task. His intellectual acuity and his personal concern can never really be properly recognized. Our conversations, including those between innings at the Oakland A's games, have been a genuine contribution to my own intellectual consciousness. Ellen Clark's contribution has been similarly overwhelming. Above all, she worked with me for several weeks, several hours a day, in the arduous task of revising the manuscript. Her intelligence and verbal sophistication are manifest throughout the text. She assisted me at every level of research and writing. She worked tirelessly in helping me to compile the bibliography. Most important, her friendship and her commitment to this book and to my broader intellectual objectives have helped me to endure the frustrations of contemporary academic life. Her patience in enduring my moods and dissatisfactions evokes a gratitude that cannot be provided in these pages.

The monumental intellectual and personal assistance of Ruth Von Blum cannot be matched. She has been involved at every stage of this enterprise. She has read and re-read every sentence and every paragraph of this book. Her analytic judgment and her editorial sense are reflected throughout *The Art of Social Conscience*. Her artistic perception was instrumental in my selection of illustrative materials to accompany my text. Her photographic expertise was employed in Mexico City during my investigation of the Mexican muralists. Her organizational talents were invaluable in meeting the seemingly endless barrage of administrative details. Finally, her devoted support and her patience in enduring my periodic craziness evoke a response from me that is best expressed in other ways and in other forums.

Index

Adams, Ansel, 186
Agonized (Baskin), *5-31,* 135
Air Raid in Bilbao, Spain (Capa), *8-7,* 193
Albright, Ivan, *5-18, 5-19,* 120–23
Alienation: Munch, *2-18,* 54; Tooker, *5-23—5-25,* 126–29
American Tragedy (Evergood), *5-17,* 119–20
Anarchism: Picasso, *4-2,* 84–85
And God Created Man in His Own Image (Albright), *5-19,* 123
Angulo 18 (Genovés), *9-1,* 212
Antal, Frederick, 4
Arbus, Diane, 186
Arneson, Robert, *9-13,* 227–28
Art Patrons (Gropper), *5-16,* 117
Atomic warfare: Baskin, *5-30,* 134–35; Shahn, *5-8—5-10,* 109–11

Baskin, Leonard, *5-29—5-31,* 126, 133–36
Beauty I Will Cherish You (Grosz), *3-13,* 76–77
Beggar on a Crutch (Picasso), 85
Beggar with a Wooden Leg (Rembrandt), *1-4,* 8–10
Beggar's Meal (Picasso), 85
Blume, Peter, *5-20,* 124
Book of Alfred Kantor, *7-8, 7-9,*174
Bourke-White, Margaret, *8-11—8-14,* 2, 200–203
Brady, Mathew, 185
Braque, Georges, 87
Breakfast Scene (Hogarth), *1-5,* 10
Brueghel, Peter, the Elder, *1-2,*6–7, 10, 48, 212
Bufano, Beniamino, *9-10,* 225–26

Bureaucracy: Tooker, *5-25,* 128–29
By the Prison Gate (Orozco), *6-13,* 160

Cadmus, Paul, *5-21, 5-22,* 125–26
Calder, Alexander, 186, 218
Callot, Jacques, 6, 7–8, 10, 42, 133, 139
Camp Commander (Haas) *7-4,* 170
Capa, Robert, 192–98, 200
The Caprices (Los Caprichos), Goya, 13–14
Cartier-Bresson, Henri, 186
Cemetery in Nam Dinh (Capa), *8-10,* 196–97
Chagall, Marc, 186
Chain Gang and Burly Police Captain (Bourke-White), *8-12,* 200
Child Bayoneted by a War Toy (Cobb), poster, *9-9,* 223, 225
Child labor: Hine, *8-1, 8-4,* 188–91; Lange, *8-18,* 200
Chwast, Seymour, *9-8,* 223
Citizen 13660, book by Okubo, 184
Clown, Rouault, *2-3,* 37
Cobb, Ron, *9-9,* 223–25
Concentration camps, 165–84; Bourke-White, *8-13,* 200; Lange, *8-19, 8-20,* 207–9
Condemned Man, Rouault, *2-7,* 42
Coney Island (Cadmus), *5-21,* 124–25
Content and form in art, 3–6
Courbet, Gustave, 165
Courts and legal institutions: Daumier *1-14, 1-15,* 28, 31; Lange, *8-21,* 209–10; Orozco, *6-9,* 153–54; Rouault, *2-7,* 42
Creation (Rivera), 144
Credo (Shahn), *5-12,* 113
Cross Section (Grosz), *3-12,* 75–76

239

Index

Daguerre, Louis, 185
Daumier, Honoré, *1-1, 1-11—1-17,* 2, 10, 11, 21–33, 34, 35, 37, 40, 48, 58, 75, 87, 116, 120, 156, 165, 210, 223
Day of the Heroic Guerrilla (Organization of Solidarity with Asia, Africa, and Latin America), *9-6,* 218, 221
Dead Mother and the Child (Munch), *2-14,* 51
Death: Lawrence, *9-2,* 213; Munch, *2-13, 2-14,* 49–51
Death Chamber (Munch) *2-13,* 49–50, 51
Death of a Spanish Loyalist (Capa), *8-6,* 192–93
Defendant (Lange), *8-21,* 209–10
De Kooning, Willem, 126
Diaz the Dictator (Siqueiros), *6-17,* 163–64
Dictator (Gropper), *5-15,* 116
Disasters of War (Goya), series, *1-9,* 19, 42, 196
Dr. Mengele (Kantor), *7-9,* 175–76
Dorra, Henri, 3–4
Dove (Picasso), *4-1,* 94–95
Drawing of an Anarchist Meeting (Picasso), *4-2,* 84–85
Dream and Lie of Franco (Picasso), *4-5a & b,* 89
Dust Storm (Okubo), *7-12,* 180

Ecce Homo (Grosz), series, *3-12—3-17,* 73–76, 125
Echo of a Scream (Siqueiros), *6-15,* 160
Election Night (Levine), *5-27,* 130
End Bad Breath (Chwast), poster, *9-8,* 223
Engineer Heartfield (Grosz), *3-11,* 70
Eternal City (Blume), *5-20,* 124
Evening Party (Grosz), *3-14,* 77
Evergood, Philip, *5-17,* 119, 120
Execution (Segal), *9-11,* 226
Executive Order 9066, book by Lange, 207

Face of the Assembly (Daumier), series, 32
Family of Charles IV (Goya), *1-7,* 15
Feast of Pure Reason (Levine), *5-26,* 129–30
Feminism: Lafollette, *9-5,* 217–18
First Night of New Arrivals (Fleischmann), *7-7,* 173

Fit for Active Service (Grosz), *3-9,* 70
Fleischmann, Karel, *7-7,* 168, 173–74
Four Prostitutes (Rouault), *2-4,* 37, 39
Franciscan Standing over Indian Supplicant (Orozco), *6-12,* 159
Fritta, Bedřich, *7-1—7-3,* 168, 169–70
Frugal Repast (Picasso), *4-3,* 85–87

Gargantua (Daumier), *1-11,* 25–26
Gendarme (student poster), *9-7,* 220
Genovés, Juan, *9-1,* 212
Gentlemen of Justice (Daumier), series, 28–31, 32
Germany's Children Are Hungry (Kollwitz), *3-6,* 67
Gluttony: Arneson, *9-13,* 227–28
Goering, the Executioner (Heartfield), *3-18,* 81–82
Gogh, Vincent van, 85
Government Bureau (Tooker), *5-25,* 128–29
Goya y Lucientes, Francisco, *1-6—1-10,* 3, 4, 11–21, 22, 28, 34, 35, 36, 42, 48, 58, 92, 96, 129, 133, 139, 160, 196, 210
Goyescas (Shahn), 113
Grandfather and Grandchildren Awaiting Evacuation Bus (Lange), *8-19,* 208
Greco, El, 3, 11
Gris, Juan, 87
Gropper, William, *5-13—5-15,* 115–119, 129
Grosz, George, *3-9—3-17,* 2, 14, 58, 64, 69–79, 125, 129, 133
Guernica (Picasso), *4-8,* 19, 84, 90–93, 124, 193
Guernica Studies and "Postcripts" (Picasso) *4-6, 4-7,* 90–92

Haas, Leo, *7-4, 7-5,* 170–71
Handball (Shahn), *5-5,* 105–6
Hanged Man (Posada), *6-2,* 139
Hanging (Callot), *1-3,* 8
Heartfield, John, *3-11, 3-18—3-20,* 58, 79–82
Heavy the Oar . . . (Albright), *5-18,* 123
Hidalgo (Orozco), *6-3,* 140
Hine, Lewis, *8-1—8-5,* 186–92
Hofmann, Hans, 126

241 Index

Hogarth, William, *1-5*, 6, 10, 11, 21, 48, 60, 212
Horse and Mother with Dead Child (Picasso), *4-7*, 91–92
Horse's Head (Picasso), *4-6*, 91
Hydrogen Man (Baskin), *5-30*, 134–35

In Memory of Richard Wagner (Grosz), *3-16*, 78
Invasion (Levine), *5-28*, 131
It Is Hard to Live (Rouault), *2-8*, 42–45
Italian Family with Their Bundled Belongings (Hine), *8-3*, 187–188

J'Accuse No. 8 (White), *9-3*, 214–17
Jealousy (Munch), *2-15*, 51–52

Kantor, Alfred, *7-8*, *7-9*, 168, 174
Kienholz, Edward, *9-12*, 226–27
Killed in Action (Kollwitz), *3-4*, 62
Kline, Franz, 126
Kollwitz, Käthe, *3-1—3-8*, 2, 10, 35, 49, 58, 59–68, 87, 105, 133, 154, 196, 212, 218

Lafollette, Rosemary, *9-5*, 217–18
Land and Liberty (Rivera), *6-6*, 148–50
Landing at Vera Cruz (Rivera), *6-8*, 151
Landscape with Figures (Tooker), *5-24*, 128, 129
Lange, Dorothea, *8-15—8-21*, 203–10
Last Soldier To Die (Capa), *8-9*, 196
Latin America (Orozco), *6-10*, 155–56
Latrine (Kantor), *7-8*, 174
Law and Justice (Orozco), *6-9*, 153–54
Lawrence, Jacob, *9-2*, 2, 212–13
Leaders and Masses (Orozco), *6-1*, 156
Le Corbusier, 186
Legislative Belly (Daumier), *1-12*, 26, 117
Leo, 48 Inches High . . . (Hine), *8-4*, 188
Levine, Jack, *5-26—5-28*, 126, 129–31, 135
Life in Migrant Labor Camp (Lange), *8-17*, 206–7
Lucky Dragon (Shahn), series, 109–10, 113
Lucky Dragon (Shahn), *5-9*, 110
Lust (Munch), *2-16*, 52, 54
Lynching: Cadmus, *5-22*, 125–126

McCarthyism: 107–9, 119; Baskin, *5-29*, 133–34
Madonna from Madison Avenue (Lafollette), *9-5*, 217–18
Male-female relationships: Grosz, *3-15*, 76–78; Hogarth, *1-5*, 10; Lafollette, *9-5*, 217–18; Munch, *2-1*, *2-15*, *2-16*, 51–53
Man At the Crossroads . . . (Rivera), 145
Man Is Wolf to Man (Rouault), *2-12*, 47–48
Man of Peace (Baskin), *5-29*, 133–34
Manzanar Relocation Center (Lange), *8-20*, 209
Marriage à la Mode (Hogarth), series, *1-5*, 10, 60
Marsh, Reginald, 119
Massacre in Korea (Picasso), *4-9*, 96–97
Massacre of the Innocents (Brueghel), *1-2*, 6–7
Memorial to Karl Liebknecht (Kollwitz), *3-1*, 66
Mental institutions: Kienholz, *9-12*, 226–27
Mexico Tomorrow (Rivera), *6-7*, 150–51
Migrant Mother (Lange), *8-16*, 204–5
Migration (Lawrence), series, *9-2*, 213
Miners' Wives (Shahn), *5-7*, 107
Miró, Joan, 88, 218
Miserere et Guerre (Rouault), series, *2-8*, *2-10—2-12*, 42–47
Miseries of War (Callot), series, 7, 42
Moving In (Okubo), *7-11*, 180
Munch, Edvard, *2-1*, *2-13—2-20*, 2, 34–35, 47–57, 91, 133
Muybridge, Eadweard, 185
My Land (Reed), *9-4*, 217

Nadar, Paul, 185
Nast, Thomas, 100, 223
Never Again War (Kollwitz), *3-5*, 63
New Democracy (Siqueiros), *6-16*, 163
New Freedom (Rivera), *6-5*, 145
Night of the Poor (Rivera), *6-4a*, 144
Night of the Rich (Rivera), *6-4b*, 144
Novak, Josef, *7-10*, 177–78

Oklahoma Child with Cotton Sack (Lange), *8-18*, 207

Okubo, Miné, *7-11—7-14,* 179–84
Old Man with Rope (Kollwitz), *3-7,* 67
Orozco, José Clemente, *6-1, 6-9—6-12,* 35, 137, 139, 142–44, 152–59, 160, 164, 212
Outbreak (Kollwitz), *3-3,* 61
Outstretched Arms (Fritta), *7-1,* 169–70

Panel 55, Migration series (Lawrence), *9-2,* 213
Passion of Sacco and Vanzetti (Shahn), 104
Peace (Bufano), *9-10,* 225
Peace (Picasso), 97
Peasant War (Kollwitz), series, *3-3,* 61
Personal suffering: Albright, *5-18, 5-19,* 123; Baskin, *5-31,* 135; Lange, *8-15—8-18,* 204–7; Munch, *2-17,* 54; Rouault, *2-2, 2-3, 2-8,* 36–38, 42–45; Shahn, *5-7,* 107; Siqueiros, *6-14,* 160; White, *9-3,* 214–17
Picasso, Pablo, *4-1—4-9,* 2, 19, 83–98, 124, 193, 218
Police brutality: Daumier, *1-13,* 28; Evergood, *5-17,* 119–20; Paris, 1968, *9-7,* 220
Pollock, Jackson, 126
Poor Quarter (Rouault), *2-6,* 40
Populace (Goya), *1-9,* 19
Portrait of an Old Woman (Ungar), *7-6,* 173
Portrait of a Small Child (Capa), *8-8,* 194, 196
Posada, José, 137–39
Poverty: Bourke-White, *8-11,* 200; Hine, *8-2, 8-5,* 187, 191; Kollwitz, *3-2, 3-6, 3-7,* 60, 66–67; Lange, *8-15—8-18,* 204–7; Picasso, *4-3, 4-4,* 85–87; Rembrandt, *1-4,* 8–10; Rivera, *6-4a,* 144; Rouault, *2-6,* 40; Shahn, *5-1, 5-5,* 105–7
Poverty (Kollwitz), *3-2,* 60
Prisoner (Goya), *1-10,* 21
Prisons and prisoners: Bourke-White, *8-12,* 200; Goya, *1-10,* 21; Siqueiros, *6-13,* 160
Proletarian Victim (Siqueiros), *6-14,* 160
Prometheus (Orozco), 154–55
Proverbs (Los Proverbios) (Goya), 21
Public Defender, series (Lange), *8-21,* 210

Rake's Progress (Hogarth), 60
Rebellion: Kollwitz, *3-3,* 59–62
Reed, Jerry, *9-4,* 217
Refugees (Rouault), *2-5,* 40
Rembrandt van Rijn, *1-4,* 6, 8–10, 22, 87
Reichsbishop Shapes up the Church (Heartfield), *3-19,* 82
Republic (Daumier), *1-17,* 31–32
Republican Automatons (Grosz), *3-10,* 70
Rivera, Diego, *6-4—6-8,* 2, 10, 105, 137, 139, 143, 144–152, 156, 160, 164, 212
Rothko, Mark, 126
Rouault, Georges, *2-2—2-12,* 2, 10, 34–47, 48, 87, 133, 154, 160, 210
Row of Tenements (Hine), *8-2,* 187
Rue Transonain, April 15, 1834 (Daumier), *1-13,* 28, 120

Sacco and Vanzetti (Shahn), *5-2,* 102–3
Sacco-Vanzetti case, *5-2—5-4,* 101–4
Satire
 legislators: Daumier, *1-12,* 26–28; Gropper, *5-13,* 116
 masses: Cadmus, *5-21,* 125; Orozco, *6-1,* 156
 middle class and bourgeoisie: Gropper: *5-14, 5-16,* 116; Grosz, *3-10, 3-14,* 70, 77; Levine, *5-26, 5-27,* 129–31; Munch, *2-19,* 55; Rouault, *2-8,* 45–46
 militarism: Cobb, *9-9,* 223, 225; Grosz, *3-9,* 69–70
 political leaders: Blume, *5-20,* 124; Daumier, *1-11,* 25–26; Goya, *1-7,* 15–16; Gropper, *5-15,* 116; Heartfield, *3-18,* 81–82; Picasso, *4-5a & b,* 89; Siqueiros, *6-17,* 164
 professions: Daumier, *1-15, 1-16,* 30–31; Grosz, *3-11,* 70; Orozco, *6-9, 6-11,* 153–54, 156
Savagery: Grosz, *3-16,* 78; Rouault, *2-12,* 47
Scott's Run, West Virginia (Shahn), *5-1,* 105
Scream (Munch), *2-17,* 54, 91
Second of May, 1808, (Goya), 16
Segal, George, *9-11,* 226
Senate (Gropper), *5-13,* 116
Sex Murder on Ackerstrasse (Grosz), *3-16,* 78

243 Index

Shahn, Ben, *5-1—5-12*, 100–13, 123, 133, 134, 192, 212
Siqueiros, David Alfaro, *6-13—6-17*, 2, 35, 137, 143, 159–64, 165
Six Witnesses Who Bought Eels from Vanzetti (Shahn), *5-3*, 103
Sleep of Reason Produces Monsters (Goya), *1-6*, 14
Slum (Rouault), *2-6*, 40
Smorgi-Bob, the Cook (Arneson), *9-13*, 227–28
Society Lady Fancies She Has a Reserved Seat in Heaven (Rouault), *2-9*, 45–46
Soldier's Widow (Orozco), 154
Solidarity: The Propeller Song (Kollwitz), *3-8*, 67–68
Soyer, Moses, 119
Soyer, Raphael, 119
Spring Awakening (Grosz), *3-15*, 76–78
Spring Evening on Karl Johan Street (Munch), *2-18*, 54
State Hospital (Kienholz), *9-12*, 226–27
Stieglitz, Alfred, 185–86
Stillborn Education (Orozco), *6-11*, 156
Street Beggar, Belgrade, Serbia (Hine), *8-5*, 191
Subway (Tooker), *5-23*, 126–28
Survivors of Buchenwald (Bourke-White), *8-13*, 200

Thanks to Society (Munch), *2-19*, 55
Theresienstadt, 166–178
Third-Class Carriage (Daumier), *1-1*, 32
Third of May, 1808 (Goya), *1-8*, 3, 16–18, 28, 92, 129
This is Nazi Brutality (Shahn), *5-6*, 107
This Will Be the Last Time . . . (Rouault), *2-10*, 46–47
Through Light to Dark (Heartfield), *3-20*, 82
Tooker, George, *5-23—5-25*, 2, 126–29
To the Lynching! (Cadmus), *5-22*, 125–26
Toulouse-Lautrec, Henri de, 85
Tragic Clown (Rouault), *2-2*, 36–37
Transport to the East (Haas), *7-5*, 171

Trek, illustrated magazine covers (Okubo), *7-13*, *7-14*, 181
Two Miners (Bourke-White), *8-14*, 200–203
Tycoon (Gropper), *5-14*, 116

Ungar, Otto, *7-6*, 168, 171–73

Vance, a Trapper Boy (Hine), *8-1*, 188–91
Velásquez, Diego, 11

War
  General: 7; Capa, *8-6—8-10*, 192–97; Genovés, *9-1*, 212; Goya, *1-9*, 18–21; Kollwitz, *3-4*, *3-5*, 62–64; Picasso, *4-6*, *4-7*, 90–93; Rouault, *2-10*, *2-11*, 46–47; Siqueiros, *6-15*, 160
  Brutality against civilians: Brueghel, *1-2*, 6; Goya, *1-8*, 16–18; Picasso, *4-8*, *4-9*, 89–93, 95–97; Rivera, *6-8*, 151; Shahn, *5-6*, 107
  Executions: Callot, *1-3*, 8; Goya, *1-8*, 16–18; Posada, *6-2*, 139; Segal, *9-11*, 226
  Refugees: Rouault, *2-5*, 40
  Vietnam: Capa, *8-10*, 196; Chwast, *9-8*, 223; Levine, *5-28*, 131
War (Picasso), 97
Washerwoman (Daumier), 87
Weavers (Kollwitz), series, 59–61
We Did Not Know What Happened to Us (Shahn), *5-8*, 110
Welders (Shahn), 107
White Angel Breadline (Lange), *8-15*, 204
White, Charles, *9-3*, 214–17
Why (Shahn), *5-11*, 110
Woman Ironing (Picasso), *4-4*, 87
Workers: Bourke-White, *8-14*, 201–3; Munch, *2-20*, 55; Picasso, *4-4*, 87
Workers Returning Home (Munch), *2-20*, 55

You Are Free to Speak (Daumier), *1-14*, 28
Young Farm Boy Using Newspapers on Wall (Bourke-White), *8-11*, 200
You've Lost Your Case (Daumier), *1-16*, 31